IRISES

A Gardener's Encyclopedia

CLAIRE AUSTIN

Foreword by James W. Waddick

TIMBER PRESS

Half title page: *Iris* 'Concertina'; frontispiece: *Iris* 'King-fisher'; above: *Iris* 'Circus Dancer'.

All photos by author unless otherwise indicated.

Published in 2005 by

Timber Press, Inc.
The Haseltine Building
133 S.W. Second Avenue, Suite 450
Portland, Oregon 97204-3527, U.S.A.

www.timberpress.com

For contact information for editorial, marketing, sales, and distribution in the United Kingdom, see www.timberpress.com/uk

Printed through Colorcraft Ltd., Hong Kong
Designed by Susan Applegate

Library of Congress Cataloguing-in-Publication Data

Austin, Claire, 1957–
  Irises: a gardener's encyclopedia / Claire Austin; foreword by James W. Waddick.
     p. cm.
  Includes bibliographical references and index.
  ISBN 0-88192-730-9 (hardcover)
  1. Irises (Plants) I. Title.
  SB413.I8.A973 2005
  635.9'3438—dc22
                                        2005005286

A catalogue record for this book is also available from the British Library.

yarn Corner
1/2012

CONTENTS

FOREWORD

Iris may be the least known of our well-known garden plants, but this book offers new vistas. The bearded irises of various sizes are familiar to most gardeners, some of whom may even grow Siberian or Dutch irises. The adventurous will recognize a species such as the yellow-flowered *Iris pseudacorus*. However, many gardeners do not realize the wide range of size, habit, and situation that is encountered in this group of plants. Even when you seek an unusual or special plant like *I. unguicularis*, you often cannot find a picture of it or the picture you find only offers a glimpse of the plant and nothing more. If this has been your experience, prepare to encounter the outer edges of "iris-dom" within these covers and be warned of symptoms of iris lust.

This book is truly encyclopedic in its presentation of irises. Some of them are suited for planting in a desert, others in a pond. Some are a mere 2 to 3 inches (5–7 cm) tall, while others tower at 6 feet (2 m) or more.

There are irises for the rock garden, containers, or the perennial bed. The text invites, no dares, you to try more and different kinds of iris. From the bulbous and so-un-iris-like Junos or the new "Eye Shadow" hybrids that are easy to grow and very hardy, most gardeners will find something new and different. The text will inspire and urge you to seek plants in catalogs and garden centers. Even familiar kinds of iris will no doubt be seen here in a newer and wider variety than most of us encounter in one place. The familiar bearded irises from tall to dwarf are represented in abundance befitting their overall popularity. Many award winners are given special emphasis. The Japanese, Louisiana, Siberian, Spuria, and Pacific Coast irises are shown as are the wild species, selections, and new and old hybrids. Historical varieties add a timely dimension to the array of irises discussed. Even less common irises such as English and Spanish iris, *Iris verna*, and crested iris are given their places and much more. Literally there is no room here to hint at the variety in the following pages.

Irises are divided into scientific groupings in this book, but that should not bother the "botany-phobic," because the pictures and explanatory text invite all readers. Sections of text cover basic cultivation, diseases and pests, fertilizing, even the fundamentals of hybridizing to produce still more new iris types. Once enticed by the bait within these pages, you will be tempted to try more and new irises; conveniently there is a list of sources covering numerous countries and specialty nurseries.

In highlighting the text, I hope I have not overemphasized the value of the information presented, since there is enough to warrant a book without illustrations, but the photos bring this book to a new level. They are the center of the book and may well be the major lure for gardeners. Over 1100 color pictures show irises of almost all types as well as in almost every possible situation. Even the smallest of the thumbnail pictures is large enough to be useful in identifying the plant and noting specific characters of each iris. Beautiful full-page portraits are scattered throughout the book and add serious information, not simply decoration. Claire Austin has done a monumental job in documenting the array of irises in all their glory.

So this is a book to study and dream about. Not every iris will grow in your climate, and some groups are far more difficult to cultivate than others. The focus is the author's wide experience in the midlands of England, so the cultivation may need some changes to fit your exact climate. In the end, you will find some new species or variety that demands space in your garden. Accept iris lust and let yourself explore.

James W. Waddick
Kansas City, Missouri

PREFACE

Wherever I have travelled in the world I have seen irises. In India, Oncocyclus irises are carved into the marble walls of the Taj Mahal. On the beaches of Cyprus, bulbous irises pop up through the sand in February. In Melbourne, Australia, irises line the road leading away from the airport, and in Florida, a state where only one type of iris grows in the wild, a large picture of bearded irises adorns a wall in one of the concourses at the Orlando airport. Irises must be among the world's favourite flowers, and there are many of them.

In fact, there are irises for all tastes and for every location in the garden. In addition to the hundreds of wild iris species and their forms, gardeners today can select from many thousands of hybrids produced in the past one hundred years. The most popular among these are the bearded or pogon irises, but there are many Siberian, Japanese, and Louisiana hybrids, together with a more limited number of Spuria and Californian irises. In addition, different species have been crossed to produce a beautiful, although not often available, range of irises. Since the 1920s the most active hybridizing has been in North America, but many wonderful introductions have also come from Australia, France, Germany, Italy, Japan, South Africa, and Britain.

In this book I have not attempted to include every species, as some are very rare, while others are difficult to cultivate. Dedicated iris enthusiasts and those who would like to know more about iris species should consult the wonderful books already published, including those by Brian Mathew (1981) and Fritz Köhlein (1987). Both make enthralling reading.

Likewise, with so many hybrids to choose from, I have not attempted to produce a definitive work on irises. It would take thousands of pages to include just ten percent of known irises. Instead, this book is intended merely as a snapshot of this wonderful genus.

In selecting plants for this encyclopedia, I turned to the people who are most passionate about irises—those gardeners involved in the many iris societies and the iris growers and breeders themselves. The American Iris Society and affiliated groups, such as the Median Society, along with the British Iris Society have provided me with much inspiration. I have also included many plants that are important in the development of the hybrids. Visits to nurseries in America, Australia, and Britain were immensely helpful, and iris catalogues from France, Canada, and Germany gave me more valuable information. Finally, I included those plants I simply could not live without. With so many to choose from, please forgive me if I have omitted one of your favourite irises.

ACKNOWLEDGEMENTS

I WOULD LIKE TO SINCERELY THANK the following people for their generosity in allowing me to take up their time, either with taking photographs, lending me photographs, checking over a specific chapter, or freely sharing their knowledge. In Australia, Barry and Lesley Blyth at Tempo Two. In California, George and Margaret Sutton and Lorraine and Gordon Nicholson. In Oregon, Keith Keppel for passing a critical eye over the photographs; David Schreiner, Paul Black, Thomas Johnson, Jim and Vicki Craig, Barbara Aitken, Will and Tracy Plotner, Chad Harris, and the American Median Iris Society. In Maryland, Carol Warner and Bruce Hornstein for letting me photograph their Japanese irises. In Britain, Kim Davis with his sibirica irises and Jennifer Hewitt for reading the Siberian iris chapter and both Jennifer and Sydney Linnegar for lending me photographs; Christine Murphy at Middleton House; Jim Almond with his wonderful Onco and Juno irises and for looking over the text; and Tony Hall at the Royal Botanic Gardens Kew. And finally my children, Ellen and Robert, for being neglected at an important time of their life and, by no means least, my husband, Ric, for sharing my iris passion. Without him I could not have done this book.

INTRODUCTION

Irises, the Rainbow Flower
[a Rainbow], Flower-de-Luce

Phillip Miller
Gardener's Dictionary, 1732

AROUND THE WORLD, approximately 270 iris species are known plus hundreds of subspecies, collected forms, and natural hybrids. All come from the Northern Hemisphere and can be found growing as far north as Scandinavia and as far south as Florida, from Europe to Japan, as well as in many parts of North America. Their habitats range from mountainsides to deserts, open grasslands, dense woodland, and sandy coastal areas. Irises grow from 5 to 200 cm (2 in. to 6 ft.) tall and bloom from late winter to late summer. With just a small selection, a garden can have irises in bloom from the dark days of winter until summer turns to autumn.

Iris flowers come in a breathtaking array of colours ranging from white, yellow, and orange through every tone of blue, purple, pink, and brown to black. There are even green and red tones. All have six petals; the three upper petals are known as the standards, and the three lower ones as the falls. The base of the fall, the part of the petal that is narrower and constricted, is known as the haft or shoulder. The flowers bring into the garden not only colour but also scent. This fragrance can be fruity, musky, and spicy, like honey, and occasionally unpleasant.

Irises also produce very handsome linear foliage that contrasts perfectly against plants with differently shaped foliage, such as lungworts (*Pulmonaria* spp.), elephant's ears (*Bergenia* spp.), dead nettles (*Laminum* spp.), and hardy geraniums (*Geranium* spp.).

Irises are easy to grow, tolerating a wide range of conditions from very cold climates, where winter freezes the ground hard, right through to subtropical climates. Some irises like bright sunny borders with well-drained soil, others grow in dappled shade, and a handful thrive in full shade. Although some irises like acid soil, most grow in soil that is slightly acid to alkaline. Some like poor dry, stony soils, others grow in damp soil. Perhaps the best-known irises are those that grow in water.

The Plant and Flowers

Irises have been used symbolically for centuries in Europe and Asia. In Greek mythology Iris was the name of the rainbow goddess who passed messages between the heavens and earth. In doing so, she let her scarf scatter the fields below with the colours of the rainbow.

In another version of the myth, Iris was the messenger to Zeus born on the Greek island of Crete where the earliest known depiction of irises exists. About 2100 B.C. a fresco was painted on the walls of the Minoan palace of Knossos in Crete, depicting a young man holding an iris. Some think it could be a Xiphium iris, but it could easily be a Juno iris. After all, Juno, the Roman goddess of the moon, was married to Zeus's Roman equivalent, Jupiter.

Irises have also been used in heraldry, an art form that developed to aid medieval knights in recognizing each other during battle. Accounts vary on how the

Differently shaped foliage

name 'Fleur-de-lis' came about. According to one legend the name dates back to the end of the fifth century, during a time when Clovis, the king of the Franks, a people who lived along the lower part of the Rhine, was at battle with the Goths. Being hemmed in, Clovis was shown where to safely cross the Rhine by the presence of the yellow flag iris, *Iris pseudacorus*. Afterwards he took it as a mascot. Later, during the twelfth century, the iris was incorporated by the French king Louis VII into the royal coat of arms and renamed the 'Fleur-de-Louis'. Then, during the fourteenth century the English king Edward III added the iris to his royal coat of arms during the battles to gain the throne from the French king Phillip VI. The iris remained in the British coat of arms until 1801.

IRISES IN ART

In their abstract form irises can be found in ancient Persian embroidery and on tiles and pottery. In Japan irises have been used for centuries during festivals, and they have frequently been incorporated into embroideries and paintings, as well as being carved into crystal and jade.

Irises have often been portrayed in religious paintings, particularly those of the Virgin Mary and the birth of Christ. These include works by the most famous of painters, Leonardo da Vinci, Albrecht Durer, and Hugo van der Goes. Irises can be seen in vases, strewn across tables, and in a bunch of flowers together with lilies and columbines. In a painting of Queen Elizabeth I, which celebrates England's victory over Spain by the Armada, the virgin queen of England wears a dress embroidered with irises.

The iris is a flower of great beauty. The petals are translucent enough to allow light to shine through, brilliantly coloured, and three-dimensional in form. For these reasons irises have been used not only in religious iconology but also as subjects for many of Europe's famous painters. Dutch artists of the seventeenth century often combined bulbous irises with other cut flowers in their famous flower paintings, which nurserymen reportedly used as an early catalogue. In the nineteenth century, irises were featured in paintings by Auguste Renoir, Paul Cézanne, Vincent van Gogh, Odilon Redon, Paul Gauguin, and Claude Monet, whose garden at Giverny in France still attracts many visitors during the iris flowering season. Elizabeth Blackadder, a well-known modern Scottish painter, has produced many beautiful watercolours with irises and cats.

Irises are also mentioned in literature. William Shakespeare's play *Anthony and Cleopatra* refers to the iris as the 'vagabond flag', which indeed it is. Lord Byron, the nineteenth-century English poet, also mentioned iris in his poem, 'Childe Harold's Pilgrimage':

> Heaven is free
> From clouds, but of all colours seems to be
> Melted to one vast Iris of the West,
> Where the day joins the past eternity

IRISES IN MEDICINE

For centuries irises have been used in Europe and North America for medicine. *Iris versicolor* and *I. pseudacorus* produce iridin, or irisin, an odourless, bitter-tasting compound. In the United States, *I. versicolor* is known medicinally as blue flag. At one time it was used in a cure for syphilis, infections of the skin, and dropsy (edema). Today it is still an official drug used to purge the liver.

The roots of *Iris* 'Florentina', which is the white form of *I. pallida*, and *I. germanica* are known as orris root. In medieval times orris root was generally mixed with other herbs, such as hyssop, and honey, and used to treat stomach problems and skin disorders such as scrofula, which causes boils on the neck. In the mid-seventeenth century Nicolas Culpeper and John Gerard, writers of famous herbal books, documented the different ways in which orris root was used. It could be made into a potion to clear the body of phlegm, cramps, convulsions, and dropsy, and to cure choler (a liver dysfunction) and snakebites. To make the potion more palatable, it could be weakened with ale or wine. A poultice of orris root mixed with verdigris (a green substance that forms on copper), honey, and the root of the wild centaury was made to extract splinters from wounds.

During the nineteenth century orris root was cut into beads and bandaged on wounds that needed to be kept open. It was also used to alleviate bad breath. Servants who needed to disguise the smell of tobacco would chew chips of orris root, while wealthy gentlemen could suck lozenges. Chopped into thin sticks, the root was given to babies to chew during teething. Today it is still grown commercially in southern Europe and Morocco and used in toothpaste, tooth powder, and teething rings, but its most common use is in cosmetics and perfumes.

IRISES FOR SCENT

When freshly cut, iris roots have an earthy smell, but orris root contains irone, which, when dried over a long period, produces an ephemeral fragrance that is similar to violets. Pliny the Elder, a Roman scholar, mentioned that *Iris pallida* was used as an ingredient in perfume for wealthy people. It is still used today by the perfume industry as an essential oil and a fixative for other scents. It can be included in potpourri and scented sachets.

Author Gwendolyn Anley (1946) described a method for drying orris root so that it could be used in sachets to freshen linens and clothes in storage. She recommended lifting the rhizomes of *Iris* 'Florentina' or *I. pallida* in late July, washing them, and trimming the ends. Once cleaned up the roots should be peeled and then sliced into chips the width of a coin. The slices should then be laid on a wire rack to dry in a sunny spot that will not get rain, such as a greenhouse or cold frame. The chips must be turned occasionally until they are dry, then stored in an airtight bottle until required. The fragrance in dried orris root will last up to two years.

IRISES FOR COLOURING AND FLAVOURING

The flowers of irises have been used as a yellow dye and, when mixed with iron sulphate, the roots produce a black dye that is black enough to be used as a printing ink.

Irises have also been used as flavouring. Chianti, a local wine of Florence, was once flavoured with orris root. A piece of the root was placed into the vats to flavour the wine as it aged. The root has been used to flavour vermouth, gin, and some aromatic brandies. As a cooking ingredient, the leaves make a good sauce for fish, and the seeds, if peeled and roasted, can be used as a substitute for coffee.

IRISES FOR CUT FLOWERS

As both a housekeeper and a gardener, I love flowers in the house. Many types of irises make good cut flowers. All the bearded irises, including the aptly named Table (Miniature Tall Bearded) irises, can be used. Although each flower lasts only a day or two, there are many more flowers to follow.

Irises should be cut before the bud unfurls. This is particularly important with bearded irises as they have delicate petals which tear easily. Place cut stems immediately into a bucket of water. Once indoors in a vase, keep the stems tidy by daily removing old flowers.

The Xiphium irises, which include Dutch irises, have been bred for the cut flower market and bloom during June. Spuria irises, which bear a resemblance to Dutch irises, bloom later in July and are also good for cutting, as are Japanese, Siberian, Sino-Siberian, Pacific Coast, and Louisiana irises. Indeed, in Japan, irises have been used for centuries for indoor decoration.

Reblooming irises cut for autumn decoration: *Iris* 'Medway Valley', *I.* 'Pink Reprise', and *I.* 'Cordoba'

Botany and Classification

To better understand how irises differ from each other and from other groups of flowers, it is important to have a basic understanding of plant structure and plant relationships.

ROOTS

Irises grow from two types of roots, bulbous and rhizomatous. By far the largest number of species produce rhizomes, or underground stems, that create a storage system to enable the plants to survive in extreme conditions. The rhizomes can be large, as in the case of bearded irises, or small, as in the case of Siberian irises.

In some kinds of irises it is hard to see the rhizome, particularly when it comes to the water-loving types. All rhizomous irises produce fibrous roots, which die back each year so that new roots can be produced.

Bulbous irises also produce slender roots, but these emerge from the bottom of bulbs. Sometimes they are covered with a papery or netted overcoat. In the case of Juno irises, the roots are thick and fleshy.

LEAVES

Irises produce handsome leaves which can form broad clumps, upright tufts, or even creep along the ground. Bearded irises produce long, flat, sword-like leaves that are generally soft blue-green and create a fan. Others,

Roots of *Iris pseudacorus*

Bearded iris roots

Siberian iris roots

Bulbs of a Reticulata iris

Roots of *Iris* 'Dardanus', an aril iris

such as the Japonica irises, produce long dark green evergreen leaves. Siberian irises have slender, grassy leaves, while bulbous irises possess long, channelled leaves. Some irises have leaves that are tinted with purple at the base.

FLOWERS

All iris flowers have at least six petals, although some Japanese irises produce more. The petals vary in size and shape from thin and strap-like to broad and rounded. Some flowers have beards sitting at the back

Leaves of Tall Bearded irises

Iris 'Snowy Owl', a Tall Bearded iris with white beards

Roots of *Iris graeberiana*, a Juno iris

Leaves of Dutch irises in early spring

Iris tectorum, a crested iris

A seedling Siberian iris (from Jennifer Hewitt)

Iris 'Crystal Halo', a beardless Japanese iris

of the falls. Others, such as some aril irises, have beards on both the falls and the standards. All these plants are referred to as bearded irises, while those without beards are logically called beardless irises. Instead of beards they have colourful signals, raised ridges or crests. The style arms can also add a further dimension to the beauty of the iris flower. Most iris blooms are borne on tall, upright, branched stems; however, some of the smallest types are stemless.

The range of flower colours in irises is simply amazing—from white, yellow, orange, pink, and lilac to purple, blue, brown, and black with many tones and combinations of colour in between. No iris flower is truly red, although the Louisianas have orange-red tones.

In addition, the falls can be one colour, the standards another. The colours can be speckled, dotted, lined, and washed or layered over the petals. Among bearded or pogon irises the many different colour patterns have been given individual names, some of which are listed here. Occasionally these names are used to describe beardless and bulbous irises as well.

Amoena: White standards and coloured falls. Examples: *Iris* 'Crimson Snow', *I.* 'Seakist'.
Bicolour: Standards one colour, falls another. Examples: *Iris* 'Edith Wolford', *I.* 'Instant Hit'.
Luminata: Flower with an area of clear colour, which could be white, yellow, pink, or orange, and which surrounds the beard and shows as pale veining on darker falls. These flowers usually have petals with pale edges and style arms that are unmarked. Examples: *Iris* 'Fancy Dress', *I.* 'New Leaf'.
Plicata: Light-coloured flower with darker-coloured stipples and lines around the edge of the petals. Examples: *Iris* 'Going My Way', *I.* 'Queen In Calico'.
Self: Whole flower the same colour. Examples: *Iris* 'Mesmerizer', *I.* 'War Chief'.
Variegata: Yellow standards and red falls. Examples: *Iris* 'Bengal Tiger', *I.* 'Blatant'.

When it comes to the shape of the petal, iris flowers range from flat, where all the petals are horizontal to the flower stems, to very upright. The petals can also be ruffled, some more extravagantly than others. The Tall Bearded iris 'Rare Treat' has ruffled petals, while the petals of Japanese irises 'Electric Rays' and 'Kaleido-show' are large and spreading, and those of Siberian irises 'Caezar' and 'Nora Distin' are both upright (standards) and drooping (falls).

Finally, iris flowers can be extremely fragrant. Despite what some authorities say, most Tall Bearded irises possess some kind of scent. Often it is thick and sweet, like honey, but it can be flowery, spicy, or as sharp as citrus fruit. Sometimes it is unpleasant and smells

Iris 'Mesmerizer', a self

Iris 'Seakist', an amoena

Iris 'Instant Hit', a bicolour

Iris 'Kaleidoshow', a Japanese iris with large, spreading petals

Iris 'Nora Distin', a typical Siberian iris with upright standards and drooping falls

Iris 'Rare Treat', a Tall Bearded iris with ruffled petals

like cats. On a warm day a field of bearded irises can be quite overpowering. Reticulata irises are said to have a violet scent. *Iris graminea*, a dwarf Spuria, is commonly known as the plum tart iris because of its fragrance. Some Juno irises smell like peaches, at least to me. It must be remembered, however, that scent is very personal and, like colour, everyone interprets these things differently.

CHROMOSOMES

Occasionally chromosomes are mentioned in the plant descriptions. For those, like myself, who are not botanically minded, chromosomes are the little rod-shaped bodies in the nucleus of a cell that carry the genes. Chromosomes come in sets referred to in this book as 'diploid' and 'tetraploid'. Diploid plants have two sets of chromosomes, while tetraploids have four sets. Hybridizers find it useful to know the chromosome count of the plants they are working with as plants with differing chromosome counts are difficult to cross-pollinate. Otherwise chromosomes help the gardener recognize certain types of plants. Diploid plants tend to be more delicate with smaller flowers and flower stems. Tetraploid plants often have bigger flowers with petals of greater substance, thicker stems, and a wider range of colours.

CLASSIFICATION

Many people think of plants simply as being there: growing every day, needing to be planted, watered, picked, eaten, or weeded out. To the botanist, plants present many fascinating questions, such as how do they relate to each other and, if plants look similar to one another, do they belong to the same family. To help answer these questions botanists devise family trees, but because plants cannot tell us their history in the same way humans can pass on their history from one generation to the next, these family trees are continually reassessed when new plants are discovered or new ways of looking at plants are developed. This system, known as classification, can also help the gardener. Classification tells us not only where a plant comes from but also where it can be grown and with which plants it will cross-pollinate to produce new hybrids.

Irises are members of the family Iridaceae, which includes, among others, crocuses, crocosmias, moraeas, and sisyrinchiums. Although the irises in this book originate from the Northern Hemisphere, other family members come from the Southern Hemisphere. Botanists divide the genus *Iris* into six subgenera. Plants are assigned to a subgenus based on their root system, form of the flower, seeds, seed pods, and distribution in nature. The first subgenus is once again called *Iris* and includes the bearded irises, sometimes called pogon irises, *pogon* being Greek for 'beard'. Next is subgenus *Limniris*, which includes the beardless irises, also called apogon irises, followed by four smaller subgenera: *Nepalenis* (not included in this book) and three bulbous subgenera, *Xiphium*, *Scorpiris* (Juno irises), and *Hermodatyloides* (Reticulata irises). Each subgenus may be divided into sections, which in turn are divided into species. Still smaller units of classification may be used. These categories are listed and defined here.

Genus: a group of closely related species
Subgenus: a division of the genus
Section: a division of the subgenus
Species: the wild forms of a genus
Subspecies: a form of a species
Variety: a selected or man-made plant grown in cultivation
Cultivar: a cultivated variety

Throughout the text I have usually used the word *variety* in its non-technical sense to mean *cultivar* as it is the more commonly used term.

Swedish botanist Carl Linnaeus first devised the botanical system in current use. He listed no more than 13 of the *Iris* species we know today. Over the years many new species have been described and included in the classification. Some were discovered to be hybrids of species and have since been removed. Further confusion can be created when botanists draw up alternative classifications.

The basic classification of genus *Iris* used today is based on work done by English botanist William Rickatson Dykes, who published *The Genus* Iris in 1912. Other eminent iris authorities have since modified the classification. The subsequent work of George H. M. Lawrence (1953) and Georgi I. Rodionenko (1961) resulted in a reshuffling of Dykes's classification. Lawrence shifted the bearded irises into one section, including the aril irises with the pogon irises. A few years later Rodionenko, a Russian botanist of great note, split the irises further, placing the bulbous species of section *Xiphium* (commonly known as Dutch and English irises) and the Juno irises into separate genera.

The story, however, does not stop there. In *The Iris* (1981), Brian Mathew drew up a further classification based largely on Dykes's work, but incorporating some alterations made by Lawrence and Rodionenko. An authority on irises, Mathew moved the Juno and Xiphium irises back into the genus *Iris*. In the present volume, I have followed Mathew's classification:

Subgenus *Iris*
　Section *Iris* (bearded irises or pogons)
　Section *Psammiris*
　Section *Oncocyclus*
　Section *Regelia*
　Section *Hexapogon*
　Section *Pseudoregelia*

Subgenus *Limniris* (beardless irises, or apogons)
　Section *Lophiris* (Evansia irises)
　Section *Limniris*
　　Series *Chinenses*
　　Series *Vernae*
　　Series *Ruthenicae*
　　Series *Tripetalae*
　　Series *Sibiricae* (Siberica irises)
　　Series *Californicae* (Pacific Coast irises)
　　Series *Longipetalae*
　　Series *Laevigatae* (Laevigata irises)
　　Series *Hexagonae* (Louisiana irises)
　　Series *Prismaticae*
　　Series *Spuriae* (Spuria irises)
　　Series *Foetidissimae* (*Iris foetidissima*)
　　Series *Tenuifoliae*
　　Series *Ensatae*
　　Series *Syriacae*
　　Series *Unguiculares* (*Iris unguicularis*)
Subgenus *Nepalensis*
Subgenus *Xiphium* (Dutch, Spanish, and English irises)
Subgenus *Scorpiris* (Juno irises)
Subgenus *Hermodactyloides* (Reticulata iris)

About This Book

This book arranges iris descriptions in three separate groups: bearded irises, beardless irises, and bulbous irises. These groups are subdivided into still smaller groups following the botanical classification of the genus.

In each chapter, the first plants to be described are the wild forms or species of the group, listed in alphabetical order by scientific name. The name of a species is always written in *italics*, as are the names of subspecies (subsp.), varieties (var.), and formas (f.).

Following the plant name is the name of the person who first discovered it and the year in which the plant name was published. In some cases in the past, the plant may have been known by another name, referred to as a synonym. The name in the text, however, is the current botanically correct name.

After the collector's name comes the country or countries in which the plant grows in the wild. The plant description follows.

All species can vary greatly, particularly if plants are distributed across a wide region. Colours, height, petal shape, and flower stems can be markedly different; however, the plants within a group of irises will have something in common, usually the shape of the seed. Therefore the flower description is as broad as possible.

Each species plant description concludes with the plant's height and flowering time in the wild. My main reference for this data was *A Guide to Species Irises* (1997), published by the Species Group of the British Iris Society. I have tried to be as general as possible when giving flowering times. This is because even here in Britain the blooming period of say, Tall Bearded irises, can vary by two to four weeks depending on where you live in the country. Britain being an island has a warm, wet oceanic climate and can have irises in bloom from midwinter to midautumn, which is generally from January to October. The bulbous Reticulata irises start the season and the reblooming, or remontanting, Tall Bearded irises end it. Most irises bloom from late spring to high summer, which is from May to mid-July in Britain. For those who garden in continental climates, where the winters come earlier and last longer, the flowering period may be more concentrated.

The second part of each chapter presents descriptions of the hybrids of the group, again in alphabetical order by scientific name. Hybrid names appear in regular font (not italics) and are enclosed by single quotation marks. The name of the hybridizer and the year the plant was registered follow the plant name and are enclosed in parenthesis. I have chosen to mention the year of registration rather than introduction as this information is more readily available, particularly for older cultivars. In most cases this information comes from documents filed at the time the iris was registered. Most of these details are logged with the American Iris Society and supplied by the hybridizer. They can be found in the American Iris Society registration Web site.

Following the description of the flower are the plant's height and flowering time. These data are very general as plants can vary when grown in different parts of the world. The flowering season is noted as early, mid, or late season. Early season hybrids open first; midseason hybrids, which tend to be in the majority, produce flowers in the middle part of a flowering period; and late season hybrids open towards the end of the main flowering period.

Hybrid plant descriptions end with the plant's parentage. The presence of a number of parenthesis indicates that some of the parents have not been introduced. The term 'sibling' is also used for irises that have not been registered but are related to plants from the same cross that have been introduced; the name of the known cross precedes the word 'sibling'. The parentage is given, not only as a general guide for those wishing to make their own crosses, but as a part of a hybrid's history. For those interested enough, the book contains varieties with parents that have also been described. By looking at these, it is possible to see where a plant gets its characteristics.

Iris Societies and Awards

Iris societies exist worldwide and are full of enthusiastic plant lovers. The British Iris Society, founded in 1922, and the American Iris Society, established in 1927, were among the earliest. Since then many more societies have been created. Some of these are very specialized, aimed only at a specific type of iris, while others are more general and often include all types of irises. Such groups are a wonderful way of meeting like-minded people and include individuals who breed and grow irises commercially. These societies usually produce informative bulletins, hold shows throughout the flowering season, and organize symposiums annually to enable iris lovers to exchange and gain information.

Iris societies also hand out awards to recognize members who are involved in the society and the best new plants. Although medals are awarded to all types of irises, the most important is the Dykes Medal. Irises to be judged are grown in trial grounds for several years and awarded points for their flowers and performance during the growing season. Awards are then given to the plants with the greatest number of points.

Showing irises at a local British Iris Society show

PART ONE BEARDED IRISES

The bearded iris gains its name from the line of thick hairs that emerges from the throat of the flower. These hairs form a long, furry caterpillar towards the back of the falls, and their purpose is to guide insects, such as bees, towards the pollen. Bearded irises are the largest group with the greatest number of cultivated varieties. They are also the most popular group of irises for garden use.

In the wild, bearded irises grow in an area that stretches from the Mediterranean to Southeast Asia and from the Arabian Peninsula north to southern Russia. They usually are found in a sunny place where the soil is poor and well drained. The flowers, which always have large petals, are borne on stiff stems above broad, sword-like, and usually soft green leaves. These form a handsome clump that is invaluable in a garden.

The bearded group is divided into two smaller groups: the pogon irises and aril irises. Pogon irises are the bearded irises we all know and love. They are cultivated throughout Europe, in North America in states that are north of Florida, and in Australia and New Zealand. The arils, which have both beards and rhizomes, are distinguished by the white appendage that is attached to the seed. These are very exotic, but difficult to grow in the countries where pogon irises grow as they need almost desert conditions to thrive. Arils include the Oncocyclus, Regelia, and Pseudoregelia irises. This latter group is not included in this book as so few plants are available to gardeners; however, the beauty of the flowers has been so admired by hybridizers that crosses between these and pogon irises have produced plants called arilbreds.

The information given here is for bearded or pogon irises of garden origin.

Horticultural Classification of Bearded Irises

By the 1950s the number of bearded cultivars was so large and varied that the American Iris Society decided to separate the hybrids into different categories, using both height and flowering time. This classification has changed slightly over the years and is now recognized throughout the world. Although the system was created by iris breeders, it has become a useful tool for gardeners to help choose the right iris for the right spot and to select plants that will extend the flowering period in the garden.

Miniature Dwarf Bearded (MDB): These grow up to 20 cm (8 in.) tall and bloom during midspring. They are the first bearded irises to flower and form low, spreading clumps with a mass of small blooms. They are useful for growing in rockeries and alpine gardens.

Standard Dwarf Bearded (SDB): These grow 20–38 cm (8–15 in.) tall and bloom in midspring after the MDB irises. The flowers are borne just above a broad clump of leaves. These irises are ideal for growing at the front of a border.

Iris 'Apricot Drops', a Miniature Tall Bearded iris

Intermediate Bearded (IB): These grow 38–71 cm (15–28½ in.) tall and bloom after SDB irises. The flowers are borne above the foliage. These irises are vigorous enough to grow in a border with other perennials.

Border Bearded (BB): These grow 38–71 cm (15–28½ in.) tall and bloom after the IB irises at the same time as the MTB and TB irises. They are smaller forms of TB irises, but like IB irises are vigorous enough grow in a mixed border.

Miniature Tall Bearded (MTB): These grow 38–71 cm (15–28½ in.) tall and bloom at the same time as BB and TB irises. They produce delicate flowers and flower stems but do not grow as vigorously as the BB and TB irises. When grown in a border they should not be allowed to be swamped by other plants.

Tall Bearded (TB): These grow more than 71 cm (28½ in.) tall and are the largest, most glamorous bearded irises and the last group to bloom. They can be grown in a flowerbed of their own, as a focal point, or combined with other plants; however, they must be given space so the rhizomes get enough sun to create flowers for the following season.

Cultivation and Maintenance

Although bearded irises are easy to grow, they do need to be grown correctly. The rhizomes need to be baked by the sun to produce flowers the following flowering season. When planting bearded irises, make sure they are spaced so that neighbouring plants will not encroach on them.

Many of the older Tall Bearded cultivars thrive with partial shade and, in climates where the summers are very hot, a partially shady site can be advantageous. The soil in all situations must be well drained. If it is wet, the rhizome will rot. In heavier soils, dig in sand, grit, or well-rotted compost before planting to allow the soil to drain. In very wet soils, particularly those that are wet during the winter or those that contain a lot of clay, plant bearded irises on a well-drained slope or in a raised bed. The soil needs to be balanced and not too

Iris 'Az Ap', an Intermediate Bearded iris

Iris 'Blackbeard', a Border Bearded iris

Standard Dwarf Bearded irises on trial at the Royal Horticultural Society Garden, Wisley, Surrey, England

Iris 'Coral Carpet', a Miniature Dwarf Bearded iris

Iris pallida, a Tall Bearded iris

rich. Bearded irises can cope with a small amount of acidity, but a very acid soil will cause the rhizomes to rot.

PLANTING DISTANCE

Generally Tall Bearded irises should be spaced at least 30 cm (12½ in.) apart. Smaller varieties can be placed as close as 23 cm (9 in.) apart. For the best effect, plant Tall Bearded irises in groups of odd numbers, preferably in threes. If they are being planted in a border with other perennials, place them in a triangle or circle with the nonfoliage ends of the rhizomes pointing inwards, towards each other. This gives the plants an open central area so the sun can get to the rhizomes and provide a barrier to prevent other plants from creeping over and between them.

PLANTING TIME

The best time to plant bearded irises is just before the new roots start to grow. Traditionally this is about six weeks after flowering; however, I feel it is much better to divide and replant bearded irises in early autumn or after the hottest and driest part of the summer. At this time the rhizomes are fully mature, they have become dormant, and the ground is damper and still warm. Bearded irises can also be planted in spring, although doing so means they are unlikely to flower the same summer.

TRIMMING FOR PLANTING

When planting a bearded iris, first trim the foliage back to the length of a hand and, again this is traditional, into a pointed V shape. This stops the plant from popping out of the ground in windy conditions and reduces water loss after planting. Also trim back the old, long roots. As these roots die back after the plant flowers, they are simply there to anchor the rhizome into the ground until the new roots grow. Trimming old roots not only makes it easier to plant the rhizome, but also stops birds, such as rooks, from pulling at stray roots that resemble worms and uprooting the plants.

HOW TO PLANT

Many books will tell you to dig a shallow hole, leave a small hump in the middle of the hole, put the rhizome on this with the roots spread out to each side, back fill the hole, and firm the soil well. I see no reason to do this. At our nursery we plant bearded irises by machine. The machine makes a furrow, drops the iris in, then pushes soil back over the plant. Therefore a simpler method of planting bearded irises is to dig a hole deep enough to accommodate the root, put the roots in the hole making sure to leave no gap under the base of the rhizome, and then back fill the hole with soil.

PLANTING DEPTH

The depth a rhizome is planted is important. Summers in Britain are not as sunny as those of hotter regions; therefore, English gardeners need to plant the rhizome at soil level so that it gets the maximum amount of sun. In other areas where the summers are hot and sunny, the rhizome should be planted up to 2.5 cm (1 in.) below soil level. Finally, in gardens that are frequently irrigated or in areas with high rainfall, the rhizome should be planted high up, on a mound of soil, so that water will not sit around the rhizome. If planted a little too deeply, a rhizome tends to push itself back up to the surface, that is, if it does not rot first.

WATERING AT PLANTING TIME

In areas with high rainfall it is not necessary to water the rhizome after planting. If no rainfall is expected, watering will stimulate new root growth and be beneficial to the plant. In my experience, only a third to a half of all bearded irises will produce flowers the following year, but all should flower by their second season. If they do not, make sure the irises are in full sun, get water during the time they produce the flower stems, are not planted too deeply, and face no competition from surrounding plants.

FERTILIZING

Because irises are vigorous plants, it is beneficial, though not critical, to fertilize them twice a year, particularly if they are growing in a poor soil or have been in the same spot for more than a year. Do this once in spring when plants are putting on new leaf growth, as it will help the production of strong flower spikes and foliage, and again after plants have bloomed, when new roots are being produced. A granular slow-release fertilizer low in nitrogen is ideal. Fertilizers made from seaweed are also okay, as is a dressing of four parts bone meal, two parts superphosphate of lime, and one part each of sulphate of ammonia and sulphate of potash. Mix these ingredients thoroughly and apply at a rate of 60 to 75 g per square meter (2–2½ oz. per square yard). Over fertilization will produce soft growth, which can lead to rhizome rot. Too much nitrogen, too much water, or an acid soil will have the same effect on iris rhizomes.

DIVIDING

Bearded irises need to be lifted and divided at least every three years. Failure to do so will lead to fewer flowers. Some varieties, particularly smaller ones like the Miniature Dwarf Bearded irises and the more vigorous Standard Dwarf Bearded irises, should be divided every two years. To do this, ease the old clump out of the ground with a fork. Shake off the soil and snap the new rhizomes from the old central rhizome, discarding the old rhizome. Tall Bearded irises can be left out of the ground for up to a month; however, rhizomes of smaller types may not last that long and should be planted soon after lifting.

TIDYING UP AND PREVENTING DISEASE

To prevent disease it is important to keep bearded irises tidy. Remove dead, dying, and diseased leaves frequently, and snap off spent flowers stems at the base. It is not necessary to cut the foliage back in the autumn, but old leaves do harbour fungal spores, slugs, and snails during the winter.

WINTER PROTECTION

Bearded irises are very tough, particularly the older hybrids. In mild and temperate areas they do not need winter protection. Elsewhere severe frosts can uproot the rhizomes, therefore bearded irises should be protected by piling the soil up around the rhizome or by covering it with layers of straw and leaves. Be sure to remove this covering in spring.

New rhizomes attached to old rhizomes

Untidy leaves

CHAPTER 1

Tall Bearded Irises

OF ALL THE IRISES FOUND in gardens, the Tall Bearded irises are the most common and certainly the most dramatic. They are the last group of bearded irises to bloom, producing large three-dimensional flowers on strong stems high above broad, sword-shaped leaves. Each stem can be branched up to four times, with the most modern varieties producing as many as 13 flowers in one flowering session. The blooming period usually begins as the Intermediate Bearded irises start to fade and continues for two or three weeks; however, some modern varieties produce flowers for up to four weeks at a time. The flower stems of Tall Bearded irises grow from 70 to 102 cm (27–41 in.) tall. The flowers are 10–17 cm (4–7 in.) across and, like all bearded irises, can be found in an infinite range and combination of colours.

Early Hybridizers of Tall Bearded Irises

Although Tall Bearded irises have been grown in Europe for hundreds of years, mainly for their medicinal properties, it was not until the nineteenth century that named varieties started to appear. At this time they

were not known as Tall Bearded irises. The plants were raised from seed pollinated by bees. Most of the plants were crosses between *Iris pallida* and *I. variegata*. Flower colours were often murky, but as so many variations occurred, hundreds of varieties were introduced, the majority of which are no longer grown.

Around 1822 a Frenchman called de Bure named the first hybrid, a plicata called *Iris* 'Buriensis'. Other influential hybridizers of the time include Lémon, Jacques, and Verdier. Although the French first dominated the iris market, elsewhere in Europe hybridizers were at work. In Germany, the nurseries of Von Berg and of Goos and Koenemann added iris hybrids to the ever-increasing list of names, and in Belgium Louis van Houtte introduced plants. Later, during the latter half of the century, British breeders also began to introduce bearded irises, Peter Barr and Amos Perry being the most important of these. By the end of the nineteenth century, so many new named hybrids had come on the market that hybridizers believed irises could be developed no further. How wrong could they have been?

SIR MICHAEL FOSTER

The most important developments in nineteenth-century iris hybridization were due to biologists not nurserymen. During the latter part of the century new species were introduced to Europe from Asia Minor. In Britain, botanist Michael Foster, a professor of physiology at Cambridge, collected and grew as many iris species as he could, including newly found plants sent to Britain by missionaries travelling through Asia Minor. Most of these plants arrived without names, but two of them in particular caught the eye of both French and British iris growers. One was called *Iris* 'Ricardi' after the person who collected it in Palestine. Foster named the other *I.* 'Amas', after Amasia, the area in which the plant was found. Unbeknown to hybridists then, *I. germanica* 'Amas' and *I.* 'Ricardi' were tetraploids. Up until this time all bearded irises had been diploids with small blooms, delicate petals, and slender stems. The new species, when crossed with diploids, produced varieties with larger flowers, thick and velvety petals, and stronger stems.

Foster took advantage of these new species and became one of the first hybridizers to use scientific knowledge in his crosses. Unfortunately, he did not record the parentage of his plants. After Foster's death in 1907, nurseryman Robert Wallace of Essex, England, introduced many of Foster's plants to the gardening world. Most have since disappeared, but *Iris* 'Mrs George Darwin', *I.* 'Mrs Horace Darwin', and *I.* 'Kashmir White' can still be obtained. These were just a few of the varieties exported to the United States, and Foster's work inspired many future iris lovers on both sides of the Atlantic. Foster was respected not only for his work but also for his generous sharing of so much of his knowledge with others, a tradition that continues among iris hybridizers today.

ARTHUR BLISS

When Foster died, he left behind a large collection of notes which Ellen Willmott loaned to William R. Dykes, the author of *The Genus* Iris. The notes outlined Foster's work and helped Dykes investigate the species

Iris 'Susan Bliss'

further. Dykes believed that many bearded species were hybrids and to test this theory asked a friend, retired engineer Arthur Bliss, to make crosses between them. Among the plants Dykes sent Bliss were plicatas, amoenas, neglectas, asiaticas, and *I. squalens*.

Bliss crossed an asiatica with a Tall Bearded hybrid named *Iris* 'Cordelia'. The asiatica parent died but is thought to have been 'Amas' or something similar. The cross, however, resulted in one of the most important irises ever raised: *I.* 'Dominion' was introduced in 1912. Nearly twenty-five years later, in 1936, F. X. Schreiner, the owner of a well-known iris nursery in the United States, considered *I.* 'Dominion' to be the most important landmark in the history of iris hybridizing. The petals of this hybrid were more velvety and thicker than those of any hybrid previously introduced. Robert Wallace included *I.* 'Dominion' in his catalogue, selling it for the vast sum of five guineas.

Iris 'Dominion' went on to parent *I.* 'Depute Nomblot' (F. Cayeux 1929) and *I.* 'Dauntless' (Connell 1927), both of which became important parents themselves. Years later Melba Hamblen (Warburton and Hamblen 1978) commented that Bliss was the greatest hybridizer of the transitional period of iris breeding.

The Early Twentieth Century

Bliss was not the only breeder to produce hybrids that included the newly discovered tetraploid species. In France, Vilmorin introduced *Iris* 'Alcazar' in 1910 and, due to the Great War of 1914 to 1918, delayed introducing *I.* 'Ambassadeur' until 1920. By that time the plant's stock had multiplied so much that *I.* 'Ambassadeur' could be bought very cheaply, and within a few years it was grown

throughout France, Britain, and the United States.

The period just before and after the Great War saw massive improvements in the quality of the bearded iris flower. Wister summed up the situation perfectly in *The World of Irises* (Warburton and Hamblen 1978) when he said that iris lovers 'cannot realise the thrills that came in the two and three years after the close of the First World War to those who had known only the poorer iris of the past century.'

It was the Americans who did most to improve the Tall Bearded iris during the early years of the twentieth century. Amateur enthusiast Bertrand Farr, the owner of a music shop in Pennsylvania, saw Peter Barr's catalogue from England and imported the entire collection. Farr fell in love with the modern hybrids he received and promptly sold the music shop to start his own nursery. He not only encouraged others to grow irises, but also turned his hand to producing bearded irises, one of which was *Iris* 'Quaker Lady'. Introduced in 1909, this diploid iris is still available today.

The Sass brothers, Jacob and Hans, had emigrated with their parents in 1884 from Germany to Nebraska. Hans brought with him an interest in botany, but once in America both brothers started breeding bearded irises. Over the years they introduced many varieties of historical importance. One of Hans's most important introductions was the yellow-flowered *Iris* 'King Tut', which was used to raise the famous *I.* 'Rameses'. Jacob used 'Rameses', which was awarded the Dykes Medal in 1932, to create *I.* 'Ola Kala', which won the Dykes Medal in 1948 and is still sold today. Another Sass hybrid, 'Prairie Sunset', was awarded the Dykes Medal in 1943.

By the end of the 1930s, some of the seedlings produced by the Sass brothers were producing flowers with bumpy edges to the petals. These bumps, now know as lacing, were at first considered unsightly, but soon they gained popularity, and other hybridizers, such as Agnes Whiting and David Hall, began actively introducing bearded irises with laced flowers.

Another great advance in iris breeding came in 1939 when Clara Rees introduced *Iris* 'Snow Flurry', a white-flowered hybrid with ruffles. Like *I.* 'Dominion', *I.* 'Snow Flurry' was used to develop the shape of the iris flower by introducing ruffles to the edges of the petals and thus breaking the mould of tailored, smoothly shaped flowers.

Many of today's most famous iris nurseries were established during this time. In the 1920s Frank X. Schreiner, an amateur grower, opened an iris nursery in Minnesota. He imported many of the newer European varieties including ones from Cayeux and Vilmorin in France, and Arthur Bliss in England. Schreiner was the first American grower to import *Iris* 'Dominion'. Although he never raised irises, he trained his two sons to do so. Soon after Frank's death in 1945, the family moved the nursery to Oregon where other iris growers were already established and the soil was more suitable. Three generations later Schreiner's is arguably the largest iris grower in the world. A visit to the nursery during the flowering season, when it resembles the bulb fields of Holland, is an awe-inspiring sight.

The Mid-Twentieth Century

The Second World War did much to discourage commercial European iris growers from raising new hybrids. Even Amos Perry, famous in Britain for introducing many herbaceous plants, replaced his enthusiasm for irises with growing food to aid the war effort. This was the time American iris breeders, living in relative peace, made even more advances. Size, substance, and colour choices of the flowers of Tall Bearded irises increased considerably. Breeders began to select the features they wanted to work on. In Chicago, Orville Fay introduced white hybrids with improved hardiness. Many of his hybrids are still sold today including *Iris* 'Arctic Flame', *I.* 'New Snow', and *I.* 'Cliffs of Dover'. Introduced in 1960, *I.* 'Arctic Flame' was the first white Tall Bearded iris to have red beards, the result of 10 years of effort and five generations of seedlings.

While Fay worked on white irises, David Hall, a Canadian who lived in the United States, worked on pink ones, again with red beards. At the time, pink irises were neither truly pink nor hardy. Most of them were pink-orange or pink-lilac. Hall introduced *Iris* 'Cherie', which won a Dykes Medal in 1951, 'Palomino', and 'Spring Festival'.

Another very important hybridizer during this period was Paul Cook. Known mainly for his work on shorter bearded irises, Paul also introduced many larger ones that were a great advancement on what was already available. These included *Iris* 'Deep Black' and *I.* 'Whole Cloth', an amoena admired for the width of its flaring falls and purity of colour and a winner of the Dykes Medal in 1962. Cook had a policy of not making further crosses with his introductions, but others used them extensively. *Iris* 'Whole Cloth' produced a vast range of different-coloured amoena seedlings, and today many modern hybrids contain it in their parentage including some of the black varieties raised by Schreiner's in Oregon.

Meanwhile back in Britain during the 1960s Harry Randall was doing much to promote irises. Hall generously sent pollen from one of his pink seedlings with Harry Randall to Cedric Morris in Britain. This pollen later produced a pink Tall Bearded hybrid Randall called *Iris* 'Strathmore' after the home of the then Queen Mother, Elizabeth. Randall's enthusiasm for the genus frequently took him to the United States, where he obtained pollen of the newest irises. This sharing of ideas and pollen is one of the most endearing qualities to be found among those who are passionate about irises. Hall, Fay, Blodget, Reckamp and Rudolph, all hybridizers whose irises are featured in this book, exchanged pollen during the middle years of the century.

The Late Twentieth Century

The 1960s and 1970s saw an increase in the size of Tall Bearded iris flowers, but no great advances in quality were made until the 1980s and 1990s. Among the most influential iris hybridizers in this new generation are Barry Blyth of Melbourne, Australia, and Keith Keppel of Salem, Oregon, who have been raising seedlings for 50 years. Their work and that of Joe Ghio in Santa Cruz, California, has increased the choice of flower shape, height, and colours available.

Blyth and Keppel regularly visit each other and exchange both ideas and pollen. Blyth has registered more than 800 hybrids with the American Iris Society, including Tall Bearded irises and many median irises. His plants tend to be unconventional. Many are heavily ruffled and unusual in colours with extraordinary patterning. Keppel, working first in California, became known for his plicata irises. Subsequently, he has done much to improve the luminata types.

Over the years California has been home to many famous hybridizers, such as William Mohr, who worked around the beginning of the century, and Sydney Mitchell, who continued Mohr's work. Around 1940 Jim Gibson started to hybridize for plicata-style Tall Bearded irises, a dozen of which are featured in this chapter. Another prolific hybridizer was Joe Gatty, who like David Hall worked to improve pink varieties. Many of his seedlings, which have extravagantly ruffled petals with excellent substance, were introduced by Keppel.

In the late twentieth century iris flowers have developed further than the early hybridizers could have imagined. Some plants have become exceptional. *Iris* 'Edith Wolford' (Hager 1986) epitomizes the extraordinary bicolour bearded iris. Irises with broken (that is, unstable) colours have made their way into our gardens. Brad Kasperek in Utah is largely responsible for popularizing such irises, and many of his introductions have names with an African theme. Horns and spoons extending from the beard have also, after many years, found favour. Once considered unusual, like hybrids with laced petals, hybrids sporting long extensions from the beards have been awarded the Dykes Medal in the United States. Many of these varieties can be attributed to Monty Byers.

During more recent years, Californian George Sutton has been introducing many bearded irises with elongated beards. The effect of the Dykes Medal award has been to legitimize what in the past were controversial developments among Tall Bearded irises. Lloyd Austin working in the 1960s in the United States first began introducing new hybrids which were then known as 'novelty'

or 'space age' irises. Today *Iris* 'Mesmerizer' and *I.* 'Thornbird', among other hybrids with spoons and horns, are included in lists without being segregated.

Raising new bearded irises is still very much an American affair, and much of it is being done in Oregon, home to some of the world's most active iris breeders and biggest growers such as Schreiner's, Cooley's, Paul Black, Thomas Johnson, Vicki and Jim Craig, and Keith Keppel. It is unquestionably the place to be during the iris flowering season if you are a lover of irises.

Hybridizing with Tall Bearded irises in Europe is confined to only a few individuals. In Britain, Brian Dodsworth, a retired director of Raleigh Bicycles, has had more success with his tall varieties than anyone else. In Italy it is Bianco, while in France the grandson of the founder of Cayeux irises, Richard, introduces many new varieties each year. These are grown in North America and Britain.

Those who love and breed bearded irises can be found throughout Europe, North America, Australia, and New Zealand. These hybrids are truly worldwide garden plants and generous ones, too. If it was not for the hybridizers mentioned here, and many more that I could not include, none of the following plants could be enjoyed by gardeners around the world.

TALL BEARDED IRIS SPECIES & THEIR COLLECTED FORMS

Iris biliottii M. Foster 1887
Asia Minor
The bright violet flowers have yellow markings and brown veins on the hafts. The standards are lighter in tone and nearer to blue. The flower is borne on a well-branched stem and is

scented. The leaves are dark green. Height: 91 cm (36½ in.). Bloom: early season.

Iris croatica I. Horvat 1956
North Croatia
The dark violet flowers have long, narrow falls and upright standards that are paler in colour. White veins mark the hafts. The pale blue beards are tipped with yellow. The leaves are grey-green. Height: 75 cm (30 in.). Bloom: early season.

Iris cypriana Baker & M. Foster 1888
Cyprus
The large red-lilac flowers have deeper-coloured veins on the falls, while the standards are a little paler in colour. The hafts are veined with white, and the white beards are tipped with orange. The foliage is evergreen. The rhizome is liable to rot in wet climates. Height: to 100 cm (40 in.). Bloom: June.

Iris croatica

Iris germanica 'Amas' (M. Foster 1885)
Asia Minor

This tetraploid, once known as *Iris germanica* var. *macrantha*, was used in the early twentieth century as a parent of many modern Tall Bearded irises. The flowers have blue-purple falls and light blue-purple standards. White veins appear on the hafts, and the pale blue beards are tipped with yellow. Height: to 70 cm (28 in.). Bloom: early season.

Iris kashmiriana Baker 1877
Kashmir, Afghanistan, western Pakistan

The white flowers are marked by greenish-yellow veins around the hafts, and the white beards are tipped with yellow. Each flower is carried on a stout stem with only one or two branches. This species is the most easterly growing of the bearded irises and seems to be confined to cultivation in gardens or graveyards. It is not totally hardy in Western Europe, but as a tetraploid it was a parent to our modern bearded irises. Height: to 75 cm (30 in.). Bloom: early season.

Iris mesopotamica Dykes 1913
Middle East

This bearded species can no longer be found in the wild. The flowers have soft purple falls that are deeper in colour in the centre and veined with bronze over a white ground on the hafts. The white beards become yellow at the throat. The standards are lighter than the falls. Each stem carries two or three scented flowers. Height: to 120 cm (41 in.). Bloom: early season.

Iris pallida Lambert 1789
North Italy, Slovenia, Croatia, Bosnia

Common in gardens throughout Western Europe, this perfect iris produces pale violet-blue flowers with white beards that are tipped yellow towards the back. The falls and standards, unlike those of many other bearded species, are very short and form a neatly shaped flower that is not damaged in poor weather conditions. In the wild the flower can vary from deep violet to almost pink. It is scented. The grey-green foliage is resistant to disease. Early hybridizers used this species as a parent to create other bearded irises. It is sometimes known as Dalmatian iris. Height: to 110 cm (44 in.). Bloom: early season.

Iris pallida 'Argentea Variegata'

This plant has foliage with yellow stripes, whereas *Iris pallida* 'Variegata' has white stripes. Height: 60–90 cm (24–36 in.). Bloom: early season.

Iris pallida 'Princess Beatrice' (Barr 1898)

Also known as *Iris pallida* subsp. *pallida*, this garden variety of great beauty produces flowers similar to the species but later in the season; they open just as the those of the species finish and are slightly smaller, on more slender stems. Like the species, the selection has disease-resistant foliage and is very fragrant. Height: to 97 cm (38¾ in.).

Iris pallida 'Variegata'

The foliage of this plant has white stripes. Like the yellow-striped *Iris pallida* 'Argentea Variegata', this selection does not produce a great quantity of flowers when compared with the plain-leaved forms. Both selections multiply slowly but are decorative. Height: to 91 cm (36½ in.). Bloom: early season.

Iris trojana Kerner 1887
Western Asia Minor

The large flowers have round, violet standards and dark purple-violet falls. Copper veins sit on a yellow background around the hafts. The white beards are tipped with yellow, and the flowers are borne low down on sturdy well-branched stems. Height: 70–120 cm (28–45 in.). Bloom: early season.

Iris germanica 'Amas'

Iris mesopotamica

Iris pallida

Dykes Medal

The Dykes Medal was established by the British Iris Society (BIS) to commemorate the work of Englishman William Rickartson Dykes. In 1913 Dykes published *The Genus* Iris, a book in which he reorganized the classification of the genus. Sadly, Dykes was killed in a road accident in 1926. A year later the first Dykes Medal was awarded. The BIS now presents this annual award jointly with the American Iris Society to the best iris raised in North America, and since 1983 with the Australian Iris Society to the best iris bred in both Australia and New Zealand. The BIS also awards the Dykes Medal to a British hybrid, though not every year. It was awarded in France starting in 1928 but suspended in 1938 due to the Second World War and never reinstated.

TALL BEARDED IRIS HYBRIDS

Iris 'Abbey Road' (D. Silverberg 1994) The creamy lemon, scented flowers have standards that are a deeper tone of colour than the falls. The rounded petals are very ruffled, while the standards just touch at the top. The beards are soft yellow. Height: 89 cm (35½ in.). Bloom: midseason. Parentage: 'Pleated Gown' × 'Ganges Moon'.

Iris 'Afternoon Delight' (R. Ernst 1983) This large frilly variety has laced petals that pale with age. The standards are caramel and sit above the pink-lilac falls with their matching caramel edging. The white beards are tipped with yellow towards the back. Height: 91 cm (36½ in.). Bloom: midseason. Parentage: ('Countryman' × 'Outreach') × ('Mary Frances' × 'Lombardy').

Iris pallida 'Princess Beatrice'

Iris pallida 'Variegata'

Iris 'Abbey Road'

Iris trojana

Iris 'Afternoon Delight'

Iris 'Aggressively Forward' (S. Innerst 1994)

The standards are corn yellow and the falls a softer yellow with maroon edges. The beards are gold. The flower is heavily scented. Height: 91 cm (36½ in.). Bloom: midseason. Parentage: 'Point Made' × (('Osage Buff' × 'Spinning Wheel') × 'Burgundy Brown').

Iris 'Alizes' (J. Cayeux 1991)

This bicolour produces large frilly flowers with white standards on the bluish side and soft violet-blue falls that are pale to white in the centre. The beards are yellow. The flowers are perfectly balanced on well-branched stems. Height: 84 cm (33½ in.). Bloom: early to midseason. Parentage: ((('Palomino' × 'Emma Cook') × 'Tahiti Sunrise') × 'Pink Taffeta') × 'Condottiere'.

Iris 'Allegiance' (P. Cook 1957)

The navy-blue flower has silky standards and rich velvety falls. The blue beards are tipped with yellow. Height: 97 cm (38¾ in.). Bloom: midseason. Parentage: 'Dark Boatman' × (('Distance' × blue seedling) × 'Pierre Menard'). Dykes Medal Winner USA 1964.

Iris 'Alenette' (C. DeForest 1969)

This variety has creamy white petals that are crinkled around the edges and heavily flushed with yellow on the hafts. The falls are large and droop downwards, and the large, round standards only just touch at the top. The beards are thick, bushy, and yellow. Height: 102 cm (41 in.). Bloom: midseason. Parentage: 'Coralene' × 'Cadette'.

Iris 'American Classic' (Schreiner 1996)

There are many white-violet plicata irises, but all that are included in this book have something different about them. This one has soft violet beards on broad, extremely ruffled white falls that are stippled, veined, and edged with violet. The falls are more heavily marked, and the white background can only be seen in the centre of the petals. Height: 91 cm (36½ in.). Bloom: early to late season. Parentage: ('Lorilee' × 'Raspberry Frill's) × ('Titan's Glory' × (('Rococo' × 'Belray') × 'Navy Strut')).

Iris 'America's Cup' (J. McWhirter 1988)

The pure white, lightly scented flowers are large and laced around the edges. The only additional colour is from a little yellow at the back of the white beards. Height: 102 cm (41 in.). Parentage: 'Skating Party' × 'Winterscape'.

Iris 'Amethyst Dancer' (R. Ernst 1996)

This slightly scented, laced, bitone flower has wine-purple falls with white veins on the shoulders and pale peach around the edges. The standards are peach-buff, crinkled, and washed at the base with purple. Height: 86 cm (34½ in.). Bloom: midseason. Parentage: 'Liaison' × ('Afternoon Delight' × 'Tracy Tyrene' sibling).

Iris 'Amethyst Flame' (R. Schreiner 1957)

The gently ruffled, deep lavender-blue flowers are touched with cinnamon on the hafts. The petals are laced around the edges, and the beards are soft lavender-white. Popular for over 10 years with American Iris Society members, this iris is the parent of many other hybrids. Parentage: 'Crispette' × ('Lavensque' × 'Pathfinder'). Dykes Medal Winner USA 1963.

Iris 'Aggressively Forward'

Iris 'Alizes'

Iris 'Allegiance'

Iris 'Alenette'

Iris 'Annabel Jane' (B. Dodsworth 1973) The falls of this heavily ruffled lilac-coloured flower are a little paler in colour compared with the standards, and they carry a few soft brown veins on the hafts. The flower has a spicy scent. Despite being tall, this plant withstands windy conditions in Britain. It was named after the raiser's daughter. Height: 122 cm (49 in.). Bloom: midseason. Parentage: 'Sterling Silver' × 'Champagne Music'. Dykes Medal Winner UK 1977.

Iris 'Anything Goes' (B. Hager 1995) The frilly flower has ruffled lavender-pink standards and extravagantly marked, palest yellow round falls. Soft mauve veins run about two-thirds of the way down the petal, forming a broad band of colour. The beards are rich tangerine. Height: 89 cm (35½ in.). Bloom: early to mid-season. Parentage: ((('Peach Tree' × ('Vanity' × 'Pink Persian')) × 'Silver Flow') × 'Falling in Love') × ('Presence' × (('Catalyst' × 'Perfect Accent') × 'Flaming Victory')).

Iris 'American Classic'

Iris 'Amethyst Dancer'

Iris 'Annabel Jane'

Iris 'America's Cup'

Iris 'Amethyst Flame'

Iris 'Anything Goes'

Iris 'Aplomb' (J. Ghio 1991)
This rosy violet flower has petals that are gently frilled around the edges. The beards are coppery orange and surrounded by veins of white. Height: 102 cm (41 in.). Bloom: mid to late season. Parentage: (('Act of Love' × 'Lady Friend') × 'Caption') × 'Stratagem'.

Iris 'Arabi Pasha' (G. Anley 1951)
At the time of its introduction, this hybrid was described as cornflower blue. I consider it to be evenly coloured deep violet-blue, with horizontal falls and wavy edges. The blue beards are brushed with burnt orange. Height: 76 cm (30½ in.). Bloom: midseason. Parentage: 'Mirette' × 'Blue Ensign'. Dykes Medal Winner UK 1953.

Iris 'Arcady' (H. Senior Fothergill 1959)
This strongly perfumed variety has pale blue flowers with satin-like petals. The standards are flushed with a deeper colour, and on the hafts sit short veins and soft blue beards. Height: 80 cm (32 in.). Bloom: midseason. Parentage: 'Jane Phillips' × 'Pegasus'. Dykes Medal Winner UK 1962.

Iris 'Arctic Fox' (V. Wood 1997)
The white heavily ruffled, glistening petals are frilled around the edges and decorated with dark coral beards. The flower is scented. Height: 81 cm (32½in.). Bloom: mid to late season. Parentage: 'Skyblaze' × 'Silver Fox'.

Iris 'Autumn Circus' (B. Hager 1990)
The clean white background of this gently ruffled flower provides a canvas for the violet topdressing, which is stippled and veined over the standards. The falls are boldly, but perfectly, pencilled with violet, while the beards are blue-white. The scented flower is a reliable rebloomer. Height: 86 cm (34½ in.). Bloom:

early season, then reblooming in autumn. Parentage: ('Space Odyssey' × 'Socialite') × 'Earl of Essex'.

Iris 'Autumn Echo' (J. Gibson 1973)
Cinnamon-brown is stippled across the falls and over a rich yellow background. The standards, which are entirely soft brown in colour, touch at the top. The beards are deep yellow. Height: 91 cm (36½ in.). Bloom: early season and reblooming. Parentage: 'Wild Ginger' × 'Summer Sunshine'.

Iris 'Autumn Leaves' (K. Keppel 1972)
A beautiful blend of autumn colours, the sweetly scented flowers are the colour of caramel, but the falls are overlaid with a strong blend of purple. The beards are orange-yellow. Height: 86 cm (34½ in.). Bloom: midseason. Parentage: 'Vaudeville' × 'Radiant Apogee'.

Iris 'Autumn Tryst' (J. Weiler 1993)
Like its parent *Iris* 'Earl of Essex', this plicata is a reliable rebloomer. The white flowers are large, stippled and washed with rosy violet. A glow of yellow radiates from the style arms. The flowers have bronze beards and a light, chocolate scent. The only drawback is that in windy autumns the flower can be battered. Height: 86 cm (34½ in.). Bloom: early to midseason, reblooming in late summer. Parentage: 'Lilac Stitchery' × 'Earl of Essex'.

Iris 'Ballyhoo' (K. Keppel 1968)
The ruffled flower has large lemon standards and rose-violet falls. Streaks of paler-coloured veins mark the falls, and a heavy wash of purple sits around the hafts. The white beards are tipped with yellow. Height: 97 cm (38¾ in.). Bloom: midseason. Parentage: 'Siva Siva' × 'Diplomacy'.

Iris 'Aplomb'

Iris 'Arabi Pasha'

Iris 'Arcady'

Iris 'Arctic Fox'

Iris 'Autumn Leaves'

Iris 'Bandera Waltz' (C. Tompkins 1982) The flower is basically white. The falls are heavily banded with rose purple, the colour being stippled and veined along the edge. The purple beards are brushed along the top with bronze. Height: 97 cm (38¾ in.). Bloom: midseason. 'Summer Sandman' × 'Etched Amoena'.

Iris 'Battle Royal' (J. Ghio 1994) The scented flowers are rich red-brown with fluted petals and standards that are paler in colour. The yellow beards are marked around the sides with white tiger-like veins. Each

Iris 'Autumn Circus'

Iris 'Autumn Tryst'

Iris 'Bandera Waltz'

Iris 'Autumn Echo'

Iris 'Ballyhoo'

Iris 'Battle Royal'

stem produces 8 to 10 buds. Height: 97 cm (38¾ in.). Bloom: early to mid-season. Parentage: complicated and including 'Lady Friend', 'Mulled Wine', 'Entourage', and 'New Moon'.

Iris 'Before the Storm' (S. Innerst 1988)
The flowers are deepest black with wavy edges to the petals and matching bushy black beards. Height: 91 cm (36½ in.). Bloom: mid to late season. Parentage: 'Superstition' × 'Raven's Roost'. Dykes Medal Winner USA 1996.

Iris 'Benton Cordelia' (C. Morris 1953)
Soft violet buds open into soft pink flowers with large coral beards. The scent reminds me of tobacco. Height: 91 cm (36½ in.). Bloom: midseason. 'Benton Petunia' × 'Radiations'. Dykes Medal Winner UK 1955.

Iris 'Best Bet' (Schreiner 1988)
The ruffled pale blue standards are flushed with purple around the base. The wavy falls are a glossy royal-blue in colour. White markings sit on the hafts, while the short beards are blue. Despite its lack of branching, this variety is vigorous-growing. Some growers find it will rebloom. Height: 91 cm (36½ in.). Bloom: early season. Parentage: (('Amigo's Guitar' × seedling) × ('Navy Strut' × 'Royal Regency' sibling)) × 'Titan's Glory'.

Iris 'Betty Simon' (M. Hamblen 1975)
This flower has round, gently ruffled pale lavender falls and very ruffled soft yellow standards that open out. The style arms are large and a deeper colour than the standards, while the beards are yellow. The flower has a spicy scent. Height: 81 cm (32½ in.). Bloom: mid to late season. Parentage: 'Misty Dawn' × 'Foggy Dew'.

Iris 'Beverly Sills' (B. Hager 1985)
The flower is a soft, creamy coral-pink with beards of the same tone. The petals are frilly with a thick substance and a sweet scent. The blooms are carried on short strong stems, and the plant is said to rebloom. Height: 91 cm (36½ in.). Bloom: midseason. Parentage: 'Pink Pirouette' × 'Vanity'. Dykes Medal Winner USA 1985.

Iris 'Bewilderbeast' (B. Kasperek 1995)
This flower is a psychedelic mixture of colours, including maroon, mauve, and cream. These colours sit in rivers across the white background. The standards are muted in tone, and the thin beards are dark yellow. Height: 76 cm (30½ in.). Bloom: midseason. Parentage: 'Tiger Honey' × 'Rustic Dance'.

Iris 'Big Squeeze' (P. Black 1999)
The ruffled flower is basically orange in colour, with soft peachy orange standards and truly orange falls. The beards also are orange. The flower is heavily scented. Height: 84 cm (33½ in.). Bloom: late season. Parentage: 'Victoria Falls' × 'Good Show'.

Iris 'Before the Storm'

Iris 'Benton Cordelia'

Iris 'Best Bet'

Iris 'Betty Simon'

Iris 'Big Squeeze'

Iris 'Blackout'

Iris 'Beverly Sills'

Iris 'Bewilderbeast'

Iris 'Black Tie Affair'

Iris 'Black Tie Affair' (Schreiner 1993) The large purple-black flower has shimmering, silky petals and black beards. It is lightly scented. Height: 91 cm (36½ in.). Bloom: midseason. Parentage: ('Black Dragon' × 'Titan's Glory') × (((((('Broadway Star' × 'Whole Cloth') × 'Blue Mountains') × ('Toll Gate' × 'After Dark')) × seedling) × ('Morning Hymn' × 'Louisiana Lace')).

Iris 'Blackout' (W. Luihn 1985) This gently ruffled variety has falls that are large, round, velvety, and very black. The standards are glossy and purple. The beards are dark blue and thick, and the flower has a fragrance like that of chocolate. Height: 97 cm (38¾ in.). Bloom: mid to late season. Parentage: 'By Night' × 'Navy Chant'.

Iris 'Blatant' (M. Byers 1989)
This variegata type of flower has soft yellow standards and flaring falls of rich mahogany-brown. The hafts are heavily striped with white, and the beards are rich yellow. The flower is said to rebloom and is scented. Height: 91 cm (36½ in.). Bloom: early to late season. Parentage: 'Spirit of Fiji' × 'Broadway'.

Iris 'Blenheim Royal' (Schreiner 1990)
This robust, reliable garden variety produces rich blue-purple flowers. The extravagantly ruffled petals are even in size and have a thick substance. The flaring falls are marked with brown at both sides and have white beards. The flower is lightly scented. Height: 97 cm (38¾ in.). Bloom: midseason. Parentage: (('Miriam Steel' sibling × 'Sailor's Dance') × ('Navy Strut' × 'Full Tide')) × ('Master Touch' × unknown).

Iris 'Blue Drift' (L. Brummitt 1967)
The violet-blue flowers have paler-coloured standards and flaring, fluted falls with orange beards and half-moon markings of brown. Height: 99 cm (39½ in.). Bloom: late season. Parentage: 'Starched Fabric' × 'Primrose Drift'.

Iris 'Blue Ensign' (H. Rollo Meyer 1937)
The blue-violet flowers are slightly veined with gently ruffled, flaring falls and standards that splay open. The violet beards are tipped with brown at the back. Height: 9 cm (3½ in.). Parentage: not recorded. Dykes Medal Winner UK 1949.

Iris 'Blue-Eyed Brunette' (C. C. Hall 1962)
Listed as 'Blueyed Brunette' in the American Iris Society registration sheets, this variety produces what is described as cigar-brown flowers. I would call them copper-brown. Each

Iris 'Blatant'

Iris 'Blenheim Royal'

Iris 'Blue Ensign'

Iris 'Blue Drift'

Iris 'Blue-Eyed Susan'

fall carries a large flash of blue in front of the golden beards. Height: 91 cm (36½ in.). Bloom: midseason. Parentage: 'Quechee' × 'Carnton'. Dykes Medal Winner UK 1967.

Iris **'Blue-Eyed Susan'** (L. Lauer 1998) The flower has laced, soft yellow standards and gently ruffled, white falls that are edged with a yellow band. On the hafts are wing-like markings of soft ochre. The soft blue beards end in rounded points. Height: 97¾ cm (38 in.). Bloom: mid to late season. Parentage: ('Nancy Glazier' × 'Brandy') × 'Triple Whammy'.

Iris **'Blue Note Blues'** (R. Ernst 1997) The very ruffled mid-blue flowers become paler around the edges. The white beards are tipped with orange towards the back. The flower is scented. Height: 94 cm (37 in.). Bloom: midseason. Parentage: from seedlings involving 'Navy Strut', 'Dover Beach', 'Swirling Seas', and 'Nights of Gladness'.

Iris **'Blue Rhythm'** (A. Whiting 1945) This classic variety has cornflower-blue flowers with falls that are deeper in colour than the standards. The white beards are brushed with deep yellow towards the back. A reliable hybrid, it is easy to grow and scented of lemons. Height: 110 cm (44 in.). Bloom: midseason. Parentage: 'Annabel' × 'Blue Zenith'. Dykes Medal Winner USA 1950.

Iris **'Blue Sapphire'** (Schreiner 1953) The gently ruffled pale blue flower is a paler colour in the centre of the petals, and the long soft blue beards are tipped with yellow. The standards touch at the top, while the falls are inclined to tip downwards. Height: 102 cm (41 in.). Bloom: early season. Parentage: 'Annabel' × 'Blue Zenith'. Dykes Medal Winner USA 1958.

Iris 'Blue-Eyed Brunette'

Iris 'Blue Note Blues'

Iris 'Blue Rhythm'

Iris 'Blue Sapphire'

Iris 'Blue Shimmer' (Sass 1941)
Although it is very old fashioned in
shape, this hybrid is nevertheless extremely reliable and beautifully
scented. The ivory white flowers are
speckled with dots and lines of blue.
The falls are less marked and have a
large white area in the centre. The
blue-white beards are brushed with
yellow. Height: 91 cm (36½ in.).
Bloom: early season. Parentage: 'Blue
Monarch' × unknown.

Iris 'Blue Staccato' (J. Gibson 1977)
The falls of this blue-white plicata are
almost entirely white, while the
edges are banded with violet-blue
stitching and the standards are almost covered with violet-blue spots.
The blue beards are tipped with yellow. The flowers are ruffled, fluted,
and heavily scented. Height: 102 cm
(41 in.). Bloom: early to midseason.
Parentage: 'Indigo Rim' × ('Bold
Overture' × 'Opening Night').

Iris 'Blue Suede Shoes' (Schreiner
1996)
This extravagantly ruffled variety is
rich violet-blue in colour. The blue
beards are long and just touched at
the back with yellow. The flower is
scented and some say it reblooms.
Height: 99 cm (39½ in.). Bloom: mid
to late season. Parentage: 'Breakers' ×
('Land o' Lakes' × 'Pledge Allegiance').

Iris 'Boogie Woogie' (H. Nicholls 1988)
This frilly bitone has heavily flushed
violet-blue falls that are paler in the
centre and marked with maroon on
the hafts. Over this, and around the
yellow tip, lie white stripes. The very
ruffled petals are laced around the
edge. Height: 91 cm (36½ in.).
Bloom: mid to late season. Parentage:
('Taj Rani' × 'In Tempo') × 'Song of
Spring'.

Iris 'Blue Shimmer'   Iris 'Boogie Woogie'

Iris 'Blue Staccato'

Iris 'Blue Suede Shoes'

Iris 'Boysenberry Buttercup'

Iris 'Boysenberry Buttercup' (L. Lauer 1997)
The flower has purple-violet falls and creamy ochre-yellow standards that are flushed with purple from the base. This colour continues up the central midribs. The violet beards are heavily brushed with mustard and edged by white tiger-like stripes. The flower is scented. Height: 94 cm (37 in.). Bloom: early to midseason. Parentage: 'Best Bet' × ('Edith Wolford' × 'Denney' (('Regents Row' sibling × 'Winterscape') × 'Midnight Love Affair')).

Iris 'Braggadocio' (K. Keppel 1997)
The strongly scented flowers have apricot-buff standards and velvety, wine-purple falls with bright orange beards. The petals are broad and very ruffled. Height: 76 cm (30½ in.). Bloom: mid to late season. Parentage: (('Gallant Rogue' × ('Ever After' × 'Impressionist')) × (('Tomorrow's Child' × ('Show Biz' × 'Villain')) × 'Gallant Rogue')).

Iris 'Braithwaite' (H. Randall 1952)
This tried-and-tested amoena has long, pendulous, velvety, purple falls that are paler around the edges and upright lilac-white standards that touch at the top. The short beards are yellow. Height: 84 cm (33½ in.). Bloom: late season. Parentage: 'Helen Collingwood' × 'Lothario'.

Iris 'Broken Dreams' (K. Keppel 1997)
The large, lacy, coral-pink flower has coral beards. A white flash sits below each beard. The flower is lightly scented. Height: 86 cm (34½ in.). Bloom: midseason. Parentage: ('Social Event' × 'Femme Fatale') × ('Social Event' × 'Bubble Up').

Iris 'Braggadocio'

Iris 'Braithwaite'

Iris 'Broken Dreams'

Iris 'Bronzette Star' (E. Kegerise 1990)
This copper-coloured flower has a large golden orange area in the centre of the falls on which the bright orange beards sit. Below this is a flush of blue. The flower is slightly scented. Height: 97 cm (38¾ in.). Bloom: midseason. Parentage: 'Lady Friend' × 'Steady Pace'.

Iris 'Brummit's Mauve' (L. Brummitt)
This flower has lightly ruffled petals. The falls flare out and are a vibrant colour combination: mauve with bands of russet. This colour also sits on the hafts. The centre of the falls pales to very soft lilac. The standards are a blend of violet and ochre. The flower is scented. Height: 102 cm (41 in.). Bloom: mid to late season. Parentage: unknown.

Iris 'Bubble Up' (J. Ghio 1988)
The very ruffled, salmon-pink flower has large, rounded petals and coral-red beards that end in short points. Height: 97 cm (38¾ in.). Bloom: early to late season. Parentage: 'Romantic Mood' × a complicated seedling.

Iris 'Burst' (B. Blyth 1993)
The large, vibrant golden yellow flower has large oval petals. The standards touch at the top, and the top half of the falls is heavily washed and striped with maroon. The short beards are orange. The flower is lightly scented. Height: 91 cm (36½ in.). Bloom: early to midseason. Parentage: 'Swain' × ('Mountain Melody' × 'Polished Amber').

Iris 'Buttercup Bower' (C. Tompkins 1960)
The big, lemon flowers have large white flashes on the falls, which sit in front of the short white, yellow-tipped beards. The standards are fluted, while the falls are only

slightly ruffled. Height: 97 cm (38¾ in.). Bloom: mid to very late season. Parentage: 'Bright Sight' × 'Butter-horn'.

Iris 'Cabaret Royale' (B. Blyth 1975)
This bicolour has flaring, velvety purple-black falls that are decorated with bright orange beards and short white stripes. The standards sit in stark contrast and are soft blue with a flush of violet. The style arms are tipped with brown. Height: 91 cm (36½ in.). Bloom: mid to late season. Parentage: 'Panoramic' × 'Twist and Shout'.

Iris 'Cajun Spices' (W. Maryott 1994)
The nutmeg-coloured flowers have tightly frilled edges. A few soft yellow veins surround the rich yellow beards. The flower is lightly scented. Height: 91 cm (36½ in.). Bloom: mid to late season. Parentage: a mixture of seedlings including 'Entourage' and 'Lady Friend'.

Iris 'Caliente' (W. Luihn 1967)
The rich red-brown flowers are gently ruffled and have silky petals. The rounded falls are poised horizontally to the standards. The short beards

Iris 'Bronzette Star'

Iris 'Bubble Up'

Iris 'Brummit's Mauve'

Iris 'Burst'

Iris 'Buttercup Bower'

Iris 'Caliente'

Iris 'Cabaret Royale'

Iris 'Camelot Rose'

Iris 'Cajun Spices'

Iris 'Cameo Wine'

are burnt orange. This robust variety carries the scented flowers on sturdy but not thick stems, well above a clump of healthy grey-green leaves. Height: 38 in.). Bloom: mid to late season. Parentage: ((seedling × 'Bang') × ('Oriental Glory' × 'Huntsman')) × 'Forward March'.

Iris 'Camelot Rose' (C. Tompkins 1965) The flower is a lovely combination of pink-maroon with a wash of deep maroon on the peach-coloured standards. Small white veins surround the orange beards. Height: 76 cm (30½ in.). Bloom: mid to late season. Parentage: ('Clarion Call' × reciprocal cross) × 'Balinesian'.

Iris 'Cameo Wine' (B. Blyth 1982) The very large, lightly scented pink flowers have undertones of beige to the falls, which are held horizontally. The petals have wavy edges and dark orange beards. Height: 91 cm (36½ in.). Bloom: midseason. Parentage: ('Snow Peach' × 'Martinique') × 'Embassadora'.

Iris 'Caramba' (K. Keppel 1972)
The flower has golden yellow standards and frilly flaring falls that are washed then streaked with chestnut-brown over a white background. The short beards are yellow. Height: 81 cm (32½ in.). Bloom: early to midseason. Parentage: ('Wild Ginger' × 'Siva Siva') × ((('Gene Wild' × 'Majorette') × 'Rococo') × 'Ballyhoo' sibling).

Iris 'Carnaby' (Schreiner 1973)
The rose-purple falls have frilly edges and are peach-pink in colour. The standards also are peach-pink, but they are flushed with lilac. A pale orange stripe extends from the bright orange beards. The flower is lightly scented. Height: 89 cm (35½ in.). Bloom: mid to late season. Parentage: 'Wine and Roses' × (seedling × 'Rippling Waters').

Iris 'Carnival Song' (Schreiner 1994)
The perfumed, ruffled flowers have buff-maroon standards that are washed with maroon-purple and peach falls that are broadly speckled with maroon-purple. The beards are tangerine. Height: 91 cm (36½ in.). Bloom: early to midseason. Parentage: (('Cozy Calico' × 'Grape Accent') × 'Capricious') × 'Gigolo'.

Iris 'Cayenne Pepper' (Schreiner 1986)
This ruffled chocolate-brown variety has very shiny petals that are decorated with ochre-coloured beards. The scent is similar to chocolate. Height: 94 cm (37 in.). Bloom: early to midseason. Parentage: 'Gallant Moment' × (('War Lord' × red seedlings) × (('Wild Ginger' × 'Taste of Honey') × (seedlings))).

Iris 'Cee Cee' (S. Innerst 1995)
The flowers of this tailored variety have large, round, dark ink-blue falls and wavy, sky-blue standards that touch at the top. The short beards are very dark, almost black. The flower is

Iris 'Caramba'

Iris 'Carnival Song'

Iris 'Carnaby'

Iris 'Cayenne Pepper'

Iris 'Cee Cee'

Iris 'Celebration Song'

said to be reblooming and has a spicy scent. Height: 91 cm (36½ in.). Bloom: mid to late season. Parentage: 'Codicil' × 'Best Bet'.

Iris 'Celebration Song' (Schreiner 1993)
The pastel-coloured flower has pale lilac falls and pale peach-pink standards. The beards are orange, and the petals very ruffled. The flower is scented. Many blooms are produced over a long period. Height: 94 cm (37 in.). Bloom: early to late season. Parentage: 'Lullaby of Spring' × 'Frances Gaulter'. Dykes Medal Winner USA 2003.

Iris 'Champagne Elegance' (D. Niswonger 1986)
This reliably reblooming variety has white standards that are tinted with pink and flaring falls that are soft peach-pink and edged with a white ribbon. The beards are soft orange. The edges of the petals are neatly ruffled. The flower is borne on a sturdy stem and is scented. Height: 84 cm (33½ in.). Bloom: early to mid-season and reblooming. Parentage: (('Magnetic Isle' × 'Rhythm and Blues') × 'Snowlight') × ('Coral Strand' × 'Peach Spot').

Iris 'Champagne Frost' (K. Keppel 1996)
This very ruffled variety has petals with a good substance. The falls are a very pale peach and veined with a deeper colour. The white standards are flushed with pink. The pale yellow beards are tipped with yellow. The flower is slightly scented. Height: 89 cm (35½ in.). Bloom: midseason. Parentage: 'Lucky Lemon' × 'Overjoyed'.

Iris 'Change of Pace' (Schreiner 1991)
The large flowers have sparkling, rosy standards and white falls that are broadly edged with a peppering of rosy mauve. The flower is scented. Height: 89 cm (35½ in.). Bloom: early to midseason. Parentage: 'Eagle's Flight' × 'Cinnamon Girl'.

Iris 'Chardonnay and Ice' (B. Blyth 2002)
This amoena has white standards that are flushed at the base with buff. The broad, soft neutral brown falls are decorated with even white stripes that radiate across the entire petal. The white beards are tipped with orange. The flower is strongly scented. Height: 89 cm (35½ in.). Bloom: mid to late season. Parentage: 'Crazy For You' × 'Strictly Jazz' sibling.

Iris 'Change of Pace'

Iris 'Champagne Elegance'

Iris 'Champagne Frost'

Iris 'Chardonnay and Ice'

Iris 'Chasing Rainbows' (B. Hager 1995)
A gently coloured blend, the very
ruffled flowers have soft violet falls
that are paler in the centre and edged
with a wash of buff-peach. As the
flowers open, they have a flare of
dark violet that later fades. The standards are similar in colour except
that they have a wash of lilac to the
base of the petals. The flowers have
orange beards and a strong scent.
Height: 81 cm (32½ in.). Bloom:
midseason. Parentage: ('Merry
Madrigal' × 'Mother Earth') × 'Sweet
Musette'.

Iris 'Cherie' (D. Hall 1945)
This soft peach-pink variety has
smoothly shaped falls that droop
downwards and coral-red beards. The
standards are shorter than the falls
and curve inwards but do not quite
touch at the top. Height: 76 cm (30½
in.). Bloom: early season. Parentage:
('Golden Eagle' × seedling) × 'Fantasy'. Dykes Medal Winner USA 1951.

Iris 'Chief Quinaby' (Schreiner 1991)
The red-brown flowers are smooth
and have only just a little ruffling to
the petals. The standards are silky,
the falls velvety, and the beards are
mustard coloured. The flower is
sharply scented. Height: 91 cm (36½
in.). Bloom: early to midseason.
Parentage: 'Play With Fire' × 'Deep
Fire'.

Iris 'China Moon' (Schreiner 1998)
This bright orange flower has paler-
coloured standards and petals that
are laced around the edges. The short
beards are bright orange. The flower
is scented. Height: 99 cm (39½ in.).
Bloom: midseason. Parentage:
(('Pinafore Pink' × ('Oraglow' × un-
known)) × ('Something Else' ×
(((‘Golden Ice’ × ‘Celestial Glory’) ×
‘Flaming Star’) × ‘Gold Trimmings’)))
× ‘Fireside Glow’.

Iris 'Chasing Rainbows'   Iris 'Cherie'

Iris 'Chief Quinaby'

Iris 'China Moon'   Iris 'Chivalry'

Iris 'Christmas Angel'

Iris 'Clarence'

Iris 'Classic Look'

Iris 'Circus Circus'

Iris 'City Lights'

Iris 'Chivalry' (J. Wills 1943)
This soft lilac-blue variety has broad white stripes around the white beards, which are brushed with orange. The long, smoothly shaped falls droop downwards, while the standards are larger and ruffled. Height: 76 cm (30½ in.). Bloom: midseason. Parentage: 'Missouri' × 'Great Lakes'. Dykes Medal Winner USA 1947.

Iris 'Christmas Angel' (F. DeForest 1959)
This tough plant has white flowers with wings of bright yellow on the hafts and long white, V-shaped beards which are touched with yellow. The petals are ruffled. The falls gently flare out, then tip downwards. Height: 91 cm (36½ in.). Bloom: late season. Parentage: 'Frances Kent' × 'Paradise Pink'.

Iris 'Circus Circus' (G. Sutton 1996)
This plicata has white falls banded with a broad rim of rose purple that gently spreads into a white centre. The white standards are heavily washed and speckled with lilac. The flower is slightly scented. Height: 94 cm (37 in.). Bloom: early to late sea-

son. Parentage: 'Momentum' × (('Heavenly Harmony' × 'Petite Posy') × 'French Gown').

Iris 'City Lights' (M. Dunn 1990)
The violet flowers have wide falls that carry a white spot near to the hafts on which sit white beards. The standards are flushed at the base with white, and the blooms are scented. Height: 94 cm (37 in.). Bloom: midseason. Parentage: 'Fancy Face' × 'Windsurfer'.

Iris 'Clarence' (L. Zurbrigg 1990)
A reliable rebloomer, this variety produces white standards that are flushed towards the top with soft violet. The falls are also violet but have a white area on the hafts and large cream-coloured beards. The flowers are sweetly scented. Height: 89 cm (35½ in.). Bloom: midseason and reblooming. Parentage: unknown.

Iris 'Classic Look' (Schreiner 1992)
This neatly ruffled plicata has violet stipples over a white background. The blue beards are touched with orange at the back, and the flower has a strong, soapy scent. Height: 91 cm (36½ in.). Bloom: early to mid-

season. Parentage: 'Go Around' × ((('Full Circle' × 'Rococo') × ('Arpege' sibling × ('Rococo' × 'Emma Cook'))) × 'Spinning Wheel').

Iris 'Clearwater River' (R. Ernst 1999) The thick, blue-white petals are flushed from the base with soft purple. The bushy beards are tipped with yellow in the throat and surrounded by a few tiger stripes of brown. The flower has a light scent. Height: 91 cm (36½ in.). Bloom: midseason. Parentage: 'Silverado' × 'Blue It Up'.

Iris 'Cliffs of Dover' (O. Fay 1953) This white variety has long, pendant-shaped falls and ruffled standards that stay open at the top. The soft orange beards are also long, and delicate soft green stripes decorate the hafts. Height: 89 cm (35½ in.). Bloom: midseason. Parentage: 'New Snow' × 'Cahokia'.

Iris 'Coalignition' (T. Burseen 1991) The flower has velvety, dark black-grape falls and silky, wine red standards. On the falls sitting in distinct contrast are fat, bushy, mustard-coloured beards. The flower has a sharp, spicy scent. Height: 91 cm (36½ in.). Bloom: early to midseason. Parentage: ('Fresno Calypso' × 'Lady Friend') × ('Lady Friend' × ('Gondolier' × 'Galen')).

Iris 'Codicil' (S. Innerst 1984) The soft blue flower has falls that are gently tinged with soft purple and decorated with blue-black beards. Height: 81 cm (32½ in.). Bloom: mid to late season. Parentage: ('Appalachian Spring' × 'Navy Strut') × 'Evening Echo'.

Iris 'Colette Thurillet' (J. Cayeux 1991) The standards are apricot-yellow, and the falls rose-violet, edged with a band of apricot-yellow. A flush of maroon surrounds each tangerine-col-

Iris 'Clearwater River'

Iris 'Coalignition'

Iris 'Cliffs of Dover'

Iris 'Colette Thurillet'

Iris 'Codicil'

Iris 'Color Me Blue'

oured beard. Height: 85 cm (34 in.). Bloom: mid to late season. Parentage: 'Gypsy Caravan' × 'Ringo'.

Iris 'Color Me Blue' (Schreiner 1997)
This scented variety has sky-blue, very ruffled flowers that are deeper coloured when they open. The white beards are tipped with yellow in the throat. Height: 91 cm (36½ in.). Bloom: midseason. Parentage: 'Delta Blues' × 'Riverboat Blues'.

Iris 'Conjuration' (M. Byers 1988)
This variety produces small, scented flowers balanced on slender, well-branched stems. The blooms are mainly white, but the falls are broadly edged with rose violet, while the standards are tinged with paler violet. The white beards are long, horned, and tipped with tangerine towards the back. Height: 91 cm (36½ in.). Bloom: mid to late season. Parentage: ('Sky Hooks' × 'Condottiere') × 'Alpine Castle'. Dykes Medal Winner USA 1998.

Iris 'Copatonic' (B. Blyth 1994)
The large, ruffled flowers have velvety, rich russet-brown falls that are edged by a band of deep caramel. The standards are the same caramel colour. The beards are yellow-brown, and the flower has a sweet but sharp scented. Height: 81–86 cm (32–34½ in.). Bloom: early to midseason. Parentage: 'Swain' × 'Rustler'.

Iris 'Copper Lustre' (J. Kirkland 1934)
The smoothly shaped, copper-coloured flower has drooping falls that are not as long as those of many irises in this group. The tall standards curve inwards. White stripes surround the orange beards. Height: average. Bloom: midseason. Parentage: unknown. Dykes Medal Winner USA 1938.

Iris 'Coral Point' (G. Sutton 1999)
The soft pink flower is laced and gently ruffled. Long, bushy, horn-shaped, bright coral beards dominate the bloom. The flower is slightly scented. Height: 94 cm (37 in.). Bloom: mid to late season. Parentage: 'Sky Hooks' × (('Pink Ember' × 'Playgirl') × 'Twice Thrilling').

Iris 'Conjuration'

Iris 'Copper Lustre'

Iris 'Copatonic'

Iris 'Coral Point'

Iris 'Cordoba' (J. Ghio 1997)
The rich orange flowers (called mango-orange by the hybridizer) come with flaring falls that are deeper in colour. The standards are neatly ruffled and flushed with maroon at the base. The beards are bright orange. The whole flower has a good substance to it and is strongly scented. Height: 91 cm (36½ in.). Bloom: early to late season. Parentage: 'Dawning' × 'Royal Honey'.

Iris 'Corona Gold' (W. Maryott 1997)
This heavily ruffled variety has standards that are entirely caramel. The flaring falls are also caramel, but they are paler in the centre and flushed with lilac. The flower has yellow beards and a slight scent. Height: 94 cm (37 in.). Bloom: midseason. Parentage: 'Temperance' × 'Juan Valdez'.

Iris 'Cozy Calico' (Schreiner 1980)
The ruffled flowers have red-purple standards and white falls that are broadly edged with the same colour. The white on the standards is stippled with a few white dots, and the falls are decorated with white beards that are tipped with yellow and purple. Height: 86 cm (34½ in.). Bloom: early to midseason. Parentage: ((seedling × 'Merry Ripple') × 'Jolie') × 'Rondo'.

Iris 'Cranberry Crush' (J. T. Aitken 1985)
This very ruffled flower has soft lilac standards that are heavily flushed with purple and flaring falls that are are red-violet. The short violet beards are brushed with yellow, and the flower is lightly scented. Height: 94 cm (37 in.). Bloom: mid to late season. Parentage: 'Going My Way' × 'Mystique'.

Iris 'Cranberry Tea' (G. Mapes 1988)
This large, vibrantly coloured flower

Iris 'Cordoba'

Iris 'Cozy Calico'

Iris 'Corona Gold'

Iris 'Cranberry Crush'

Iris 'Cranberry Tea'

Iris 'Crimson Snow'

Iris 'Crispette'

Iris 'Crowned Heads'

Iris 'Cross Current'

Iris 'Crushed Velvet'

has violet falls that are edged with glossy brown. On the hafts sit wings of red-brown and beards of bronze. The standards are glossy brown-purple. The flower has wavy petals and is lightly scented. Height: 97 cm (38¾ in.). Bloom: midseason. Parentage: 'Cranberry Ice' × 'Paris Lights'.

Iris 'Crimson Snow' (B. Blyth 1987)
This amoena has blue-white standards that are brushed at the base with soft peach-pink. The velvety, round falls are purple-maroon with edges bleached to almost white. Surrounding the burnt orange beards are short white stripes. The flower is strongly scented. Height: 76–78 cm (30–32 in.). Bloom: early to midseason. Parentage: 'Ambiance' × ('Tomorrow's Child' × ('Love Chant' × 'Festive Skirt')).

Iris 'Crispette' (Schreiner 1957)
The soft pink-lilac flower has evenly sized, very gently ruffled, round petals that are lightly serrated around the edges and standards that just touch at the top. The white beards are brushed with yellow and bordered, on the hafts, by yellow patches over which sit white veins. Height: 102 cm (41 in.). Bloom: midseason. Parentage: 'Harriet Thoreau' × ('Angelus' × 'Matula').

Iris 'Cross Current' (K. Keppel 1995)
This ruffled variety produces violet-blue falls that are spray-painted on the hafts with a V shape of white. The standards are soft white and flecked with patches of lilac. The flower has pale blue beards and is scented. Height: 97 cm (38¾ in.). Bloom: early to midseason. Parentage: 'God's Handiwork' × 'Armada'.

Iris 'Crowned Heads' (K. Keppel 1997)
This ruffled reverse bicolour has violet-blue standards and soft blue falls. Both the falls and the standards are veined and flecked with a deeper blue. The bushy beards are soft blue. The flower is scented. Height: 97 cm (38¾ in.). Bloom: midseason. Parentage: 'In Reverse' × 'Honky Tonk Blues'. Dykes Medal Winner USA 2004.

Iris 'Crushed Velvet' (J. Ghio 1976)
The petals of this deep rose-violet variety are gently ruffled and are serrated around the edges. The standards touch at the top, and the beards are pale blue. Height: 102 cm (41 in.).

Bloom: early to midseason. Parentage: includes 'Mulberry Wine', 'Haunting Rhapsody', 'Frosted Starlight', 'Spanish Peaks', 'Black Satin', 'Cahokia', 'Pierre Menard', 'Black Forest', 'Chivalry', 'Utah Valley', 'Melissa', and 'Warm Laughter'.

Iris 'Cup Race' (Buttrick 1962)
The white flower has a tint of blue, and the petals have ruffled edges. The white beards are touched with yellow, while the hafts exhibit thin ochre stripes. Height: 91 cm (36½ in.). Bloom: mid to late season. Parentage: ('Bluebird Blue' × 'South Pacific') × 'Concord Town'.

Iris 'Dancers Edge' (B. Blyth 2002)
This amoena-plicata combination has ruffled soft blue, almost white standards and flaring, pure white falls that are rimmed and peppered with violet-blue. The short bushy white beards are touched with yellow in the throat. 'Painted From Memory' and 'Lord of Letters' are sisters of this iris. Height: 91 cm (36½ in.). Bloom: midseason. Parentage: 'Hey Dreamer' × 'Harmonics'.

Iris 'Dancer's Veil' (R. Hutchinson 1959)
This evenly sized, neatly ruffled variety has white petals that are speckled with blue-violet dots. The standards are almost covered with violet dots, while the falls are only broadly rimmed with the colour. The white beards are tipped with bronze. Height: 91 cm (36½ in.). Bloom: mid to late season. Parentage: (seedling × 'Dancing Waters') × 'Rosy Veil'. Dykes Medal Winner UK 1963.

Iris 'Dark Passion' (Schreiner 1998)
The flowers are ruffled, very dark purple-black in colour with velvety falls and silky standards. The beards are also black, and the flower is lightly scented. Height: 89 cm (35½ in.). Bloom: midseason. Parentage: includes 'Back in Black', 'Midnight Dancer', 'Whole Cloth', 'Amethyst Flame', 'Melodrama', and 'Swazi Princess'.

Iris 'Dauntless' (C. Connell 1929)
This bicolour has rose-purple standards with softer red-maroon falls. Height: 9 cm (3½ in.). Bloom: midseason. Parentage: 'Cardinal' × 'Rose Madder'. Dykes Medal Winner USA 1929.

Iris 'Dazzling Gold' (D. Anderson 1977)
The bright orange-yellow flowers have neatly ruffled, flaring falls and very ruffled standards. The falls are heavily veined with maroon, a colour that washes further into the petals. The tight beards are orange, and the flower has a fruity scent like that of oranges. Height: 74 cm (29½ in.). Bloom: midseason. Parentage: 'Radiant Apogee' × 'West Coast'.

Iris 'Dear Jean' (F. Kerr 1996)
This ruffled flower has rich lemon standards and pale lemon falls. The edges are washed with soft mauve, and in front of the yellow beard sits a broad flash of white. The flowers are thickly scented and carried on well-branched stems. Height: 97 cm (38¾ in.). Bloom: midseason. Parentage: ('Edith Wolford' × 'Lullaby of Spring') × ('Alpine Castle' × 'Gypsy Woman').

Iris 'Deep Black' (P. Cook 1953)
The flowers have long, slender, velvety, blue-black falls that look almost pure black and round, silky, black-purple standards that touch at the top. The beards are violet, and the flowers are scented. Height: 76 cm (30½ in.). Bloom: late season. Parentage: 'Black Forest' × unknown.

Iris 'Deep Pacific' (E. Burger 1975)
The photograph does not show just how navy-blue these flowers are. The beards are mid-blue. The flowers of

Iris 'Cup Race'

Iris 'Dancers Edge'

Iris 'Dancer's Veil'

Iris 'Dark Passion'

Iris 'Dear Jean'

this robust, vigorous variety are borne on strong, thick stems. Height: 84 cm (33½ in.). Bloom: mid to late season. Parentage: 'Cup Race' × 'Royal Touch'.

Iris 'Deft Touch' (C. Tompkins 1977) This gently coloured variety has soft peach-pink flowers with ruffled petals and orange beards. Height: 99 cm (39½ in.). Bloom: mid to late season. Parentage: includes 'Tinsel Town', 'Charmaine', 'Maudie Marie', and 'Pink Pussycat'.

Iris 'Dauntless'

Iris 'Deep Black'

Iris 'Deep Pacific'

Iris 'Dazzling Gold'

Iris 'Deft Touch'

Iris 'Delta Blues' (Schreiner 1994)
The neatly ruffled, glistening, rich sky-blue flowers have light blue beards and a strong scent. Height: 91 cm (36½ in.). Bloom: midseason. Parentage: 'Breakers' × 'Tide's In'.

Iris 'Desert Song' (Fay 1946)
The small, soft lemon flowers have slightly crinkled petals and bright yellow beards. In front of the beards sits a long flash of white. Height: 91 cm (36½ in.). Bloom: midseason. Parentage: 'Snow Flurry' × 'Golden Eagle'.

Iris 'Devonshire Cream' (G. Sutton 1999)
The heavily ruffled petals of this soft cream variety are thick in substance, just as its name implies, with standards that are slightly deeper in tone. The beards are also cream and extend in long upward-facing horns. The flower is scented. Height: 94 cm (37 in.). Bloom: mid to very late season. Parentage: 'Elizabeth Poldark' × 'Simply Pretty'.

Iris 'Diabolique' (Schreiner 1997)
The scented, garnet-purple flowers are deeper coloured in the flounces of the petals. The blue beards are short. Height: 97 cm (38¾ in.). Bloom: mid to late season. Parentage: includes a 'Rosette Wine' sibling, 'Thriller' sibling, 'Amethyst Flame' × 'Melodrama'.

Iris 'Dorothea Marquart' (S. Innerst 1993)
This true yellow variety has golden yellow beards. The oval-shaped falls are ruffled, and the standards are laced. The flower is slightly scented. Height: 91 cm (36½ in.). Bloom: mid to late season. Parentage: 'Catalyst' × 'Idol's Dream'.

Iris 'Delta Blues'

Iris 'Desert Song'

Iris 'Devonshire Cream'

Iris 'Diabolique'

Iris 'Double Bubble' (J. Ghio 1997)
The falls of this pale blue self lighten
to almost cream in the centre and
carry whiskery cream-coloured
beards. The standards are laced and
flare out, while the falls are large,
round, and frilly. Height: 91 cm (36½
in.). Bloom: early to midseason.
Parentage: 'Water Ballet' × 'Quintes-
sence'.

Iris 'Double Vision' (J. Ghio 1998)
The gently ruffled, plicata flowers are
basically dark maroon. The standards
are almost entirely maroon, while the
falls have a background of cream that
is etched and lined with maroon.
This colour looks darker in the
ruffles. The beards are copper coloured, and the flower, which is said
to rebloom, is lightly scented. Height:
81 cm (32½ in.). Bloom: early to midseason and reblooming. Parentage:
includes 'Gay Parasol', 'Ponderosea',
'New Moon', 'Vanity', 'Indiscreet',
'Epicenter', and 'Shenanigan'.

Iris 'Drum Roll' (B. Hager 1992)
This extravagantly ruffled blue-violet
flower has soft blue beards that are
tipped with gold in the throat. The
flower is scented. Height: 86 cm
(34½ in.). Bloom: mid to late season.
Parentage: ((('Geometrics' × 'Ice
Sculpture') × 'Avalon Bay') × 'Ron') ×
(('Silver Flow' × 'Ruffled Ballet') ×
'Mother Earth' sibling).

Iris 'Dusky Challenger' (Schreiner
     1986)
Best described as purple-black, the
large, ruffled flowers are shiny and
have blue-black beards. The flowers
are carried on strong stems and have
a heavy, sharp scent that is reminis-
cent of hot chocolate. Height: 99 cm
(39½ in.). Bloom: mid to late season.
Parentage: unknown. Dykes Medal
Winner USA 1992.

Iris 'Dorothea Marquart'

Iris 'Drum Roll'

Iris 'Double Bubble'

Iris 'Dusky Challenger'

Iris 'Double Vision'

Iris 'Dutch Chocolate' (Schreiner 1970) This self-coloured hybrid is orange-brown and has beards of the same colour. Height: 89 cm (35½ in.). Bloom: early to midseason. Parentage: 'Gypsy Jewels' × 'Luihn' seedling.

Iris 'Eagle's Flight' (Schreiner 1985) The lightly ruffled flower has lilac standards that are washed with deeper hues and white falls that are edged with purple. A few purple eyelashes surround the tangerine beards, which are touched with white at the ends. The flower is said to be reblooming in late summer. Height: 89 cm (35½ in.). Bloom: early to midseason. Parentage: 'Circuit' × 'Spinning Wheel'.

Iris 'Earl of Essex' (L. Zurbrigg 1979) This white-and-violet plicata is a very reliable rebloomer. The large, round, white falls are veined and peppered with violet. A wash of rose violet sits across the white area. The standards are more veined than the falls, and the white beards are tipped with yellow at the back. Height: 89 cm (35½ in.). Bloom: early season and reblooming. Parentage: ((('Crinkled Ivory' × 'Autumn Sensation') × 'Grand Baroque') × ('Sky Queen' × 'Grand Baroque')) × 'Violet Classic'.

Iris 'Early Light' (N. Scopes 1983) The soft lemon flowers have falls that are heavily bleached with a large flush of white. The petals are ruffled and laced, and the beards are yellow. Height: 97 cm (38¾ in.). Bloom: mid to late season. Parentage: 'Cup Race' × 'Lemon Brocade'. Dykes Medal Winner UK 1989.

Iris 'Earth Song' (E. Kegerise 1992) Similar to *Iris* 'Edith Wolford', this hybrid has ruffled rich lemon standards and flaring, rose-purple falls. The falls are bleached to a paler colour around the edges. The beards are

golden yellow, and the bloom has a spicy scent. Height: 89–91 cm (35–36½ in.). Bloom: mid to late season. Parentage: 'Edith Wolford' × 'Helen Wanner'.

Iris 'Earthborn' (B. Hager 1992) This iris produces flowers the colour of burnt orange peel. The standards are fluted and laced around the edges, and the falls are ruffled. The beards are dark orange, and the style arms are large. Height: 84 cm (33½ in.). Bloom: midseason. Parentage: ('Fringe Benefits' sibling × 'Good Show') × ((('Golden Brilliance' × 'Glowing Ruffles') × 'Perfect Accent') × 'Flaming Victory').

Iris 'Eastertime' (Schreiner 1980) This very large, ruffled flower has cream falls that are edged with a broad yellow band. The lemon standards are deeper in colour around the edges, and the flower is lightly scented. Height: 97 cm (38¾ in.). Bloom: mid to late season. Parentage: ('White Taffeta' × (seedling × 'Arctic Flame')) × (('May Delight' × 'Christmas Time') × 'Tinsel Town').

Iris 'Echo de France' (P. Anfosso 1984) The standards of this wavy, laced flower are white, while the falls are bright yellow. The style arms are also tipped with yellow, and the golden yellow beards are surrounded by broad white veins. Height: 85 cm (34 in.). Bloom: early to midseason. Parentage: 'Snowlight' × 'Champagne Braise'.

Iris 'Edith Wolford' (B. Hager 1984) When this hybrid was introduced, the flower was considered very unusual. Since then many similar varieties have also been introduced. The flower has pale yellow standards that are flushed from the base with violet and soft violet falls that are paler around the edges. The short beards

Iris 'Dutch Chocolate'

Iris 'Eagle's Flight'

Iris 'Earl of Essex'

Iris 'Early Light'

Iris 'Eastertime'

are orange, and the petals are very ruffled. Height: 102 cm (41 in.). Bloom: midseason. Parentage: 'Merry Madrigal' × 'Freedom Road'. Dykes Medal Winner USA 1993.

***Iris* 'Eileen Louise'** (B. Dodsworth 1999) This variety produces ruffled creamy peach flowers with large white beards that are tipped with orange. The tightly ruffled petals are almost laced, and the centre of the falls is paler in colour. The flower has a good scent. Height: 91 cm (36½ in.). Bloom: mid to late season. Parentage: 'Early Light' × 'Paradise'.

Iris 'Earth Song'

Iris 'Echo de France'

Iris 'Edith Wolford'

Iris 'Earthborn'

Iris 'Eileen Louise'

Iris 'Eleanor's Pride' (E. Watkins 1952)
The pale blue flower has smoothly shaped oval falls and ruffled standards. The white beards are tipped with yellow at the back. Height: 105 cm (41 in.). Bloom: midseason. Parentage: 'Jane Phillips' × 'Blue Rhythm'. Dykes Medal Winner USA 1961.

Iris 'Electrique' (B. Blyth 1991)
The flowers of this very three-dimensional plant should be observed from above to get the full effect. The gently ruffled ochre falls are highlighted with flashes of purple. The short very upright standards are palest violet in colour and tinged with streaks of purple. The upright, violet style arms are edged with tan. The bloom is sweetly scented. Height: 96 cm (38½ in.). Bloom: very early to late season. Parentage: (('Inca Queen' × ('Tranquil Star' × ('Love Chant' × 'Festive Skirt'))) × 'Amber Snow') × ('Shine on Wine' × sibling).

Iris 'Elizabeth Poldark' (R. Nicholls 1987)
The petals of this white variety are heavily ruffled and fluted, thick in substance, and touched with yellow. The white beards are also touched with yellow and surrounded by short yellow veins. The flower is scented. Height: 97 cm (38¾ in.). Bloom: midseason. Parentage: 'Mary Frances' × 'Paradise'.

Iris 'Enhancement' (J. Ghio 1995)
The lemon-coloured lacy edged flowers have falls that are paler in front of the yellow beards and standards that are flushed with pink. The bloom is lightly scented. Height: 91 cm (36½ in.). Bloom: early to late season. Parentage: (('Mogul' sibling × 'Guadalajara') × 'Caracas') × (('Montevideo' × 'Guadalajara') × 'Peach Bisque').

Iris 'Eleanor's Pride'

Iris 'Enhancement'

Iris 'Electrique'

Iris 'English Charm'

Iris 'Elizabeth Poldark'

Iris 'English Cottage'

Iris 'Ennoble'

Iris 'Everything Plus'

Iris 'Exotic Gem'

Bloom: early season and reblooming. Parentage: (('Crinkled Ivory' × 'Autumn Sensation') × 'Grand Baroque') × 'Cross Stitch'.

Iris 'Ennoble' (J. Ghio 1998)

This rich maroon-purple flower has velvety petals that are laced around the edges. The flaring falls are lighter in colour and are covered with dark purple veins. The flower has deep russet-orange beards and a scent that is a mixture of spice and citrus fruit. Height: 84 cm (33½ in.). Bloom: mid to late season. Parentage: includes 'Lady Friend', 'Ponderosa', 'Coffee House', 'New Moon', and 'Lightening Bolt'.

Iris 'Everything Plus' (D. Niswonger 1983)

This complicated bloom has soft blue standards and white falls that are broadly edged with purple. The purple is peppered into the centre of the falls, and long lines of purple extend from the hafts. The purple beards are tipped with ginger. Height: 86 cm (34½ in.). Bloom: midseason. Parentage: 'Focus' × 'Spinning Wheel'. Dykes Medal Winner USA 1991.

Iris 'Exotic Gem' (M. Olson 1970)

The petals of this lilac flower are ruffled around the edges. The falls are smeared with a coating of blue, while the beards are the same colour as the falls. Height: 86 cm (34½ in.). Bloom: midseason. Parentage: 'Crinkled Beauty' × ('Amethyst Flame' × (('Char-Maize' × 'Bellerive') × ('Cathedral Bells' × 'Ballerina'))).

Iris 'English Charm' (B. Blyth 1989)

The gently ruffled petals are laced around the edges. The standards flare out and are soft apricot in colour, but paling around the edges; they carry tangerine beards. The cream standards are heavily veined with soft apricot-yellow, and the flower is lightly scented. Height: 86 cm (34½ in.). Bloom: midseason. Parentage: ('Love Chant' × 'Festive Skirt') × 'Cameo Wine'.

Iris 'English Cottage' (L. Zurbrigg 1976)

In the middle of England, this hybrid is the first Tall Bearded iris to bloom in summer, and it never fails to rebloom in autumn. The large white flowers have traces of violet speckling on the hafts and white beards, which are tipped with yellow towards the back. In cooler temperatures and in autumn the violet speckling is more apparent. The flower is heavily scented. Height: 98 cm (39 in.).

Iris 'Fade to Black' (Schreiner 2002)
This very purple-black flower has shiny, ruffled petals and large purple-black beards. It is heavily scented. Height: 97 cm (38¾ in.). Bloom: early to midseason. Parentage: Schreiner seedling × 'Hello Darkness'.

Iris 'Fancy Dress' (K. Keppel 1997)
The very frilly flower has flaring falls and open standards. The standards are violet with paler edges and a white line that radiates from the base. The blue-purple falls are edged with white and have a square patch of white towards the back. The white beards are brushed with orange. The flower is scented. Height: 86 cm (34½ in.). Bloom: early season. Parentage: 'Mind Reader' × 'Fancy Woman'.

Iris 'Fancy Woman' (K. Keppel 1994)
The frilly, peach-based flower is peppered with rose-purple dots. The standards are softer in tone, and the peach background is revealed around the edges. The falls, which are almost entirely rose purple, reveal the peach background through broad veins that break through the surface colour. The beards are orange, and the flower is strongly scented. Height: 97 cm (38¾ in.). Bloom: very early to midseason. Parentage: includes 'Tea Apron', 'Full Circle', 'Rococo', 'April Melody', 'Joy Ride', 'Roundup', 'Mistress', 'Peccadillo', 'Goddess').

Iris 'Fanfaron' (R. Hager 1987)
This variety produces flowers with bright yellow standards and red-brown falls that are broadly edged with the same bright yellow. The beards are bright yellow, and the slightly ruffled petals are laced around the edges. The flower is lightly scented. Height: 97 cm (38¾ in.). Bloom: midseason. Parentage:

'Dazzling Gold' × ('Santana' × (unknown seedling × ('Decolletage' × ('Sense of Humor' × 'Dancer's Veil')))).

Iris 'Fashion Statement' (J. Gatty 1996)
The greyish rose-lavender flower has a white flush to the falls. The beards are pink-coral. The petals are ruffled and laced around the edges. The flower has a spicy scent. Height: 91 cm (36½ in.). Bloom: midseason. Parentage: 'Coming Up Roses' × 'Designing Woman'.

Iris 'Fatal Attraction' (F. Kerr 1995)
The ruffled falls are velvety dark purple-blue in colour, while the standards are violet-blue and washed at the base with purple, a colour that seeps up from the falls. These are further speckled with purple. The flower has blue beards that are tipped with white and a sweet scent. Height: 91 cm (36½ in.). Bloom: early season. Parentage: 'Twist of Fate' × 'Mystique'.

Iris 'Festive Skirt' (F. Hutchings 1973)
This amoena has white standards that are flushed with salmon-pink and salmon-pink falls that are paler in colour around the edges. The beards are orange. The petals are slightly ruffled. Height: 89 cm (35½ in.). Bloom: midseason. Parentage: includes 'La Parisienne', 'Barbara Luddy', 'Just Annie', 'Golden Eagle', 'Pinnacle', 'China Gate', 'Numero Uno', and 'Sunset Snows'.

Iris 'Fine China' (J. Gatty 1985)
The pure white flowers have very ruffled petals and matching white beards. The hafts have a few yellow veins. The flower is sharply scented. Height: 91 cm (36½ in.). Bloom: early to midseason. Parentage: 'Social Whirl' × 'Dream Affair'.

Iris 'Firecracker' (D. Hall 1943)
This plicata has chestnut-brown and bright yellow flowers. The yellow background is peppered with brown, and a triangle of white emerges from the hafts, forming a background for the thin yellow beards. The round standards touch at the top and are washed almost entirely with brown. The oblong falls tip downwards. Height: 76 cm (30½ in.). Bloom: early season. Parentage: 'Orloff' × 'Elsa Sass'.

Iris 'Fade to Black'

Iris 'Fancy Dress'

Iris 'Fancy Woman'

Iris 'Fashion Statement'

Iris 'Fatal Attraction'

Iris 'Fanfaron'

Iris 'Festive Skirt'

Iris 'Fine China'

Iris 'Firecracker'

Iris **'First Interstate'** (Schreiner 1990)
This neatly ruffled flower has brilliant yellow standards and white falls edged in a yellow that matches the standards. The flower has golden yellow beards and a fruity scent. Height: 91 cm (36½ in.). Bloom: mid to late season. Parentage: ('Soft Moonbeam' × 'New Moon') × ((('Lightning Ridge' × ('Wine and Roses' × 'Gypsy Lullaby')) × ((('Imperial Lilac' sibling × 'Arctic Flame') × 'White Taffeta') × 'Launching Pad')) × 'Piping Hot').

Iris **'First Violet'** (F. DeForest 1952)
This truly violet flower is untainted by any other hue. The oval falls dip downwards and are gently ruffled, as are the standards. The beards are blue-white. Height: 97 cm (38¾ in.). Bloom: midseason. Parentage: 'Chivalry' × 'Spanish Peaks'. Dykes Medal Winner USA 1956.

Iris **'Fjord'** (R. Nelson 1996)
The gently ruffled flower of palest blue has a faint yellow wash below the pale blue beards, which are tipped with lemon. The flower is scented. Height: 94 cm (37 in.). Bloom: mid to late season. Parentage: 'Seminole Spring' × 'Silverado'.

Iris **'Fogbound'** (K. Keppel 1997)
This laced and frilly flower is almost a reverse bicolour. The standards are purple, but the colour becomes washed out by the time it reaches the top of the petals. The almost white falls are marked with bronze on the hafts, and the short white beards are touched with orange at the back. The flower is scented. Height: 107 cm (43 in.). Bloom: midseason. Parentage: 'Wishful thinking' × 'Spring Shower'.

Iris **'Fresno Calypso'** (J. Weiler 1977)
The gently ruffled flowers are soft orange in colour. White patches surround the tan-orange beards. Height: 91 cm (36½ in.). Bloom: mid to late season: Parentage: ('Ballerina' × 'Orange Crush') × seedling.

Iris **'Frost and Flame'** (D. Hall 1956)
The pure white flowers have ruffled standards and smoothly shaped, round falls that dip downwards. A few ochre veins surround the vibrant orange beards. Height: 91 cm (36½ in.). Bloom: early season. Parentage: involves two seedlings.

Iris **'Full Impact'** (Schreiner 2001)
This variety produces many glistening, silky flowers that are smaller than those of many other Tall Bearded irises introduced today. They are dusky black-violet with a patch of white radiating from the shoulders. The scented flower has a white beard that is brushed with yellow. Height: 74 cm (29½ in.). Bloom: early to late season. Parentage: ('Black Dragon' × (seedling × 'Titan's Glory')) × ('Black Dragon' × 'Titan's Glory').

Iris **'Gaelic Jig'** (B. Blyth 1999)
The very ruffled flowers have soft blue standards and rosy brown falls. The colour of the falls is smeared over a background of lilac and deepens in tone in the centre. The white beards are brushed with bronze, and the flower is scented. Height: 86 cm (34½ in.). Bloom: very early season. Parentage: 'Cast a Spell' × 'Arabian Story' sibling.

Iris **'Gala Gown'** (Corey 1958)
Not the most robust variety, this early orange introduction is vibrant in colour. The beards are even brighter and sit on a paler zone. The petals are gently ruffled, and the standards are laced at the edges. The flower is strongly scented. Height: 76 cm (30½ in.). Bloom: midseason. Parentage: ('Buneau' × (pink seedling × 'Anthea')) × 'Pink Tea'.

Iris 'First Interstate'

Iris 'First Violet'

Iris 'Fjord'

Iris 'Fogbound'

Iris 'Full Impact'

Iris 'Gala Madrid' (L. Peterson 1967)
The reddish-brown falls are round and heavily smeared with violet down the centre. In stark contrast to the falls, the very ruffled standards are the colour of butterscotch. The beards are burnt orange. Height: 76 cm (30½ in.). Bloom: mid to late season. Parentage: 'Main Event' × 'Gypsy Lullaby'.

Iris 'Gibson Girl' (J. Gibson, year uncertain)
A reliable rebloomer, this plicata is very old fashioned in shape. The long downward-drooping, soft cream falls

Iris 'Fresno Calypso'

Iris 'Gaelic Jig'

Iris 'Gala Madrid'

Iris 'Frost and Flame'

Iris 'Gala Gown'

Iris 'Gibson Girl'

are heavily peppered with rose maroon. The standards are large, inward-curving, and almost entirely rose maroon in colour. The whiskery beards are ginger coloured. This hybrid was registered in 1946, which could be the date it was introduced. Height: 91 cm (36½ in.). Bloom: midseason and reblooming. Parentage: 'Mme. Louis Aureau' × 'Tiffany'.

Iris 'Gilston Gwyneth' (Fletcher 1963)
The colour of this soft blue variety is unevenly spread across the petals. The very ruffled inward-curving standards are smeared with violet from the base, and the flaring, gently ruffled falls are flushed with violet in the centre. The white beards are tipped with yellow at the back. Height: 87 cm (34¾ in.). Bloom: midseason. Parentage: 'Pegasus' × ('Cascadian' × 'Keene Valley').

Iris 'Givendale' (B. Dodsworth 1989)
This very ruffled flower is ginger coloured, with deeper-coloured veins running down all the petals. Each fall has a violet stripe down the centre. The beards are rich orange. Height: 107 cm (43 in.). Bloom: early season. Parentage: 'Flareup' × 'Carnival Time'.

Iris 'Gnu' (B. Kasperek 1993)
The lavender falls are heavily streaked with white splashes. The beards are burnt orange. The very ruffled standards are soft lilac and stained around the edges with deeper lavender streaks. Height: 81 cm (32½ in.). Bloom: midseason. Parentage: 'Maria Tormena' × 'Eagle's Flight'.

Iris 'Gnu Again' (B. Kasperek 1993)
This flower with broken (unstable) colours has flaring falls that are velvety, rose purple and curl up at the edges. The falls are irregularly splashed with white and are deco-

rated with burnt orange beards. The ruffled standards are a softer purple in colour and have one or two white splashes. Height: 81 cm (32½ in.). Bloom: midseason. Parentage: 'Maria Tormena' × 'Eagle's Flight'.

Iris 'Gnus Flash' (B. Kasperek 1994)
Another flower with broken (unstable) colours, this hybrid combines black-violet and tan. The flaring falls are very dark violet and streaked and lined with white. The ruffled standards are basically tan in colour, but the edges are veined with brown, a colour that washes into larger streaks. The beards are soft yellow, and the flower is slightly scented. Height: 97 cm (38¾ in.). Bloom: early season. Parentage: 'Glitz 'n Glitter' × 'Tiger Honey'.

Iris 'Go Between' (G. Grosvenor 1998)
The bluish-white flower has tightly ruffled and laced petals. On opening, the standards are a distinct soft blue. The white beards are tipped with yellow. The flowers are carried on well-branched stems and are heavily scented. Height: 89½ cm (35 in.). Bloom: midseason. Parentage: 'Kuniko' × 'Silverado'.

Iris 'Godfrey Owen' (M. Owen 1986)
This frilly, neatly ruffled flower has pale lemon standards and white falls that are edged with a broad band of lemon. The beards are bright yellow. The blooms, which are borne in perfect symmetry on upright stems, have a strong lemon scent. Height: 91 cm (36½ in.). Bloom: early to late season. Parentage: 'Percy Brown' × 'Liz'.

Iris 'Godsend' (M. Byers 1988)
The flowers have mid-pink standards and pink-white falls that are stained with beige on hafts. The beards are red-orange and extend to long up-

Iris 'Gilston Gwyneth'

Iris 'Givendale'

Iris 'Gnu'

Iris 'Gnu Again'

Iris 'Godfrey Owen'

Iris 'Golden Alps'

Iris 'Gnus Flash'

Iris 'Godsend'

Iris 'Go Between'

Iris 'Going My Way'

ward-pointing amethyst horns. The flower has a strong, sweet fragrance. Height: 91 cm (36½ in.). Bloom: mid to late season. Parentage: 'Vanity' × 'Moonlit'.

Iris **'Going My Way'** (J. Gibson 1971) Popular from the time it was introduced, this plicata has standards that are almost entirely purple and falls that are white, banded with rich dark purple. The petals are ruffled and have a good substance. The flower is lightly scented. Height: 94 cm (37 in.). Bloom: midseason. Parentage: 'Border Happy' × 'Stepping Out'.

Iris **'Golden Alps'** (L. Brummitt 1952) The falls are on the greenish side of rich yellow, and the lemon-white standards are veined with dark yellow. On the hafts sit white stripes and bushy yellow beards that are darker in colour towards the throat. The style arms are edged with yellow around the crest. Height: 97 cm (38¾ in.). Bloom: midseason. Parentage: 'Admiration' × unknown. Dykes Medal Winner UK 1957.

Iris 'Golden Encore' (F. Jones 1972)
This smoothly shaped, bright yellow self has just a hint of a white flash on the falls. As a rebloomer, this hybrid never fails to produce flowers during late summer and into the autumn. Height: 89 cm (35½ in.). Bloom: early season and reblooming. Parentage: (('Happy Birthday' × 'Fall Primrose') × 'Fall Primrose') × 'Renaissance'.

Iris 'Golden Forest' (P. Hutchinson 1958)
This medium-sized flower has a form that was popular in the 1960s. It is deep straw yellow in colour with a large white flare on the falls and brown veins at the hafts. The beards are golden. The plant produces lots of very scented flowers. Height: 87 cm (34¾ in.). Bloom: midseason. Parentage: ('Dora Morris' × 'Benton Susan') × 'Dancing Sunlight'. Dykes Medal Winner UK 1969.

Iris 'Good Looking' (Schreiner 1995)
The colour is a sort of crushed black grape or maybe a dusky grey-violet with blue flashes down the midribs. The very short violet beards are tipped with ochre, and brown veins surround the hafts. The petals are ruffled and laced around the edges. The flower is slightly scented. Height: 94 cm (37 in.). Bloom: early to midseason. Parentage: 'Sultry Mood' × ('Visual Arts' × (a seedling which contains among other irises including 'Amethyst Flame')).

Iris 'Good Vibrations' (Schreiner 1997)
The short. ruffled standards are orange, and the white falls are broadly rimmed with orange. The beards are rich orange. The flower has a sharp, chocolaty scent. Height: 94 cm (37 in.). Bloom: mid to late season. Parentage: includes 'Pinafore Pink', 'Celestial Glory', 'Flaming Star', 'Flaming Light', 'Esther Fay', and 'Flaming Day'.

Iris 'G. P. Baker' (A. Perry 1930)
In its time this hybrid was a real breakthrough for British-raised plicatas. Many other plicatas lacked substance in their petals and were short, especially when compared with plicatas raised in California. The flowers are soft yellow, the falls being paler than the standards and covered with deep brown veins. Although they are small, the flowers are carried on long stems. Height: average. Bloom: midseason. Parentage: unknown. Dykes Medal Winner UK 1930.

Iris 'Great Lakes' (L. Cousins 1938)
Popular for many years, this sweetly scented variety produces deep mid-blue flowers with white beards that are tipped with orange. Height: average. Bloom: midseason. Parentage: ('Dauntless' × unknown) × ('Conquistador' × unknown). Dykes Medal Winner USA 1942.

Iris 'Gudrun' (Katherine Dykes 1925)
Very popular for many years after its introduction, this plant was valued for its large sweetly scented flowers. The large beards are white. Height: 76 cm (30½ in.). Bloom: midseason. Parentage: unknown. Dykes Medal Winner UK 1931.

Iris 'Gypsy Romance' (Schreiner 1994)
The ruffled, silky, vibrant purple flowers have maroon wing-like markings on the hafts and dark blue beards. The scent is light and spicy. Height: 94 cm (37 in.). Bloom: mid to late season. Parentage: ('Louisiana Lace' × 'Entourage') × ((seedling × 'Fabulous Frills') × 'Starcrest').

Iris 'Habit' (P. Black 1999)
This bicolour has velvety purple-black falls with frilly edges and soft lilac standards that are flecked with violet. The flower has golden yellow

Iris 'Golden Encore'

Iris 'Golden Forest'

Iris 'Good Looking'

Iris 'Good Vibrations'

Iris 'Gudrun'

beards and is scented. Height: 86 cm (34½ in.). Bloom: midseason. Parentage: 'In Town' × 'Oklahoma Crude'.

Iris 'Happenstance' (K. Keppel 2000) This bright pink iris has laced, lightly ruffled petals and standards that splay outwards. On the falls sit big, coral beards, and the flower is distinctively scented. Not known for toughness, according to Schreiner's 2003 catalogue, this pink is probably the hardiest and most vigorous variety available at the time of this writing. Height: 95 cm (38 in.). Bloom: midseason. Parentage: ('Femme

Iris 'G. P. Baker'

Iris 'Habit'

Iris 'Great Lakes'

Iris 'Gypsy Romance'

Iris 'Happenstance'

Fatale' × (('Nefertiti' × 'Playgirl') × 'Presence')) × 'Social Event'.

Iris 'Harbor Blue' (Schreiner 1954)
Vigorous growing, this variety produces violet-blue flowers with long, broad, drooping falls and shorter ruffled standards. On the hafts sits large patches of white that are lined with brown tiger-like stripes. The white beards are touched with yellow, and the flower is scented. Height: 91 cm (36½ in.). Bloom: midseason. Parentage: 'Jane Phillips' × 'Quicksilver'.

Iris 'Haute Couture' (J. Gatty 1995)
The very ruffled, blue-pink flowers are marked with peach around the coral beards. The falls are paler in colour, with darker serrated edges. The flower is lightly scented. Height: 86 cm (34½ in.). Bloom: mid to late season. Parentage: (('Nefertiti' × 'Playgirl') × 'Presence') × 'Rare Occasion'.

Iris 'Headlines' (L. Brummitt 1953)
Considering the age of this variety, its flower is still hard to beat for cleanliness of colour. The pure white standards are sometimes edged with an extremely fine line of purple, the same colour as the velvety falls and the style arms. The beard is yellow, and the flower is lightly scented. Height: 91 cm (36½ in.). Bloom: midseason. Parentage: 'Extravaganza' × 'Louise Baker'. Dykes Medal Winner UK 1959.

Iris 'Helen Dawn' (G. Grosvenor 1998)
This flouncy white flower has a faint yellow wash, and the white beards are tipped with yellow. The blooms are borne on stems with good branching, and they have a heavy, sharp scent. Height: 91 cm (36½ in.). Bloom: midseason. Parentage: 'Skating Party' × 'Scandia Delight'.

Iris 'Helen K. Armstrong' (S. Innerst 1993)
This large-flowered variety has deep violet-blue falls and sky-blue standards. The petals are visibly veined, and the scented blooms have blue beards. Height: 91 cm (36½ in.). Bloom: mid to late season. Parentage: 'Thunder Mountain' × 'Codicil'.

Iris 'Helen McGregor' (R. Graves 1946)
This soft blue-flowered variety has largely been superseded by the similar Iris 'Jane Phillips', also raised by Graves, although I. 'Helen McGregor' remained very popular in Britain and the United States for many years. It was named after the hybridizer's wife. Height: 91 cm (36½ in.). Bloom: midseason. Parentage: 'Purissima' × 'Cloud Castle'. Dykes Medal Winner USA 1949.

Iris 'Helene C' (J. Cayeux 1995)
Soft mauve-pink buds produce very frilly, ruffled soft pink flowers, a pink that is more blue than yellow. Brown veins surround the coral beards. Height: 95 cm (38 in.). Bloom: early to midseason. Parentage: 'Rosé' × 'Enchanted World'.

Iris 'Hello Darkness' (Schreiner *1992*)
This very dark variety produces purple-black flowers with velvety falls and shiny standards. The beards are also black. Height: 94 cm (37 in.). Bloom: early to midseason. Parentage: includes 'Allegiance', 'Navy Strut', 'Black Forest', 'Titan's Glory'. and 'Midnight Dancer'. Dykes Medal Winner USA 1999.

Iris 'Hell's Fire' (S. Roberts 1976)
This intensely coloured variety has old-fashioned, ruby red-brown flowers with bronze beards. Height: 91 cm (36½ in.). Bloom: early to midseason and reblooming. Parentage:('Lois Craig' × 'Edenite') × ('Adam' × 'Edenite').

Iris 'High Blue Sky' (R. Ernst 1998)
This pale blue-white flower has falls that are tinged with violet, a colour that leaks out from the veins to cover the whole falls. The standards are very ruffled, the falls less so. The beards are soft blue. Height: 89 cm (35½ in.). Bloom: midseason. Parentage: 'Proud Tradition' × 'Blue It Up'.

Iris 'High Master' (B. Blyth 2000)
The very ruffled flower has yellow standards and maroon falls with lacy, fine yellow edges. The colour on the falls breaks into fine veins over a pale yellow background. The yellow

Iris 'Harbor Blue'

Iris 'Haute Couture'

Iris 'Headlines'

Iris 'Helen McGregor'

Iris 'Hell's Fire'

Iris 'Helen Dawn'

Iris 'Helene C'

Iris 'High Blue Sky'

Iris 'Helen K. Armstrong'

Iris 'Hello Darkness'

Iris 'High Master'

is scented. Height: 102 cm (41 in.). Bloom: early to midseason. Parentage: includes 'Inca Queen', 'Tranquil Star', 'Love Chant', 'Festive Skirt', 'Amber Snow', 'Alpine Journey', 'Beachgirl', 'Coral Strand', 'Persian Smoke', and 'Chimbolam'.

Iris 'Indian Chief' (Ayers 1928)

This popular variety is still often found in gardens around England. The standards are a faded burgundy colour that is washed and veined over a yellow background. The falls are deeper in colour, a pure burgundy, and veined with maroon. The hafts have white markings, and the beards are yellow. The flower is scented. Height: 110 cm (44 in.). Bloom: early season. Parentage: 'Cardinal' × unknown.

Iris 'Indiscreet' (J. Ghio 1987)

This big, frilly mauve plicata has the colour stippled across a background of soft yellow. The standards are almost entirely mauve, while the fall have yellow edges. The beards are deep orange. Height: 97 cm (38¾ in.). Bloom: early to midseason. Parentage: includes 'Ponderosa', 'Claudia Rene', 'New Moon', 'Vanity', 'Anon', 'Flareup', and 'Osage Buff'.

Iris 'Interpol' (G. Plough 1972)

This purple-black flower has an old-fashioned shape. The tall, shiny standards touch at the top, and the long, oval, velvety falls droop downwards. The bushy beards are deep violet and are touched with mustard. The flower is sweetly scented. Height: 91 cm (36½ in.). Bloom: mid to late season. Parentage: ('Study In Black' sibling × 'Black Swan') × 'Charcoal' sibling.

Iris 'Into The Wilderness' (T. Blyth 2001)

A soft mustard-brown self, this hybrid has wide falls that are more yellow. The ruffled flowers are borne on stems with good branching. Height: 96 cm (38½ in.). Bloom: mid to late season. Parentage: lost.

Iris 'It's Magic' (W. Maryott 1994)

This bright, glowing yellow ruffled flower has large white patches on the falls, which sit in front of the deep orange beards. The beards elongate slightly into horns. Height: 91 cm (36½ in.). Bloom: midseason. Parentage: 'Lemon Fever' × 'Blowtorch'.

Iris 'I've Got Rhythm' (Schreiner 1998)

This small-flowered plicata has standards that are almost entirely rose maroon in colour, while the falls are mainly cream and rimmed with maroon. The short beards are deep tangerine. The flower is carried on a well-branched stem and has a light, spicy scent. Height: 97 cm (38¾ in.). Bloom: early to midseason. Parentage: 'Footloose' × ((('Cozy Calico' × 'Grape Accent') × 'Capricious') × 'Gigolo').

Iris 'Jaguar Blue' (G. Sutton 2001)

The unevenly coloured pale blue scented flowers have large round falls, short pale blue beards, and laced petals. Height: 91 cm (36½ in.). Bloom: late season. Parentage: 'Silver Flow' × 'Silverado'.

Iris 'Jane Phillips' (R. Graves 1946)

Entirely pale blue, the petals are lined with deeper blue veins and have the texture of crepe paper. Short brown stripes surround the white beards. The grey-green leaves are resistant to disease. Over the years this hybrid has been an important parent of many irises, including Iris 'Sapphire

Iris 'Indian Chief'

Iris 'Indiscreet'

Iris 'Interpol'

Iris 'Into The Wilderness'

Iris 'Jaguar Blue'

Hills. Height: 91 cm (36½ in.). Bloom: midseason. Parentage: 'Helen McGregor' × ('Pale Moonlight' × 'Great Lakes').

***Iris* 'Jazz Festival'** (Schreiner 1990) This large flower has broad, heavily ruffled petals. The soft buff-pink standards are washed with soft lilac, while the flaring, rose-violet falls contain a hint of maroon. The beards are violet, the distinctive style arms tan coloured. The flower is scented. Height: 102 cm (41 in.). Bloom: mid to very late season. Parentage: (('Breaking Dawn' × ('Amethyst

Iris 'It's Magic'

Iris 'Jazz Festival'

Iris 'I've Got Rhythm'

Iris 'Jane Phillips'

Flame' × (('Lavanesque' × 'Opal Beauty') × 'Wonderment'))) × 'Navajo Blanket' sibling) × (('Chapeau' × 'Bold Hour') × 'Lorilee').

Iris 'Jean Guymer' (L. Zurbrigg 1976) This reliable reblooming variety has very plain flowers by today's standards. Apricot in colour, the petals show off veining. The beards are tangerine, and the flower is slightly fragrant. Height: 91 cm (36½ in.). Bloom: early season and reblooming. 'Mary Maria' × 'Now and Later'.

Iris 'Jeanne Price' (B. Jones 1976) The rich yellow flowers have gently ruffled petals, which are delicately pinched around the edges. Below the bright yellow beards sit small white flares. The scent is strong and somewhat sickly. Height: 86 cm (34½ in.). Bloom: midseason. Parentage: 'Lemon Tree' × 'Shining Light'.

Iris 'Jennifer Rebecca' (L. Zurbrigg 1984) The ruffled flowers emerge from violet buds and open lavender-pink with violet edges. The standards are softer in tone. Buff-white veins surround the pale coral-red beards, and the flower has a pronounced, but sweet scent. Height: 89 cm (35½ in.). Bloom: midseason and reblooming. Parentage: 'Grace Thomas' × 'Vanity'.

Iris 'Jesse's Song' (B. Williamson 1979) This plicata is consistently the first Tall Bearded iris to flower in my nursery. The white petals are beautifully speckled with violet. The beards are soft violet, and the neatly ruffled flowers are borne on strong, straight stems. Height: 91 cm (36½ in.). Bloom: early to midseason. Parentage: ('Charmed Circle' × 'Kiss') × ('Smoke Rings' × 'Decolletage'). Dykes Medal Winner USA 1990.

Iris 'Jean Guymer'

Iris 'Jeanne Price'

Iris 'Jesse's Song'

Iris 'Jennifer Rebecca'

Iris 'Jitterbug'

Iris 'Jitterbug' (K. Keppel 1987)
This variety produces ruffled, bright yellow-and-brown plicata-patterned flowers. The darker colour is speckled across the falls like sandpaper, while the standards are lightly peppered with brown. The flowers are sweetly scented and have bright yellow beards. Height: 89 cm (35½ in.). Bloom: early season. Parentage: ('Rancho Rose' × 'Peccadillo' sibling) × 'Rustic Dance'.

Iris 'Joyce Terry' (T. Muhlestein 1974)
The flowers have large, round petals that are ruffled around the edges. The standards are mid yellow, and the white falls are edged with a similar colour. The beards are also yellow. Height: 97 cm (38¾ in.). Bloom: mid to late season. Parentage: 'Charmaine' × 'Launching Pad'.

Iris 'Juicy Fruit' (M. Byers 1988)
This lacy reblooming peach-pink variety has falls that are paler in colour and tangerine beards. Height: 86 cm (34½ in.). Bloom: very early to midseason and reblooming. Parentage: 'Howdy Do' × 'Coral Charmer'.

Iris 'Jurassic Park' (L. Lauer 1995)
The flowers have light mustard-yellow standards and violet falls that pale around the edges. The standards are flecked with soft purple. White tiger-like stripes on the hafts surround the sparse yellow beards. The flower is scented. Height: 91 cm (36½ in.). Bloom: early to midseason. Parentage: 'Best Bet' × ('Edith Wolford' × (('Regents' Row' sibling × 'Winterscape') × 'Midnight Love Affair')).

Iris 'Kangchenjunga' (H. Miller 1955)
The large pale, creamy white blooms have extremely ruffled petals and white beards that are tipped with yellow. The flower is highly scented. Height: 137 cm (55 in.). Bloom: midseason. Parentage: 'Desert Song' × 'Jane Phillips'. Dykes Medal Winner UK 1960.

Iris 'Kent Pride' (Hutchinson 1958)
This smoothly shaped chestnut-coloured plicata has falls that are speckled and veined with chestnut over a creamy yellow background. The beards are deep yellow. The foliage is purple at the base. Height: 91 cm (36½ in.). Bloom: midseason. Parentage: ('Dora Morris' × 'Benton Susan') × 'Dancing Sunlight'.

Iris 'Joyce Terry'

Iris 'Jurassic Park'

Iris 'Juicy Fruit'

Iris 'Kangchenjunga'

Iris 'Kent Pride'

Iris **'Kildonan'** (B. Dodsworth 1976)
The neatly ruffled mid-blue flowers have flaring falls that are slightly deeper in colour. The large standards touch at the top, and the beards are soft blue. Height: 107 cm (43 in.). Bloom: midseason. Parentage: 'Sterling Silver' × 'Pacific Panorama'. Dykes Medal Winner UK 1980.

Iris **'Kilt Lilt'** (J. Gibson 1969)
This plicata has petals that are heavily laced around the edges. The long, drooping white falls are stippled with brown, and down the centre runs a further streak of brown. On the golden hafts sit large, deep gold beards. The caramel standards are also large. Height: 102 cm (41 in.). Bloom: early to midseason. Parentage: seedling × 'Golden Filigree'. Dykes Medal Winner USA 1976.

Iris **'Kiss of Kisses'** (F. Kerr 1997)
Said to rebloom, this variety has soft lemon standards and white falls that are heavily washed around the edges with rosy violet. The beards are bright yellow, and the flower is sharply scented. Height: 89 cm (35½ in.). Bloom: midseason and reblooming. Parentage: 'Peach Picotee' × ('Gypsy Woman' × 'Condottiere').

Iris **'Laced Cotton'** (Schreiner 1978)
As the name suggests, this very lacy variety has gently ruffled, pure white petals. Even the buds are laced. The white beards are tipped with lemon. The flower is slightly scented. Height: 86 cm (34½ in.). Bloom: mid to late season. Parentage: ('Crinkled Joy' × seedling) × 'Grand Waltz'.

Iris **'Lady Essex'** (L. Zurbrigg 1990)
This reblooming variety has white petals that are veined and dotted with pale violet. The standards are paler in colour than the falls, and the white beards are just brushed with yellow.

Height: 86 cm (34½ in.). Bloom: midseason. Parentage: ('Needlecraft' × 'Earl of Essex') × ('Cross Stitch' × 'Earl of Essex').

Iris **'Lady Friend'** (J. Ghio 1980)
The ruffled flowers are hard to describe. The colour is a sort of pink-red or, perhaps as the breeder describes it, garnet-red. The beards are burnt orange. Height: 97 cm (38¾ in.). Bloom: very early to early season. Parentage: 'Indian Territory' × 'Countryman'.

Iris **'Lark Ascending'** (B. Hager 1994)
This variety produces white flowers with bright tangerine beards and ruffled petals that are laced around the edges. Height: 122 cm (49 in.). Bloom: mid to late season. Parentage: complicated and including crosses of many seedlings.

Iris **'Latin Lark'** (B. Blyth 1988)
This very ruffled flower has fluted falls that are rose maroon and rimmed with soft coral-orange. The standards and the stripes on the hafts are the same coral tone. The beards are bright orange. Height: 91 cm (36½ in.). Bloom: early to midseason. Parentage: ('Capricorn Dancer' × 'Anon') × 'Queen In Calico'.

Iris **'Latin Rock'** (Schreiner 1984)
This variety produces sweetly scented flowers in a handsome blend of colours. The soft orange standards are flushed with soft purple, while the velvety falls are pink-plum and stained with magenta. The petals are large and ruffled, and the beards are soft orange. Height: 99 cm (39½ in.). Bloom: midseason. Parentage: ('Breaking Dawn' × 'Fairy Magic') × mixed seed of unknown parentage.

Iris **'Lavensque'** (Schreiner 1953)
This pink-lilac flower has drooping

falls that pale in colour around the edges. The hafts are marked with wings of brown and veins of white, and the beards are tipped with yellow at the back. The standards are slightly paler in colour. Height: 89 cm (35½ in.). Bloom: midseason. Parentage: 'Dreamcastle' × ('Angelus' seedling × 'Matula' seedling).

Iris **'Leda's Lover'** (B. Hager 1979)
The large, very ruffled flower is pure white with yellow veins sitting at the hafts around the beards. The cream-coloured beards are touched with yellow towards the back. The flower is

Iris 'Kildonan'

Iris 'Kilt Lilt'

Iris 'Kiss of Kisses'

Iris 'Lady Friend'

Iris 'Latin Rock'

Iris 'Laced Cotton'

Iris 'Lark Ascending'

Iris 'Lavensque'

Iris 'Lady Essex'

Iris 'Latin Lark'

Iris 'Leda's Lover'

scented. Height: 97 cm (38¾ in.).
Bloom: midseason. Parentage: 'Geometrics' sibling (blue) × 'Ice Sculpture'.

Iris 'Lemon Brocade' (N. Rudolph 1973)
The laced, ruffled flowers have soft
lemon yellow standards and white
falls that are broadly edged with yellow. The petals are heavy in substance, and the white beards are
tipped with yellow. The flowers are
scented of lemon. Height: 86 cm
(34½ in.). Bloom: midseason. Parentage: 'Cream Taffeta' × seedling.

Iris 'Lightning Bolt' (J. Ghio 1992)
This sweetly scented variety is a vibrant blend of violet-blue and soft
rosy mauve with coral beards. The
petals are ruffled around the edges,
and the falls flare out horizontally,
while the standards arch inwards.
The plant produces many flowers on
well-branched stems. Height: 89 cm
(35½ in.). Bloom: early to late season.
Parentage: (('Act of Love' × 'Lady
Friend') × (('Entourage' × 'Home-
coming Queen') × 'Mulled Wine')) ×
'Stratagem'.

Iris 'Lilac Wine' (B. Blyth 1977)
The velvety, deep red-brown falls
have deeper brown veins. Above the
falls sit pale lilac standards that are
heavily flushed with beige. The
beards are yellow, and the flower is
scented. Height: 91 cm (36½ in.).
Bloom: early to midseason. Parentage: ('Barcelona' × 'Outer Limits') ×
('Snowlight' × 'Visionary' sibling).

Iris 'Lingering Love' (D. Meek 1986)
This basically white plicata flower is
flecked and veined with soft rose purple. The ruffled petals are laced
around the edges, and the burnt
orange beards are short. The flower
has a sharp fragrance. Height: 91 cm

Iris 'Lemon Brocade'

Iris 'Lingering Love'

Iris 'Lightning Bolt'

Iris 'Little John'

Iris 'Lilac Wine'

Iris 'Local Color'

(36½ in.). Bloom: mid to late season. Parentage: 'Magenta Rose' × ('Grecian Gown' × (seedling × 'Apricot Blaze')).

Iris 'Little John' (D. Spoon 1995)

This ruffled, frilly edged variety has vibrant violet falls that are tinged with blue and violet beards that are tipped with orange at the back. The standards are buff-peach, and the flowers are sharply scented. Height: 86 cm (34½ in.). Bloom: midseason. Parentage: 'Damsel' × 'Queen Dorothy'.

Iris 'Local Color' (K. Keppel 1995)

The royal purple flowers have neatly arched standards and velvety, dark purple falls that fade to a paler colour around the edges. Short soft purple stripes surround the bright orange beards. The gently ruffled flower is scented. Height: 107 cm (43 in.). Bloom: midseason. Parentage: 'Witches' Sabbath' × 'Gallant Rogue'.

Iris 'Lord of Letters' (B. Blyth 2000)

This plicata-amoena combination has flaring, laced, white falls that gently undulate around the edges. The edges are speckled with purple dots that spread a little inwards. The hafts are banded with a further stippling of purple-black and on these sit soft mustard-coloured beards. The ruffled standards are pale lilac. Height: 91 cm (36½ in.). Bloom: mid to late season. Parentage: 'Hey Dreamer' × 'Harmonics'.

Iris 'Lord Warden' (J. Taylor 1966)

The rich golden yellow flower has petals that are short and round and falls that are decorated with golden orange beards. Height: 84 cm (33½ in.). Bloom: midseason. Parentage: 'Ethel Miller' × 'Melbreak'.

Iris 'Lorilee' (Schreiner 1981)

The large, soft rosy lavender flowers have white flashes on the falls and sparsely whiskered brownish-yellow beards. The falls are lightly ruffled and flaring, the style arms short and buff coloured. The flower is scented. Height: 94 cm (37 in.). Bloom: mid to mid-late season. Parentage: ((('Amethyst Flame' × seedling) × 'Lilac Supreme') × 'Warm Laughter' sibling) × 'Cranberry Ice'.

Iris 'Lotus Land' (K. Keppel 1999)

The very lacy, gently ruffled flowers are buff-pink in colour. The centre of the flaring falls is softer in tone, while the large, bushy coral beards are paler at the tips. Height: 91 cm (36½ in.). Bloom: midseason. Parentage: ('Social Event' × 'Femme Fatale') × ('Social Event' × 'Bubble Up').

Iris 'Lord of Letters'

Iris 'Lorilee'

Iris 'Lord Warden'

Iris 'Lotus Land'

Iris 'Lovely Again' (R. G. Smith 1963)
A never-failing rebloomer, this hybrid
has lavender flowers that soften in
colour with age. The beards are pale
yellow, and the flower is scented.
Height: 76 cm (30½ in.). Bloom:
early season and reblooming. Parentage: the product of two seedlings.

Iris 'Lyme Time' (V. Messick 1995)
This variety produces large, ruffled
soft yellow flowers that are laced
around the edges and reveal pink undertone. The caramel beards are surrounded at either side by wings of the
same colour. The flower is lightly
scented. Height: 91 cm (36½ in.).
Bloom: mid to late season. Parentage:
'Fortunata' × 'Copper Lace'.

Iris 'Mabel Chadburn' (Chandron 1939)
The falls of this rich yellow self hang
downwards at first but then flare out
as the flowers age and get bigger. The
edge of the petals is serrated, and the
flower is strongly scented. Height: average. Bloom: midseason. Parentage:
'Golden Hind' × unknown. Dykes
Medal Winner UK 1941.

Iris 'Madeira Belle' (Quadros 1967)
This robust variety has lightly
scented, ruffled white flowers that
are flushed with lilac and emerge
from pale green buds. The beards are
white, and the short sturdy stems are
well branched. Height: 91 cm (36½
in.). Bloom: early to midseason.
Parentage: 'Lovilia' × 'Angel's Dream'.

Iris 'Magical Encounter' (Schreiner
1999)
The salmon-pink flower has dainty
ruffled edges, soft coral beards, and a
light nutmeg scent. Its parentage includes many award-winning irises.
Height: 89 cm (35½ in.). Bloom:
early to late season. Parentage: includes 'Amethyst Flame', 'Rippling
Waters', 'Chantilly', 'Cherie', 'Pretty
Carol', and 'Dreamsicle'.

Iris 'Lovely Again'

Iris 'Mabel Chadburn'

Iris 'Lyme Time'

Iris 'Magical Encounter'

Iris 'Madeira Belle'

Iris 'Maisie Lowe'

Iris 'Maisie Lowe' (J. L. Gibson 1930)
This variety produces very large flowers with silky, gently ruffled, deep purple standards and velvety, slightly wavy, royal purple falls. The blue beards are tipped with orange. Height: unknown. Bloom: mid to late season. Parentage: 'Dominion' × 'Souvenir de Mme. Gaudichau'. Dykes Medal Winner UK 1948.

Iris 'Mallow Dramatic' (J. Gatty 1995)
The lacy, rosy violet flowers have overtones of beige. The standards sit straight up, while the falls flare out and have a small, light blue flash in front of the white beards. The beards are heavily brushed with coral. The flowers have a light but sharp scent. Height: 91 cm (36½ in.). Bloom: midseason. Parentage: 'Coming Up Roses' × 'Designing Woman'.

Iris 'Mandela' (J. Ghio 1998)
The petals are very ruffled and frilly around the edge. The rosy lavender falls are pale in the centre. The standards are almost white, but these are stained by a flush of lavender that emerges from the bottom of the petals. The dark orange beards fade to almost white at the tip. Height: 81 cm (32½ in.). Bloom: mid to late season. Parentage: ('Pink Ballerina' × ('Newlywed' × 'Caption')) × 'Boudoir' sibling.

Iris 'Mary Frances' (L. Gaulter 1971)
The lavender flowers are ruffled around the edge with flaring falls and round standards that just touch at the sides. All the petals are paler in the centre. The white beards are brushed with yellow. Height: 97 cm (38¾ in.). Bloom: midseason. Parentage: 'Town and Country' × ('Marie Phillips' × 'Sterling Silver'). Dykes Medal Winner USA 1979.

Iris 'Mary Geddes' (T. Stahlman-Washington 1931)
The simple flowers have copper standards and russet falls. Yellow veins run halfway down the petals, and the beards are yellow. Height: average. Bloom: mid to late season. Parentage: 'Dejazet' × 'Sherbert'. Dykes Medal Winner USA 1936.

Iris 'Mallow Dramatic'

Iris 'Mary Frances'

Iris 'Mary Geddes'

Iris 'Mandela'

Iris 'May Melody' (M. Hamblen 1964)
The bright yellow flower has flaring falls that are essentially white and rimmed with yellow. On them sit bright orange beards. The petals are toothed around the edges. Height: 91 cm (36½ in.). Bloom: early to late season. Parentage: (yellow sibling to 'Valimar' × 'June's Sister') × 'Cotlet'.

Iris 'Melbreak' (H. Randall 1958)
Well respected at the time of its introduction, this variety was considered to be a new look in the colour category of pink. The colour, however, is really not pink at all, but rather buff peach. The hafts have soft brown veins, and the beards are tangerine. Height: 91 cm (36½ in.). Bloom: midseason. Parentage: ('Cherie' × 'Angela Borgia') × 'Mary Randall'.

Iris 'Melted Butter' (Chun Fan 1992)
The ruffled standards are white and flushed with yellow from the base, while the large, round falls are butter yellow, a colour that is more concentrated in certain areas. The white beards are tipped with orange, and the flower is sweetly scented. Height: 99 cm (39½ in.). Bloom: mid to late season. Parentage: 'Cup Race' × 'Coral Beauty'.

Iris 'Memphis Delight' (E.Kegerise1977)
The petals of this soft pink self are ruffled, round, and serrated along the edges. The falls display short tangerine beards below which a lighter patch of colour streaks the centre. Height: 86 cm (34½ in.). Bloom: late season. Parentage: 'Pink Taffeta' × 'Point Clear'.

Iris 'Men in Black' (L. Lauer 1998)
The flowers are glossy and very dark purple. As the petals unfurl, they look almost black. The dark purple beards are tipped with copper. The falls wave gently around the edges and the standards are ruffled. The

Iris 'May Melody'

Iris 'Melbreak'

Iris 'Melted Butter'

Iris 'Memphis Delight'

Iris 'Men in Black'

flower is very lightly scented. Height: 86 cm (34½ in.). Bloom: mid to late season. Parentage: 'Witches' Sabbath' × 'Black Fantasy'.

***Iris* 'Mescal'** (J. & V. Craig 1996)
This very ruffled, gently laced variety has soft lemon standards and creamy white falls that are edged with a rim of yellow speckles. The hafts are peppered with corn yellow. Yellow wings are evident on either side of the whiskery yellow beards. The scent is light and sweet. Height: 102 cm (41 in.). Bloom: late season. Parentage: unknown.

***Iris* 'Mesmerizer'** (M. Byers 1990)
The unusual flower has ruffled pure white petals that are just touched with cream. It produces long spoon-like flounces from its orange-tinted white beards. Unfortunately, it is not the most stable of varieties, and I have found blue as well as white flowers blooming on the same plant. Height: 91 cm (36½ in.). Bloom: midseason. Parentage: ('Sky Hook's × 'Condottiere') × 'Branching Out'. Dykes Medal Winner USA 2002.

***Iris* 'Midnight Oil'** (K. Keppel 1997)
This very black variety has gently ruffled petals that are thick in substance. The short standards open outwards, and bushy dark blue beards sit on the round falls. The flower is lightly scented. Height: 91 cm (36½ in.). Bloom: mid to late season. Parentage: (('Snowbrook' × 'Blackout') × 'Light Show' sibling) × 'Before the Storm'.

***Iris* 'Millennium Falcon'** (B. Kasperek 1998)
This bicolour with broken (unstable) colours has standards that splay outwards and falls that are semi-flaring. Both are gently ruffled. The soft violet-blue flowers are streaked with

Iris 'Mescal'

Iris 'Midnight Oil'

Iris 'Mesmerizer'

Iris 'Millennium Falcon'

white as are the rich purple falls. The beards are orange, and the flower is slightly scented. Height: 97 cm (38¾ in.). Bloom: midseason. Parentage: 'Gnus Flash' × ('Batik' × ('Rustic Dance' × 'Maria Tormena')).

Iris 'Mission Sunset' (C. Reckamp 1962)
The falls are burnt orange and shorter than the very upright gold standards. The beards are vivid yellow, and the flower is scented. Like many varieties from this period, this hybrid has poorly branched stems. Height: 97 cm (38¾ in.). Bloom: midseason. Parentage: ('Techny Chimes' × 'Fleeta') × 'Celestial Glory'.

Iris 'Missouri' (J. Grinter 1933)
This parent of many irises was greatly admired at the time of its introduction but is now considered a very old fashioned style of iris. The violet falls are paler around the edges. The V-shaped whiskery, white beards are tipped with yellow in the throat, and thick brown veins emerge from the throat. The standards are soft lilac in colour. Height: 102 cm (41 in.). Bloom: midseason. Parentage: 'Blue Ribbon' × 'Sensation'. Dykes Medal Winner USA 1937.

Iris 'Mlle Yvonne Pelletier' (unknown)
This variety is sometimes listed as *Iris* 'Yvonne Pelletier'. Graham Thomas, the famous horticulturist, gave me this charming plant in the late 1980s. I am amused to read that as far back as 1959 Graham finds irises like this one far preferable to the modern irises with flaring falls (Berrisford 1961). Very like *Iris pallida*, this hybrid has small, very pale violet-blue flowers and long white beards that are tipped with yellow. The flowers are borne on slender, well-branched stems with very clean foliage. Height: 114 cm (46 in.). Bloom: just after *I. pallida*. Parentage: unknown.

Iris 'Mme Chereau' (Lémon 1844)
One of the oldest named varieties, this hybrid is still available from iris nurseries. The very small flowers are carried on tall, upright, well-branched stems. They are white, with a broad band of violet stitched around the ruffled standards. The standards touch at the top. The falls are the same colour as the standards, but they have more obvious violet stitching. Height: 91 cm (36½ in.). Bloom: early season. Parentage: unknown.

Iris 'Mulberry Punch' (Schreiner 1992)
This dusky purple self has large petals that are ruffled and laced around the edges. The colour is uneven, and the beards are short. The flower has a spicy scent. Height: 99 cm (39½ in.). Bloom: mid to late season. Parentage: unknown.

Iris 'Mulled Wine' (K. Keppel 1981)
The flowers are rosy mauve with bushy deep orange beards. The petals are laced around the edges, and the flower is scented. Height: 91 cm (36½ in.). Bloom: late season. Parentage: ((('Amigo's Guitar' × ('Rippling Waters' × 'Gypsy Lullaby')) × (seedling × ('Marquesan Skies' × 'Babbling Brook'))) × 'Salmon River') × 'Maraschino'.

Iris 'Muriel Neville' (H. Senior Fothergill 1969)
When registered, this flower was described as being crimson, but it really has no red. I would describe it as mahogany-brown with velvety falls and silky standards. The petals are gently ruffled. The beards are burnt ginger, and the flower is strongly scented. Height: 107 cm (43 in.). Bloom: mid to late season. Parentage: ('Quechee' × 'Great Day') × (('Sequatchie' × 'Blood Carnelian') × ('Mexican Magic' × 'Benton Mochal')) × 'Ebony Echo'. Dykes Medal Winner UK 1973.

Iris 'Mission Sunset'

Iris 'Missouri'

Iris 'Mme Chereau'

Iris 'Mlle Yvonne Pelletier'

Iris 'Must Unite' (G. Grosvenor 1998)
This dark purple self has very ruffled, broad, shiny petals and purple-blue beards. Height: 99 cm (39½ in.). Bloom: mid to late season. Parentage: 'Holy Night' × 'Larry Gaulter'.

Iris 'Mute Swan' (B. Dodsworth 1985)
The pure white flowers have petals that are ruffled and laced around the edges. The large, whiskery beards are brushed with tangerine at the back. Height: 97 cm (38¾ in.). Bloom: midseason. Parentage: 'Princess' × 'Vanity'.

Iris 'Mulberry Punch'

Iris 'Muriel Neville'

Iris 'Must Unite'

Iris 'Mulled Wine'

Iris 'Mute Swan'

Iris 'My Honeycomb' (J. Gibson 1958)
Largely orange-yellow in colour, the flower is peppered with dark brown dots. The dots are softly scattered over the bottom of the falls and the standards, but they are much heavier around the hafts. A patch of white sits in the centre of each fall. The beards are yellow. Height: short. Bloom: midseason. Parentage: unknown.

Iris 'Mystique' (J. Ghio 1972)
The Bay View Gardens catalogue of 1981 described this iris as 'a sensation from its maiden bloom in 1971 to its pinnacle recognition in 1980, the Dykes Medal, on its first year of eligibility'. The falls are rose purple, while the soft blue standards are washed with blue from the base. The beards are soft blue, and the petals are ruffled. Height: 91 cm (36½ in.). Bloom: early to late season. Parentage: (((('Frosted Starlight' × ('Spanish Peaks' × 'Black Satin')) × (('Cahokia × Pierre Menard') × ('Black Forest × Chivalry'))) × 'Penthouse') × ('Mahalo' × 'Diplomacy')) × 'Veneration'. Dykes Medal Winner USA 1980.

Iris 'Nashborough' (J. Wills 1957)
The falls are velvety, deep mahogany-brown with bushy golden yellow beards. The dark yellow standards remain closed at the top. Height: 91 cm (36½ in.). Bloom: early to midseason. Parentage: includes 'Brown Thrasher', 'Hermitage', 'Hernani', 'Marvellous', 'Jerry', and 'Gay Troubadour'.

Iris 'New Leaf' (J. Ghio 1996)
This heavily laced, gently ruffled flower has flaring maroon-coloured, velvety falls that are edged with pale peach. Each fall has a patch of white on which sits a white beard. The pale peach standards are heavily washed with rose violet. Height: 81 cm (32½

Iris 'My Honeycomb'

Iris 'Mystique'

Iris 'New Leaf'

Iris 'Nashborough'

Iris 'New Moon'

in.). Bloom: midseason. Parentage: sibling to 'Skipalong'.

Iris 'New Moon' (N. Sexton 1968)
The flowers have large pure yellow petals that pale around the edges, orange beards, and a lemon scent. Height: 91 cm (36½ in.). Bloom: midseason. Parentage: 'Moon River' × 'New Frontier'. Dykes Medal Winner USA 1973.

Iris 'Nigerian Raspberry' (B. Kasperek 1994)
Basically pink in colour, the falls are heavily flecked with an uneven wash of maroon and decorated with bushy tangerine beards. The standards are also flecked but less so. The gently ruffled petals are laced around the edges, and the flowers are strongly scented. Height: 91 cm (36½ in.). Bloom: midseason. Parentage: 'Maria Tormena' × 'Bygone Era'.

Iris 'Night Ruler' (Schreiner 1990)
This ruffled, deep purple-black flower has fat, deep blue-black beards. The standards are shiny and touch at the top, while the falls are velvety and flare out. All the petals are tightly ruffled, and the flower is scented. The base of the leaves is stained with purple. Height: 99 cm (39½ in.). Bloom: midseason. Parentage: ((((('Black Onyx' × seedling) × 'Grand Ball' sibling) × 'Matinata') × 'Navy Strut') × ('Miriam Steel' × 'Ermine Robe').

Iris 'Ocelot' (J. Ghio 1997)
This laced and very ruffled flower has velvety, deep maroon falls and apricot-caramel standards. The beards are orange, and the flower is slightly scented. Height: 91 cm (36½ in.). Bloom: early to midseason. Parentage: 'Chinese New Year' × 'Romantic Evening'.

Iris 'Nigerian Raspberry'

Iris 'Night Ruler'

Iris 'Ocelot'

Iris 'Oh Jamaica' (Schreiner 1995)
The large flower has rose-maroon falls and peach standards that are flushed with a wash of maroon. The beards are deep orange. The bud count is excellent, and the plant produces flowers long after all other irises have finished. Despite being tall, the stems remain upright even in strong winds and heavy rain. The flower is lightly scented. Height: 102 cm (41 in.). Bloom: mid to very late season. Parentage: ((((('October Ale' × 'Hi Top') × (('Wild Ginger' × 'Taste of Honey') × (('Olympic

Iris 'Oh Jamaica'

Torch' × 'Brass Accents' sibling) × ((((seedling × 'Casa Morena') × 'Inca Chief') × 'Dark Chocolate')))) × 'Copper Nugget') × 'San Jose').

Iris 'Ola Kala' (J. Sass 1941)
The bright yellow flowers are smoothly shaped and small. The falls flare out slightly and sit below standards that are closed at the top. Light brown veins surround the deep yellow beards. This is a robust plant with scented flowers. Bloom: late season. Parentage: ('Prairie Sunset' × unknown) × ('Golden Age' × unknown). Dykes Medal Winner USA 1948.

Iris 'Old Black Magic' (Schreiner 1996)
The silky, purple-black flower has ochre beards and short standards that open out. It is sharply scented. Height: 91 cm (36½ in.). Bloom: early to midseason. Parentage: 'Midnight Dancer' × 'Back in Black'.

Iris 'Olympic Torch' (Schreiner 1956)
The flowers at first appear to be rich golden bronze, but this hue when closely inspected is the result of different layers of colour. Basically a layer of orange is smeared over a yellow background. The rocket-shaped blooms have gently curved standards that just touch at the top and slightly ruffled falls that arch down. On either side of the bronze beard sit zebra stripes of brown. The flowers have a distinctive sweet scent. Height: short. Bloom: midseason. Parentage: 'Inca Chief' × seedling involving 'Prairie Sunset', 'Bryce Canyon', 'Watchfire'.

Iris 'Ominous Stranger' (S. Innerst 1992)
The pale lemon petals of this plicata have grey-violet markings, and the blue-white beards are brushed with bronze. The flowers appear from subtle purple spathes and have a spicy, orange scent. Height: 86 cm (34½ in.). Bloom: midseason. Parentage: 'Point Made' × sibling.

Iris 'Orange Order' (B. Dodsworth 1995)
The gently ruffled pure orange flower has bushy tangerine beards. Height: 91 cm (36½ in.). Bloom: late season. Parentage: 'Orange Dawn' × 'Fresno Calypso'.

Iris 'Orange Slices' (Niswonger 1986)
The flowers are melon-orange and have short fat coral beards. Height: 84 cm (33½ in.). Bloom: midseason. Parentage: 'Far Corners' × 'Copper Classic'.

Iris 'Oriental Glory' (Salbach 1952)
The colour of these flowers is essentially rose violet, but the falls are heavily smeared with dollops of dusky violet over a background of wine red. The beards are bright orange, and the smooth petals are broad and evenly proportioned, while the flaring standards are small. The flower is scented. Height: 91 cm (36½ in.). Bloom: late season. Parentage: unknown.

Iris 'Osaka' (J. Ghio 1991)
This variety has mauve falls and white standards that are washed from the base with lemon. The yellow beards are surrounded by white stripes on the haft. The scent is light and spicy. Height: 107 cm (43 in.). Bloom: early to midseason. Parentage: ('Success Story' × ('Fancy Tales' × 'Alpine Castle')) × ((('Entourage' × ('Carved Cameo' × 'Louise Watts')) × 'Marauder' sibling) × 'Bristo Magic').

Iris 'Ostentatious' (J. Ghio 1997)
The flowers have glossy, burgundy-maroon standards and velvety, corn yellow falls that are edged with maroon. White veins surround the brown beards, and the flowers are lightly scented. Height: 97 cm (38¾ in.). Bloom: mid to late season. Parentage: includes many of Ghio's favourite irises such as 'Goddess', Rancho Rose', 'Flareup', 'Osage Buff', 'Vanity', 'Anon', 'Gay Parasol', 'Mystique', 'Ponderosa', 'Claudia Rene', 'New Moon', 'Gigolo', and 'Epicenter'.

Iris 'Out of Control' (W. Maryott 1994)
The gently ruffled flower is a combination of purple and white, which is streaked and splashed across the

Iris 'Ola Kala'

Iris 'Old Black Magic'

Iris 'Olympic Torch'

Iris 'Orange Slices'

Iris 'Ominous Stranger'

Iris 'Oriental Glory'

Iris 'Ostentatious'

Iris 'Orange Order'

Iris 'Osaka'

Iris 'Out of Control'

petals. The beards are soft blue, and the flower has a light, spicy scent. Height: 86–89 cm (34–35 in.). Bloom: mid to late season. Parentage: 'Colours' × 'Batik'.

Iris 'Out Yonder' (G. Wickersham 1969)
This smoothly shaped, gently ruffled flower has flaring violet-blue falls and pale blue standards. The white beards are brushed at the back with soft yellow. Height: 91 cm (36½ in.). Bloom: midseason. Parentage: unknown.

Iris 'Overjoyed' (J. Gatty 1993)
The large frilly flower has cream standards that are washed with soft yellow and lemon falls that are paler around. The beards are soft lemon yellow. The flower is sharply scented. Height: 89 cm (35½ in.). Bloom: midseason. Parentage: 'Perfect Interlude' × 'Sunny and Warm'.

Iris 'Owyhee Desert' (L. Pinkston 1996)
The flowers are the colour of vanilla ice cream. The petals, which are of a good substance, are drizzled with a netting of honeycomb and edged further with a rim of white. The falls flare out horizontally. The beards are light lemon, and the flowers have a strong fragrance. Height: 91 cm (36½ in.). Bloom: mid to late season. Parentage: 'Wild Jasmine' × unknown.

Iris 'Pacific Mist' (Schreiner 1979)
The petals of this pale blue variety are washed with violet, and the soft blue beards are tipped with soft yellow. The blooms are carried on a well-branched stem. Height: 91 cm (36½ in.). Bloom: mid to late season. Parentage: 'Apropos' × seedling.

Iris 'Pagan Dance' (B. Blyth 1989)
This variety produces flowers with round, deep black-violet falls that are broadly edged with deep lavender. The standards are lavender-purple, and the beards are deep orange. The flower is scented and said to rebloom. Height: 81 cm (32½ in.). Bloom: early to late season, reblooming. Parentage: 'Cameo Wine' × 'In Smoke'.

Iris 'Paint It Black' (Schreiner 1994)
The ruffled flowers are purple-black with black beards, and they are sweetly scented. Height: 91 cm (36½ in.). Bloom: mid to late season. Parentage: ('Black Dragon' × (((('Dark Boatman' × seedling) × 'Black Swan') × 'Navy Strut' sibling) × 'Storm Flurry')) × 'Back in Black' sibling.

Iris 'Painted From Memory' (B. Blyth 2000)
This plicata has broad, ruffled petals. The standards are essentially lilac-coloured, but the colour is heavily speckled across a white background. The white falls are heavily rimmed, then broadly banded with violet, a colour that ekes into the central area. The lilac beards are tipped with yellow. Height: 87 cm (34¾ in.). Bloom: midseason. Parentage: 'Hey Dreamer' × 'Harmonics'.

Iris 'Palace Gossip' (B. Blyth 1981)
The burgundy standards show almost nothing of the plicata patterning visible in the white falls with their broad burgundy borders. The soft purple beards are tipped with bronze. Height: 86 cm (34½ in.). Bloom: early to midseason. Parentage: 'Going My Way' × 'Caramba'.

Iris 'Palomino' (D. Hall 1952)
This pale pink flower represents the earliest of the pink Tall Bearded irises. Although not entirely pink, it was in its time as near to pink as any Tall Bearded iris could get. The upright, oval standards are soft pink,

Iris 'Out Yonder'

Iris 'Overjoyed'

Iris 'Owyhee Desert'

Iris 'Pacific Mist'

Iris 'Painted From Memory'

Iris 'Panama Hattie'

Iris 'Pagan Dance'

Iris 'Palace Gossip'

while the long downward-pointing falls are creamy peach. The beards are soft orange. Height: 75 cm (30 in.). Bloom: early season. Parentage: 'Hi Time' × unknown.

Iris 'Panama Hattie' (J. Begley 1995) This tall flower has floppy, pale pink falls that are heavily etched with maroon, a colour that forms veins around the bright orange beards. The soft pink standards are flushed with pale mauve, and the flower has a chocolate scent. Height: 91 cm (36½ in.). Bloom: early to midseason. Parentage: 'Queen In Calico' × 'Rustic Dance'.

Iris 'Paint It Black'

Iris 'Palomino'

Iris 'Patina' (K. Keppel 1976)
The breeder notes in the British Iris Society yearbook of 1980 that although this Tall Bearded iris is 'of little garden value, it is an excellent example of an iris one either likes or hates'. Perhaps that is still true today. The variety may not be as prolific as many others, but I think it is quite a lovely thing. The delicate soft yellow colouring of the flower is suffused with soft brown. The stems are soft green, and the buds are tinged purple. Height: 89 cm (35½ in.). Bloom: midseason. Parentage: 'Limerick' × 'Roundup'.

Iris 'Peacetime' (L. Blyth 2001)
This very ruffled variety has soft blue-white standards that are flushed violet along the midrib and round lavender falls that are paler in the centre around the pale lavender beards. Height: 97 cm (38¾ in.). Bloom: mid to late season. Parentage: 'Coming Up Roses' × 'Born At Dawn'.

Iris 'Peach Float' (O. Brown 1973)
The pink-apricot flowers have standards that are a purer pink than the falls. The beards are deep orange. Height: 97 cm (38¾ in.). Bloom: mid to late season. Parentage: involves (pinks × 'Chinese Coral') × 'Flaming Heart'.

Iris 'Peach Spot' (G. Shoop 1973)
The flowers have soft peach-white standards that are flushed with orange-peach from the base and peach falls that are rimmed with peach-white. The beards are tangerine. Height: 91 cm (36½ in.). Bloom: midseason. Parentage: 'Snow Peach' × sibling.

Iris 'Pearls of Autumn' (B. Hager 1992)
This greyish-white self has gently wavy, laced petals. The falls and hafts have a pale yellow cast. The flower is scented and is said to rebloom in California. Height: 81 cm (32½ in.). Bloom: midseason and reblooming. Parentage: 'Mother Earth' × 'Bonus Mama'.

Iris 'Perfect Gift' (K. Keppel 1995)
This variety has scented, tightly ruffled, soft pink flowers. The standards are short, while the horizontal falls boast a paler flash of pink that extends the length of the petals. The beards are coral. Height: 86 cm (34½ in.). Bloom: midseason. Parentage: 'Social Event' × 'Femme Fatale'.

Iris 'Persian Berry' (L. Gaulter 1976)
This rosy lavender variety has ruffled petals that are laced around the edges. A paler tone extends down the centre of the falls below the tangerine beards. Originally the plant was registered simply as 'Berry'. Height: 89 cm (35½ in.). Bloom: midseason. Parentage: 'Holiday House' × 'Tiburon'.

Iris 'Pillow Fight' (D. Meek 1995)
This variety produces frilly, soft peach-pink flowers with paler falls and white beards that are touched with burnt orange at the back. Height: 86 cm (34½ in.). Bloom: early to midseason. Parentage: 'Magic' × 'Sugartime'.

Iris 'Pink Sleigh' (N. Rudolph 1970)
The lacy, pale pink flowers have coral beards and a spicy scent. Like many early pink varieties, this one is not a strong grower, but hybridizers have used it as a parent to produce pink irises. Height: 76 cm (30½ in.). Bloom: midseason. Parentage: seedling × 'Pink Taffeta'.

Iris 'Pinnacle' (J. Stevens 1949)
This yellow amoena is described in *The World of Irises* (Warburton and Hamblen 1978) as a white variety with yellow added to the falls. The white beards are tipped with yellow and surrounded by white veins. Height: 91 cm (36½ in.). Bloom: midseason. Parentage: ((('Rangatira' × 'Lady Morvyth') × 'Gudrun') × 'Lagos') × 'Magnolia'.

Iris 'Pipes of Pan' (O. Brown 1963)
The mauve falls are paler around the edges and have white stripes on the shoulders, behind long, bushy coral beards. The buff standards are washed with mauve towards the base. Height: 99 cm (39½ in.). Bloom: mid to late season. Parentage: ('Pinnacle' × pink seedling) × 'Gypsy Lullaby'.

Iris 'Patina'

Iris 'Peacetime'

Iris 'Peach Float'

Iris 'Perfect Gift'

Iris 'Pink Sleigh'

Iris 'Peach Spot'

Iris 'Persian Berry'

Iris 'Pinnacle'

Iris 'Pearls of Autumn'

Iris 'Pillow Fight'

Iris 'Pipes of Pan'

Iris 'Pledge Allegiance' (Schreiner 1983)

This ruffled, mid-blue flower has falls that are richer in colour than the standards and beards that are soft blue. Height: 124 cm (50 in.). Bloom: midseason. Parentage: (((seedlings) × 'Black Swan') × 'Navy Strut') × (seedling × 'Neptune's Pool').

Iris 'Poem Of Ecstasy' (B. Hager 1997)

A feminine sort of flower, this hybrid has pure pink standards and deep lavender falls. The petals are large, fluted, and ruffled, while the beards are a soft tangerine colour. Height: 91 cm (36½ in.). Bloom: midseason. Parentage: ('Merry Madrigal' × 'Mother Earth') × 'Adventuress'.

Iris 'Poetess' (B. Blyth 1999)

Although the hybridizer calls the colour of this flower coffee rose, I would describe it as fudge or coffee. The laced standards are flushed from the base with lavender, and the ruffled falls are paler below the tangerine beards. The flower is sweetly scented. Height: 97 cm (38¾ in.). Bloom: mid to late season. Parentage: 'Plume d'Or' sibling × 'Bygone Era'.

Iris 'Pond Lily' (E. Jones 1994)

Lilac-pink when they open, the flowers pale to pastel pink with a soft violet flush. The white beards are tipped with orange, and the lightly scented flowers are tightly borne on well-branched stems. Height: 97 cm (38¾ in.). Bloom: midseason. Parentage: includes 'Lullaby of Spring', 'Heather Blush', 'So Rare', 'Lilac Champagne', 'Betty Simon', 'Spanish Affair', 'Marilyn C', 'Orange Chariot', and 'Pink Sleigh'.

Iris 'Prairie Sunset' (H. P. Sass 1939)

A breakthrough in the colour pink at the time, this hybrid has proved to be a good parent. In colour it can hardly

Iris 'Pledge Allegiance'

Iris 'Poem Of Ecstasy'

Iris 'Pond Lily'

Iris 'Poetess'

Iris 'Prairie Sunset'

Iris 'Pretender'

be considered pink today, but more of a pink-copper with standards that are almost translucent and falls that are thicker in substance. White veins surround the whiskery golden beards. Height: average. Bloom: early season. Parentage: 'Sandalwood' × 'Amitola'. Dykes Medal Winner USA 1943.

Iris 'Pretender' (Cook 1951)
The falls are dark purple and the edges are bleached a paler colour. On the hafts sit prominent white veins and yellow beards that match the yellow standards. These are darker in

colour around the base of the petals. The flower is strongly scented. Height: 74 cm (29½ in.). Bloom: late season. Parentage: unknown.

Iris 'Primrose Drift' (L. Brummitt 1960)
This rich yellow self has slightly ruffled petals. The falls have small flares of white extending from the deep yellow beards. Height: 107 cm (43 in.). Bloom: mid to late season. Parentage: 'Arabi Pasha' × 'Cosmetic'. Dykes Medal Winner UK 1964.

Iris 'Private Treasure' (G. Shoop 1993)
The tangerine flowers have standards that are deeper in colour and falls that are more yellow. On these sit short coral beards that are surrounded by an area of white. The flowers are fairly small and gently ruffled and have a fruity fragrance. Height: 91 cm (36½ in.). Bloom: midseason. Parentage: 'Blazing Light' × 'Edna's Wish'.

Iris 'Prosper Laugier' (Verdier pre-1910)
I cannot recall how I came by this plant—it was probably through the Hardy Plant Society—and I am assuming it to be correctly named, as I cannot find any description so that it can be cross-referenced. The maroon falls are touched at the base with violet and edged with a small rim of buff. The buff standards are flushed with maroon-violet. The whiskery beards are yellow, and the hafts have white veins. Height: 91 cm (36½ in.). Bloom: midseason. Parentage: unknown.

Iris 'Proud Tradition' (Schreiner 1990)
The large, ruffled flowers have soft blue standards and round, dark blue falls. The beards are blue and tipped with yellow. The flowers open all the way down the strong stems. Height: 91 cm (36½ in.). Bloom: early to midseason. Parentage: (('First Violet' × 'King's Choice') × ('Allegiance' ×

Iris 'Prosper Laugier'

Iris 'Primrose Drift'

Iris 'Proud Tradition'

Iris 'Private Treasure'

((‘Pierre Menard’ × ‘Blue Ensign’) ×
‘Harbor Blue’)) × ((‘First Violet’ ×
‘Arabi Pasha’) × (‘Salem’ × ‘Bluebird
Blue’)) × ‘Navy Strut’) × ‘Royal Cru-
sader’.

Iris ‘Provencal’ (J. Cayeux 1978)

This rich chocolate-brown plicata has
a background of yellow that is heavily
speckled with brown. The standards
are almost solid in colour, and the
short beards are bronze. The petals are
thick in substance. Height: 91 cm
(36½ in.). Bloom: early to midseason.
Parentage: ‘Radiant Apogee’ × ‘High
Life’.

Iris ‘P. T. Barnam’ (J. Meek 1979)

The lightly ruffled, broad flowers
have tan standards and velvety, deep
wine red falls. The beards are golden
yellow. Height: 91 cm (36½ in.).
Bloom: mid to late season. Parentage:
‘Flaming Star’ × ‘Barcelona’.

Iris ‘Pumpkin Cheesecake’ (D. Nis-
wonger 1995)

Many of Dave Niswonger’s irises are
orange in colour, and this hybrid is
no exception. The flaring falls are soft
orange, and the white standards are
flushed with orange. The beards are
also orange, and the flower has a
sharp scent. Height: 76 cm (30½ in.).
Bloom: midseason. Parentage: ‘Apricot Frosty’ × (‘Ambrosia Delight’ ×
(‘Coral Beauty’ × pink amoena ‘Marmalade Skies’ sibling)).

Iris ‘Purple Pepper’ (D. Nearpass 1986)

This plicata has standards that are almost a solid violet colour, while the
falls are white and heavily freckled
with violet. All the petals are lightly
ruffled. The beards are yellow.
Height: 89 cm (35½ in.). Bloom:
midseason. Parentage: ‘Spinning
Wheel’ × ‘Easy Street’.

Iris ‘Provencal’

Iris ‘P. T. Barnam’

Iris ‘Purple Pepper’

Iris ‘Pumpkin Cheesecake’

Iris ‘Quaker Lady’

Iris 'Queen In Calico'

Iris 'Quaker Lady' (Farr 1909)
This subtly coloured flower has soft tan standards and pale lilac falls that are washed soft tan around the rims. White patches on the hafts are veined with brown, and the big beards are yellow. Height: 69 cm (27½ in.). Bloom: mid to late season. Parentage: unknown.

Iris 'Queen In Calico' (J. Gibson 1979)
In this ruffled plicata, the petals have a yellow background and are rivered with speckles of muted violet. The beards are deep orange. Height: 87 cm (34¾ in.). Bloom: midseason.

Iris 'Quito'

Iris 'Rameses'

Iris 'Rajah'

Iris 'Rapture in Blue'

Parentage: ('Orange Plush' × 'Anon') × ('Orange Plush' × a seedling).

Iris 'Quito' (J. Ghio 1992)
This burnt orange flower is tinged with deep brown at the hafts and in the depths of the ruffles. The large style arms are distinctive, and the sweetly scented flower has deep orange beards. Height: 102 cm (41 in.). Bloom: early to late season. Parentage: ('Esmeralda' sibling × 'Stratagem' sibling) × 'Bogota'.

Iris 'Rajah' (K. Smith 1942)
This smoothly shaped variegata has bright yellow standards and long, oval falls that are heavily covered with maroon-brown. The only yellow visible on the falls is around the edges. The bright orange-yellow beards have white stripes. Height: 91 cm (36½ in.). Bloom: midseason. Parentage: unknown.

Iris 'Rameses' (H. Sass 1928)
The flowers of this old award-winning iris have copper-coloured standards that arch outwards. They are deeper in colour at the top and yellow at the base. The falls are rose purple halfway up, then become yellow towards the hafts. Brown veins surround the long yellow beards. Height: 81 cm (32½ in.). Bloom: mid to late season. Parentage: 'King Tut' × 'Baldwin'. Dykes Medal Winner USA 1932.

Iris 'Rapture in Blue' (Schreiner 1990)
This variety produces large, heavily ruffled, sky-blue flowers with white beards and a light scent. Height: 91 cm (36½ in.). Bloom: midseason. Parentage: includes 'Sailor's Dance', 'Pacific Panorama', 'Parisian Blue', 'Sapphire Hills', 'Violet Harmony', 'Swan Ballet', 'Snowy Heron', and 'Tide's In'.

Iris 'Rare Quality' (Schreiner 1999)
The touching standards of this plicata would be purple if it was not for a large area of white in the centre. The falls are almost white except for a fine band of purple that is stitched into the white. Height: 91 cm (36½ in.). Bloom: midseason. Parentage: unknown × 'Honky Tonky Blues'.

Iris 'Raspberry Fudge' (K. Keppel 1988)
The background colour of this plicata flower is caramel. Speckled over this colour are dots and streaks of dark wine red, a similar colour to that of a good merlot wine. The beards are dark orange, and the flower is lightly scented. Height: 91 cm (36½ in.). Bloom: early to midseason. Parentage: 'Gigolo' × 'Columbia the Gem'.

Iris 'Raven Hill' (F. Carr 1973)
This black-blue self has flaring, gently ruffled, velvety falls that carry dark violet beards. The standards splay open. Height: 91 cm (36½ in.). Bloom: mid to late season. Parentage: ('Licorice Stick' × 'Dark Splendor') × 'Royal Touch'.

Iris 'Red Revival' (F. Preston 1975)
One of our most reliable reblooming varieties, this hybrid has pink-bronze standards and soft brown falls. The hafts are heavily veined with yellow and white, and the beards are deep orange. Height: 76 cm (30½ in.). Bloom: early to midseason and reblooming. Parentage: 'Fall Primrose' × 'Cayenne Capers'.

Iris 'Regal Affair' (G. Shoop 1989)
This slightly scented, ruffled bitone has purple-blue falls that are bleached white around the edges. The blue-white standards are tinged blue along the edges, and the hafts are heavily, but evenly, marked with white veins. The short beards are orange, and the flower is lightly scented. Height: 91 cm (36½ in.).

Bloom: midseason. Parentage: ('Condottiere' × 'Delphi') × seedling.

Iris 'Rime Frost' (L. Zurbrigg 1976)
The scented, white flowers, as they open, are just touched with blue. The blue fades rapidly, leaving the flower pure white. The flower has lightly ruffled petals and a little veining at the sides of the short white beards. Height: 89 cm (35½ in.). Bloom: midseason and reblooming. Parentage: 'Winter Olympics' × 'Grand Baroque'.

Iris 'Ringo' (G. Shoop 1979)
The gently ruffled flowers have white standards and rose-purple falls that are rimmed with white. The standards have a small flush of rose purple on their midribs. The beards are tangerine. Height: 91 cm (36½ in.). Bloom: midseason. Parentage: from seedlings of 'Behold', 'Fanfare Orchid', and 'Royal Host').

Iris 'Rippling River' (Schreiner 1995)
The velvety, deep royal-blue flower has petals that are tightly and extravagantly ruffled, glistening in the light. The beards are pale blue. The flower has a light, sweet scent. Height: 91 cm (36½ in.). Bloom: midseason.

Parentage: includes 'Shipshape', 'Sailor's Dance', 'Land o'Lakes', 'Pacific Panorama', 'Parisian Blue', 'Sapphire Hills', 'Neptune's Pool', 'Royal Regency', and 'Jean Hoffmeister').

Iris 'River Avon' (G. Sutton 1995)
This variety has strongly scented, gently ruffled, pale blue flowers with a paler centre to the falls and bushy violet-blue beards. Height: 99 cm (39½ in.). Bloom: early to late season. Parentage: 'Demi et Demi' × 'Chico Maid'.

Iris 'Role Model' (D. Denney by J. McWhirter 1988)
This variety produces a rosy copper-coloured flower with standards that are softer in colour compared with the falls. The hafts are decorated with neat copper veins, which form a butterfly-shaped pattern down the falls. The flower has tangerine beards and a spicy fragrance. Height: 91 cm (36½ in.). Bloom: early to midseason. Parentage: ('Spectacular Bid' × 'Brandy') × 'All That Jazz'.

Iris 'Roman Rhythm' (B. Blyth 1984)
The flower has velvety, rich burgundy-purple falls and rose-white standards. The burnt orange beards

Iris 'Rare Quality'

Iris 'Raspberry Fudge'

Iris 'Raven Hill'

Iris 'Rime Frost'

Iris 'River Avon'

Iris 'Red Revival'

Iris 'Ringo'

Iris 'Role Model'

Iris 'Regal Affair'

Iris 'Rippling River'

Iris 'Roman Rhythm'

have tips that are washed with ochre. Height: 91 cm (36½ in.). Bloom: early to midseason. Parentage: 'Tomorrow's Child' × ('Love Chant' × 'Festive Skirt').

Iris **'Romantic Evening'** (J. Ghio 1994) The lightly laced and ruffled flower has flaring, velvety, very dark deep purple falls and dark violet standards. The beards are deep copper, the style arms striped with deep purple, and the flower is lightly scented. Height: 91 cm (36½ in.). Bloom: mid to late season. Parentage: includes 'Success Story', 'Fancy Tales', 'Alpine Castle', 'Persian Smoke', 'Entourage', 'Strawberry Sensation', 'Artiste', 'Tupelo Honey', 'Costa Rica', and 'Witch's Wand').

Iris **'Rosalie Figge'** (J. McKnew 1991) This very gently ruffled, dark purple flower has a few white veins around its self-coloured beard. The flower has a good scent and is said to rebloom. Height: 99 cm (39½ in.). Bloom: midseason and reblooming. Parentage: 'Titan's Glory' × 'Violet Miracle'.

Iris **'Roseplic'** (J. Cayeux 1990) The basic colour of this gently ruffled plicata is white. The standards are almost solidly speckled with small dots of soft pink, while the falls are broadly edged with a light dotting of soft purple-pink. Height: 85 cm (34 in.). Bloom: mid to late season. Parentage: 'Pink Taffeta' × 'Schiaparelli'.

Iris **'Rosette Wine'** (Schreiner 1988) This ruffled, rosy-violet flower has a flush of bronze staining the midribs of the standards and the edges of the falls. Extending down the middle of the falls, from the violet-white beard, is a flare of white. Height: 91 cm (36½ in.). Bloom: early to late season.

Iris 'Romantic Evening'

Iris 'Rosalie Figge'

Iris 'Roseplic'

Iris 'Rosette Wine'

Iris 'Ruban Bleu'

Parentage: 'Lorilee' × 'Raspberry Frills' sibling.

***Iris* 'Ruban Bleu'** (J. Cayeux by R. Cayeux 1997)
The scented flower has white standards and ink-blue falls. A patch of white sits in front of the orange beards. Height: 85 cm (34 in.). Bloom: mid to late season. Parentage: ('Alizes' sibling × 'Love Bandit') × ('Condottiere' × 'Delphi').

***Iris* 'Ruby Mine'** (Schreiner 1961)
The smoothly shaped dark ruby red self has copper-coloured beards. The falls gently flare out below standards that open outwards. Height: 102 cm (41 in.). Bloom: mid to late season. Parentage: (('Pacemaker' × 'Argus') × 'Inca Chief') × 'Trim'.

***Iris* 'Rustic Cedar'** (Schreiner 1981)
This ruffled, copper-coloured flower has large petals and golden copper beards that are surrounded by butterfly wings of russet-brown veins. Height: 89 cm (35½ in.). Bloom: mid to late season. Parentage: (('Wild Ginger' × 'Taste of Honey') × 'Dutch Chocolate') × 'Hi Top'.

***Iris* 'Rustler'** (K. Keppel 1987)
The ruffled standards are orange-brown, and the chestnut-brown falls are caramel around the gently ruffled edges. White stripes appear on the hafts surrounding the orange beards. The flower has a sweet fragrance. Height: 94 cm (37 in.). Bloom: midseason. Parentage: 'Laredo' × 'Dazzling Gold'.

***Iris* 'Sable'** (P. Cook 1938)
The velvety, violet-black flowers have long falls with plain edges and dark violet standards that arch inwards. The violet beards are touched with yellow. Height: 91 cm (36½ in.). Bloom: early to midseason. Parentage: includes 'Innocenza', 'Blue Boy', 'Cinnabar', and 'Seminole'.

Iris 'Ruby Mine'

Iris 'Rustler'

Iris 'Rustic Cedar'

Iris 'Sable'

Iris 'Select Circle' (J. Ghio 1996)
Each fall of this rich, dark plum-purple plicata has a white spot, a yellow flush, and purple stitching. The standards are fluted and more purple than cream. The neatly ruffled flower is scented of nutmeg. Height: 97 cm (38¾ in.). Bloom: early to late season. Parentage: 'Epicenter' sibling × 'Somersault' sibling.

Iris 'Serene Moment' (Schreiner 1998)
This glowing, glistening flower has frilly petals that are basically lavender, edged with russet-pink and flushed with pale blue and white. Russet-brown patches at the hafts surround the orange beards. The flower is sweetly scented. Height: 97 cm (38¾ in.). Bloom: midseason. Parentage: 'Grape Ice' × 'Mulberry Punch'.

Iris 'Shipshape' (S. Babson 1968)
Cobalt-blue in colour, the ruffled flowers are borne on well-branched stems and have short white beards. The petals are shiny, and the flowers are lightly scented. Height: 97 cm (38¾ in.). Bloom: midseason. Parentage: 'Pacific Panorama' × 'Epic'. Dykes Medal Winner USA 1974.

Iris 'Shurton Inn' (C. Bartlett 1994)
Named after a pub the hybridizer frequented, this hybrid has white standards that are flushed with ochre. The falls are also white, but this colour almost disappears under a large patch of ochre. The beards are dark yellow, and the petals are ruffled. Height: 86 cm (34½ in.). Bloom: mid to late season. Parentage: ((((('Chimbolam' × 'Walter Bruce') × ('Chimbolam' × inv. 'Tracey')) × ('Champagne Braise' × ('Alpine Sunshine' × 'Sun King'))) × 'Echo de France') × 'Fritillary Flight'.

Iris 'Select Circle'

Iris 'Shurton Inn'

Iris 'Serene Moment'

Iris 'Sierra Blue'

Iris 'Shipshape'

Iris 'Silk Brocade'

Iris 'Silverado'

Iris 'Siva Siva'

Iris 'Skating Party'

Iris 'Skier's Delight'

Iris 'Sierra Blue' (E. Essig 1932)
This old variety has pale blue petals. The flowers are unruffled with standards that close up at the top and falls that droop downwards. Height: average. Bloom: midseason. Parentage: 'Souvenir de Mme. Gaudichau' × 'Sta. Barbara'. Dykes Medal Winner USA 1935.

Iris 'Silk Brocade' (K. Keppel 1998)
This plicata has rosy mauve markings peppered into rivers across a background that reminds me of a strawberry milkshake. The standards are almost entirely rosy mauve, while the beards are orange. The flower is sharply scented. Height: 89 cm (35½ in.). Bloom: early to midseason. Parentage: (('Highland Haze' × 'Change of Heart' sibling) × ('Ever After' × 'Lorilee')) × 'Dawn Sky'.

Iris 'Silverado' (Schreiner 1987)
This soft blue self produces large, slightly scented flowers with purple touches here and there. The hafts have distinctive brown veins. Height: 97 cm (38¾ in.). Bloom: midseason. Parentage: ('Starina' × 'Navy Strut') × 'Carriage Trade'. Dykes Medal Winner USA 1994.

Iris 'Siva Siva' (J. Gibson 1961)
The standards of this ruffled plicata are almost entirely ginger, a colour that is stippled tightly across a yellow background. The falls are white and speckled with mahogany-brown. The beards are soft yellow. Height: 91 cm (36½ in.). Bloom: midseason. Parentage: 'My Honeycombe' × seedling.

Iris 'Skating Party' (L. Gaulter 1983)
This large, ruffled, blue-white flower has yellow-stained falls that exhibit just a few brown veins sitting below the surface of the petals. The beards are white, and the flower is lightly scented. Height: 86 cm (34½ in.). Bloom: mid to late season. Parentage: ('Portrait of Larrie' × 'Carriage Trade') × sibling.

Iris 'Skier's Delight' (Schreiner 1982)
This pure white flower has very ruffled and fluted petals. The beards are also pure white. Height: 91 cm (36½ in.). Bloom: early to midseason. Parentage: 'Miriam Steel' × (('Sylvan Stream' × seedling) × ('Curl'd Cloud' × 'Florence Bellis')).

***Iris* 'Sky Hooks'** (M. Osborne 1979)
This hybrid was introduced as a
'space age' iris because of the rich
orange-yellow beards that end in
large hooks. The ruffled flowers have
soft yellow falls and laced standards.
Height: 97 cm (38¾ in.). Bloom:
midseason. Parentage: 'Wedding
Vow' × 'Moon Mistress'.

***Iris* 'Skylark Song'** (Schreiner 1996)
The blue-white ruffled flowers are
flushed with pale blue throughout
the falls and short white beards. The
stems are well branched, and the
flower is slightly scented. Height: 91
cm (36½ in.). Bloom: mid to late season. Parentage: 'Overnight Sensation' × 'Oregon Skies'.

***Iris* 'Smoke Rings'** (J. Gibson 1971)
This ruffled cream-white plicata is
stippled with pale plum and amber.
The flower is very fragrant. Height:
94 cm (37 in.). Bloom: midseason.
Parentage: ((seedling × 'Rococo') ×
'April Melody') × seedling.

***Iris* 'Sneezy'** (K. Keppel 1996)
The overall colour of the standards is
soft orange. This colour is flecked
with purple, while the falls, which
vary from soft orange through cream
to white, are finely sanded with purple. The beards are bright orange,
and the scented flowers are held on
well-branched stems. Height: 74 cm
(29½ in.). Bloom: midseason. Parentage: includes 'Light Show', 'Morocco',
'Broadway', 'Theatre', 'Anon', and
'April Melody'.

***Iris* 'Snow Mound'** (Schreiner 1976)
This bicolour has rich blue-purple
falls and pure white standards. The
white beards are tipped with yellow
towards that back, and short white
stripes surround the beards. Height:
91 cm (36½ in.). Bloom: midseason.
Parentage: (('Indiglow' × 'Toll Gate')

Iris 'Sky Hooks'

Iris 'Skylark Song

Iris 'Smoke Rings'

Iris 'Sneezy'

Iris 'Snowy Owl'

Iris 'Snow Mound'

Iris 'Social Event'

Iris 'Snowed In'

Iris 'Social Graces'

× ('After Dark' × seedling)) × ((seed-lings) × ('Merry Ripple' × seedling)).

Iris 'Snowed In' (J. Ghio 1998)
The velvety, purple-black falls have fluted edges and white tiger-like stripes that cover nearly half of the petal. The ruffled, white standards are very finely edged with tan, a colour that is also flushed across the style arms. The bushy beards are tangerine. Height: 86 cm (34½ in.). Bloom: early to late season. Parentage: includes 'Notorious', 'Success Story', 'Fancy Tales', 'Alpine Castle', 'Persian Smoke', 'Entourage', 'Strawberry Sundae', 'Artiste', 'Tupelo Honey', and 'Romantic Evening'.

Iris 'Snowy Owl' (R. Blodgett 1977)
This ruffled flower is almost entirely pure white, but at the back of the hafts sit fine deep yellow veins. The white beards are very gently brushed with yellow. Height: 97 cm (38¾ in.). Bloom: midseason. Parentage: 'White Vision' × 'Winter Olympics'.

Iris 'Social Event' (K. Keppel 1990)
The tightly ruffled cream-pink flowers have short standards and flaring falls. The beards are coral, and the heavily scented flowers are carried on well-branched stems. Height: 91 cm (36½ in.). Bloom: midseason. Parentage: ('Maraschino' sibling × 'Thelma Rudolph') × 'Satin Siren sibling'.

Iris 'Social Graces' (K. Keppel 2000)
The very laced and tightly ruffled flowers are rosy lilac in colour, with a flush of blue smeared down the falls and coral beards. The scent is like that of newly cut grass. Height: 97 cm (38¾ in.). Bloom: mid to late season. Parentage: 'Happenstance' sibling: ('Femme Fatale' × ('Nefertiti' × 'Playgirl' × 'Presence)) × 'Social Event'.

Iris 'Somerset Blue' (C. Bartlett 1997)
The mid violet-blue flowers have thick, ruffled petals that are finely veined with deep blue. Patches of white speckles and veins sit in a V shape at the top of the falls. The white beards are tipped with yellow in the throat, and the flower has a slight, sweet fragrance. Height: 94 cm (37 in.). Bloom: midseason. Parentage: 'Pledge Allegiance' × 'Breakers'.

Iris 'Song Of Norway' (W. Luihn 1977)
This very pale blue flower is almost white with very gently ruffled petals. Mid-blue beards are tipped with white. Height: 97 cm (38¾ in.). Bloom: mid to late season. Parentage: 'Nobleman' × 'Blue Luster'. Dykes Medal Winner USA 1986.

Iris 'Sostenique' (B. Blyth 1975)
The flowers have soft apricot standards and vibrant pink-violet falls. The falls flare out and are deeper in colour along the edges. Burnt orange patches on the hafts are covered with white veins, and the beards are tangerine. Height: 99 cm (39½ in.). Bloom: midseason. Parentage: ('Lilac Champagne' × 'Bon Vivant') × 'Latin Tempo'. Dykes Medal Winner Australia 1986.

Iris 'Spice Lord' (B. Blyth 2002)
The thick, velvety white falls are broadly rimmed and peppered with a heavy covering of oxblood red. The standards are the same colour as the falls, but muted in tone. The white beards are lightly brushed with ginger. Height: 91 cm (36½ in.). Bloom: midseason. Parentage: 'Copatonic' × 'Power Surge'.

Iris 'Spiced Custard' (J. Weiler 1987)
This bicolour has cream standards that are veined with yellow and falls that are cinnamon-orange. Freckled cream veins surround the tangerine beards, and the flower is lightly

scented. Height: 81 cm (32½ in.). Bloom: mid to late season. Parentage: ('Misty Moonscape' × 'Miss Goldilocks') × ('Trudy' × greenish amoena seedling).

Iris 'Spiced Tiger' (B. Kasperek 1994)
This flower with broken (unstable) colours has mahogany-brown falls, a colour that is streaked over a base of soft yellow and is thicker towards the lower part of the petals. The slim beards are copper coloured. The very ruffled standards are the colour of brown sugar mixed with streaks of soft yellow. The flower is strongly scented. Height: 79 cm (31½ in.). Bloom: early season. Parentage: 'Hot Streak' × 'Tiger Honey'.

Iris 'Splashacata' (R. Tasco 1997)
This gently ruffled flower has pale violet standards and white falls that are heavily peppered with purple. The purple dots are more concentrated around the edges, and the fat white beards are tipped with golden yellow. Height: 89 cm (35½ in.). Bloom: midseason. Parentage: 'Purple Pepper' × ('Snowbrook' × 'Jesse's Song').

Iris 'Spring Festival' (D. Hall 1957)
The standards of this near pure pink, gently ruffled flower are laced around the edges and the falls are a creamy tone of pink. Just visible on the hafts are short veins of orange-brown that sit on either side of the bright orange beards. Height: 107 cm (43 in.). Bloom: midseason. Parentage: seedling × 'May Hall'.

Iris 'Stairway To Heaven' (L. Lauer 1992)
The standards are creamy white and flushed with lavender up the midribs. The large, rounded falls are lavender-blue, paling around the edges, and the white beards are tipped with yellow. This plant produces many buds on open, strong stems. Height:

102 cm (41 in.). Bloom: early to midseason. Parentage: 'Edith Wolford' × 'Breakers'. Dykes Medal Winner USA 2000.

Iris 'Star Quality' (J. Ghio 1995)
The ruffled, laced blooms are rich plum in colour with orange beards. The flowers are borne on good, straight stems. Height: 89 cm (35½ in.). Bloom: mid to late season. Parentage: includes 'Romantic Mood', 'Ponderosa', 'Pink Sleigh', 'Champagne Music', 'New Moon, and 'Crystal Dawn'.

Iris 'Somerset Blue'

Iris 'Song Of Norway'

Iris 'Sostenique'

Iris 'Spiced Tiger'

Iris 'Spring Festival'

Iris 'Spice Lord'

Iris 'Splashacata'

Iris 'Stairway To Heaven'

Iris 'Spiced Custard'

Iris 'Star Quality'

Iris 'Superstition' (Schreiner 1977)
This very dark flower is purple-black, as are the beards. Etched on either side of the beard are violet speckles. The flower has velvety falls and silky standards. Height: 91 cm (36½ in.). Bloom: midseason. Parentage: (2 seedlings) × 'Navy Strut'.

Iris 'Supreme Sultan' (Schreiner 1987)
This extremely large, ruffled flower has red-brown falls and deep golden yellow standards. The beards also are deep golden yellow. Height: 102 cm (41 in.). Bloom: mid to late season. Parentage: 'Gallant Moment' × 'Peking Summer'.

Iris 'Swazi Princess' (Schreiner 1978)
One of many dark purple-black varieties, this iris has small flowers with velvety falls and silky standards. The beards are black. Height: 91 cm (36½ in.). Bloom: midseason. Parentage: involves a number of seedlings and ('Black Swan' × 'Tuxedo' sibling).

Iris 'Sweet Musette' (Schreiner 1986)
As laced and frilled as a saucy Victorian lady's underwear, the standards of this hybrid are also serrated along the edges. The peach-coloured standards are flushed with lavender, while the falls are pink-lavender, and the beards are coral-red. Height: 94 cm (37 in.). Bloom: mid to late season. Parentage: (seedling ('Son of Star' × seedling) × 'Sandberry') × (('Rippling Waters' × seedling) × ('Dreamtime' × seedling)).

Iris 'Sweeter Than Wine' (Schreiner 1988)
The ruffled flowers have white standards that are flushed with soft pink and flaring, velvety, mauve-purple falls that are edged with a paler wash of mauve. The petals are laced around the edges, and the beards are dark orange. Height: 89 cm (35½

Iris 'Superstition'

Iris 'Sweet Musette'

Iris 'Supreme Sultan'

Iris 'Swazi Princess'

Iris 'Sweeter Than Wine'

Iris 'Swingtown'

in.). Bloom: early to midseason. Parentage: 'Latin Lady' × 'Bristo Magic' sibling.

Iris **'Swingtown'** (Schreiner 1996)
The very ruffled, vibrant blue-purple flower is slightly paler around the dark purple V-shaped beards. The flowers are held on well-branched stems and are heavily scented. Height: 91 cm (36½ in.). Bloom: late season. Parentage: 'Sultry Mood' × (('Cranberry Ice' × (('Dream Time' sibling × 'Mulberry Wine') × ('Sky-watch' × ('Amethyst Flame' × 'Silver-tone'))))).

Iris **'Sylvia Murray'** (Norton 1943)
The flowers are a very pale powder-blue and old fashioned in shape with long, drooping falls and rocket-shaped standards. Stripes of ochre sit on the hafts. The white beards are tipped with orange, and the flower is strongly scented. Height: 97 cm (38¾ in.). Bloom: midseason. Parentage: 'Great Lakes' × 'Shining Waters'.

Iris **'Syncopation'** (J. Gatty 1983)
The standards and beards are tan gold, a colour that washes down to and around the violet falls. The plant does not produce many blooms, and the flowers are carried on straight, poorly branched stems. Height: 97 cm (38¾ in.). Bloom: midseason. Parentage: 'Velvet Flame' × 'Show Biz'.

Iris **'Tall Chief'** (F. DeForest 1955)
An even mahogany-brown in colour, the flowers are barely ruffled and have ginger beards. On the falls sit very small veins of yellow at either side of the beards. Height: 91 cm (36½ in.). Bloom: mid to late season. Parentage: 'Bright Gem' × unknown.

Iris **'Tall Ships'** (J. T. Aitken 1993)
The flower has mid violet-blue standards and falls. The colour of the falls is broken by rivers of white that emerge from the white patch at the back of the petals. The beards are white, and the flower is slightly scented. Height: 97 cm (38¾ in.). Bloom: mid to late season. Parentage: 'Victoria Falls' × 'Sea Wolf'.

Iris 'Sylvia Murray'

Iris 'Tall Chief'

Iris 'Syncopation'

Iris 'Tall Ships'

Iris 'Tangerine Sky' (Schreiner 1976)
The rich tangerine flower has ruffled petals with serrated edges. The beards are a red-tangerine colour. Height: 91 cm (36½ in.). Bloom: late season. Parentage: ('Carla' × 'Celestial Glory') × 'Alaskan Sunset'.

Iris 'Tanzanian Tangerine' (B. Kasperek 1994)
This well-formed flower has petals with a base colour of dark peachy-orange. The falls are sanded with dark maroon, while the peachy orange standards are just occasionally flecked with mauve. The flowers are borne on well-branched stems. Height: 97 cm (38¾ in.). Bloom: early to midseason. Parentage: 'Tiger Honey' × 'Jitterbug'.

Iris 'Tennessee Woman' (S. Innerst 1989)
The white falls are neatly edged with plum stitching, while the standards are the colour of caramel. The style arms are also caramel, and the short beards are bronze. The flower is slightly scented. Height: 91 cm (36½ in.). Bloom: early to midseason. Parentage: 'Colortrak' × 'Ted Shiner'.

Iris 'Tennison Ridge' (J. Begley by J. McWhirter 1988)
The standards are solid burgundy, while the white falls are heavily stitched with a broad edge of burgundy, a colour that is speckled across the falls. The beards are bronze, and the flower, which is said to rebloom, is scented. Height: 97 cm (38¾ in.). Bloom: early to midseason and reblooming. Parentage: 'Splash O' Wine' × 'Cozy Calico'.

Iris 'Terra Rosa' (Schreiner 1998)
The flowers have red-brown falls and glossy, smoky brown standards. The red-brown beards are tipped with ochre. The plant produces small,

Iris 'Tangerine Sky'

Iris 'Tennison Ridge'

Iris 'Tanzanian Tangerine'

Iris 'Terra Rosa'

Iris 'Tennessee Woman'

Iris 'Thornbird'

sharply scented flowers on excellently branching stems. Height: 99 cm (39½ in.). Bloom: midseason. Parentage: includes 'Danger', 'October Ale', 'Credit Card', 'Olympic Torch', 'Inca Chief', 'Dark Chocolate', 'Copper Nugget', 'San Jose', and many seedlings.

Iris 'Thornbird' (M. Byers 1988)

The gently ruffled flowers of this plant are either loved or hated. They are a rather murky collection of colours. The standards are pale ecru, and the flaring falls are a sort of green-tan with smears of violet and deep brown veins. The violet beards are heavily brushed with gold and lengthen into long upwards-pointing violet horns. The sweetly scented flowers are elegantly carried on well-branched stems. Height: 89 cm (35½ in.). Bloom: midseason. Parentage: 'Art of Raphael' × ('Cease-Fire' × 'Sky Hooks'). Dykes Medal Winner USA 1997.

Iris 'Thriller' (Schreiner 1988)

The silky pure purple flowers appear to be purple-black in the ruffles. At the sides of the pure purple beards sit patches of mahogany-brown. The flower has a spicy scent. Height: 91 cm (36½ in.). Bloom: mid to late season. Parentage: ('Lorilee' × 'Lady X') × (('Sailor's Dance' × seedling) × (seedling × 'Royal Regency' sibling)).

Iris 'Tiger Honey' (B. Kasperek 1993)

This flower with broken (unstable) colours has gently ruffled butterscotch standards that are randomly flecked with soft violet and deep yellow. The flaring ginger- and caramel-coloured falls have white streaks and ruffled edges. Brown veins surround the golden yellow beards. The flower is slightly scented. Height: 97 cm (38¾ in.). Bloom: early to midseason. Parentage: 'Desert Realm' × 'Maria Tormena'.

Iris 'Titan's Glory' (Schreiner 1981)

This plant produces big, glossy, dark blue-purple flowers with matching beards that are carried on sturdy stems. Despite the size of the flower, the stems do not collapse in poor weather. Height: 94 cm (37 in.). Bloom: early to midseason. Parentage: 'Navy Strut' × ((seedlings) × ('Rococo' × 'Prince Indigo')). Dykes Medal Winner USA 1988.

Iris 'Tom Johnson' (P. Black 1996)

The very ruffled flowers have shiny, dark purple standards and velvety, very dark purple falls. The bushy beards are bright orange, and the flowers are slightly scented. Height: 89 cm (35½ in.). Bloom: early season. Parentage: 'Witches' Sabbath' × 'In Town'.

Iris 'Thriller'

Iris 'Titan's Glory'

Iris 'Tiger Honey'

Iris 'Tom Johnson'

Iris 'Touch of Mahogany' (B. Blyth 1999)
The colour of coffee, the petals are large, ruffled, and laced around the edges. The falls are softer in colour and decorated with broad wings of red-brown on either side of the dark ginger beards. The flower is scented. Height: 91 cm (36½ in.). Bloom: mid to late season. Parentage: 'Chestnut Avenue' × 'Copatonic'.

Iris 'Tut's Gold' (Schreiner 1979)
The pure bright yellow flower has matching beards and gently ruffled petals. Height: 94 cm (37 in.). Bloom: mid to late season. Parentage: 'Saffron Robe' × unknown.

Iris 'Unfinished Business' (W. & M. Griner 1998)
The flower has flaring pale blue standards and frilly, flaring purple falls. The falls are marked with broad, white veins that radiate halfway down the petals. The long, horned beards are made up of many colours, consisting of purple and white with yellow at the tips. The flower has a chocolate scent. Height: 117 cm (46 in.). Bloom: mid to late season. Parentage: 'Miss Pretty' × 'Conjuration'.

Iris 'Vanity' (B. Hager 1974)
This important pink variety has been much used as a parent. The very pale pink flowers have softer-coloured falls with white veins around the light coral-red beards. The standards are tissue thin, and the strongly scented flowers are carried on well-branched stems. Height: 91 cm (36½ in.). Bloom: early to late season. Parentage: 'Cherub Choir' × 'Pink Taffeta'. Dykes Medal Winner USA 1982.

Iris 'Vanity's Child' (T. Olson 1985)
An obvious child of *Iris* 'Vanity', this hybrid has blue-pink standards and coral-pink falls. The petals are gently ruffled and laced around the edges. The beards are bright coral, and the flower is sweetly scented. Height: 73 cm (29 in.). Bloom: mid to late season. Parentage: 'Pink Sleigh' × 'Vanity'.

Iris 'Vibrant' (P. Black 1999)
The neat, very ruffled intensely yellow flowers have large, golden yellow beards and are lightly scented. Height: 86 cm (34½ in.). Bloom: early to midseason. Parentage: 'Good Show' × 'Goldkist'.

Iris 'Vibrations' (M. Dunn 1989)
The burgundy flower has standards that are a dusky version of the rich rose-maroon falls. Long white streaks radiate down the petals. The white beards are heavily brushed with ginger. Height: 86 cm (34½ in.). Bloom: midseason. Parentage: ((('Graceline' × 'Rippling Waters') × 'Apropos') × 'Gala Madrid') × 'Rancho Rose'.

Iris 'Victoria Falls' (Schreiner 1977)
The very ruffled, soft lilac flowers have falls with a white patch and white beards. Because the tall stems produce so many flowers, they have a tendency to topple over in windy weather. Therefore this iris is sometimes affectionately known as 'Victoria Falls Down'. Height: 102 cm (41 in.). Bloom: early to late season. Parentage: ('White Pride' × seedling) × 'Violet Favor'. Dykes Medal Winner USA 1984.

Iris 'Violet Classic' (L. Zurbrigg 1976)
The standards of the deep violet flower are paler than the richly coloured, flaring falls. The beards are white, and the petals are ruffled along the edges. The flower is said to rebloom. Height: 84 cm (33½ in.). Bloom: mid to late season and reblooming. Parentage: 'Violet Supreme' × 'Jolly Goliath'.

Iris 'Touch of Mahogany'

Iris 'Tut's Gold'

Iris 'Unfinished Business'

Iris 'Vanity'

Iris 'Vibrations'

Iris **'Violet Harmony'** (Mrs F. Lowry 1948)

The ruffled flower has violet petals with falls that are white at the top and become paler down the centre of the falls. On the falls sit beards that are orange at the back and white at the front. Height: average. Bloom: midseason. Parentage: 'Snow Flurry' × 'Cloud Castle'. Dykes Medal Winner USA 1957.

Iris **'Violet Rings'** (J. Gibson 1985)

The colour of this plicata is muted. The large, fluted standards are almost solidly pink-lilac with a few

Iris 'Vanity's Child'

Iris 'Victoria Falls'

Iris 'Violet Harmony'

Iris 'Vibrant'

Iris 'Violet Classic'

Iris 'Violet Rings'

white speckles towards the base. The soft white falls are rimmed with a neat band of deeper violet and curl underneath. The white beards are tipped with yellow-orange. Height: 96 cm (38½ in.). Bloom: midseason. Parentage: (('Smoke Rings' × 'Blueberry Trim') × 'Smoke Rings') × ('Smoke Rings' × ('Smoke Rings' × seedling)).

Iris 'Viva Mexico' (W. Maryott 1995)
The falls open bright orange, fading to salmon-orange with age. The standards are paler in colour, and the whole bloom is laced and ruffled. The big beards are orange, and the flower is strongly scented. In California it is known to rebloom. Height: 91–94 cm (36–37 in.). Bloom: midseason and reblooming. Parentage: 'Radiant Energy' × 'Peach Bisque'.

Iris 'Vizier' (J. Ghio 1997)
The petals of this glossy vibrant mauve flower are tightly ruffled, giving the edges a deeper tone of colour. The beard is orange, and the flower has a rather unpleasant, sharp scent. Height: 91 cm (36½ in.). Bloom: early to midseason. Parentage: 'Reality' × 'Star Quality'.

Iris 'Volatile' (J. & V. Craig 1996)
The small, ruffled flowers are soft blue in colour. The petals are washed with violet from the hafts, and the soft blue beards are tipped with yellow towards the back. The flowers are scented and carried on well-branched stems. Height: 81 cm (32½ in.). Bloom: midseason. Parentage: involves 'Bold Crystal', 'Odyssey', 'Stepping Out', 'Deborah Suzanne', 'Shipshape', 'Rimfire', 'Cedarcrest', 'Lovely Letty', 'Pinwheel', and 'Patina'.

Iris 'Wabash' (M. Williamson 1936)
This simply shaped flower has smooth, purple falls that are rimmed with a white line. The large white standards are touched with yellow and touch at the top. White stripes surround the yellow beards. Height: 101 cm (40½ in.). Bloom: early to midseason. Parentage: 'Dorothy Dietz' × 'Cantabile'. Dykes Medal Winner USA 1940.

Iris 'Waiting for George' (B. Blyth 1997)
This ruffled plicata has flaring, creamy white falls that are speckled and stitched around the edges with smoky, rose-pink. The standards are more intensely marked with smoky, rose-pink. The beards are a burnt tangerine colour, and the flower is lightly scented. Height: 91 cm (36½ in.). Bloom: midseason. Parentage: 'Lemon Silence' × ('Bama Berry' × 'Holiday Lover').

Iris 'War Chief' (Schreiner 1992)
This plant produces gently ruffled, smooth, red-mahogany flowers with bright yellow beards. The flowers are carried on well-branched stems in profusion. Schreiner's has introduced several varieties similar to this one, including Iris 'Warrior King' and I. 'War Sails'. Height: 94 cm (37 in.). Bloom: early to midseason. Parentage: 'Minisa' × ('Sultan's Palace' × 'Gallant Moment').

Iris 'Wearing Rubies' (B. Blyth 2001)
The neatly ruffled flower has deep purple-pink, flaring standards and velvety, rich burgundy falls. The beards are bright coral-red with short stripes of white at either side. The style arms are burnt orange. Height: 94 cm (37 in.). Bloom: mid to late season. Parentage: (('Holiday Lover' × 'Love Comes') × 'Bygone Era') × 'Who's Your Daddy'.

Iris 'Wedding Vow' (J. Ghio 1970)
Pure white when open, the flowers are at first tinged with blue. This col-

Iris 'Viva Mexico'

Iris 'Vizier'

Iris 'Volatile'

Iris 'Wabash'

Iris 'Wearing Rubies'

Iris 'Waiting for George'

Iris 'Wedding Vow'

our fades as the bloom matures. The beards are also white but touched with yellow at the back. Height: 94 cm (37 in.). Bloom: early season. Parentage: ('Patricia Craig' × ('First Courtship' × 'Nina's Delight' sibling)) × ('G Junior Prom' sibling × ('Nina's Delight' sibling × 'First Courtship')).

Iris **'Wench'** (L. Miller 1991)
The velvety falls are deep rosy maroon, and the standards are peach coloured. White tiger-like stripes surround the burnt orange beards. The well-branched stems produce many buds, and the flowers are lightly scented. Height: 86 cm (34½ in.). Bloom: early to midseason. Parentage: 'Colortart' × 'Ringo'.

Iris **'White City'** (O. Murrell 1937)
This smoothly shaped white flower is touched with a hint of blue. The standards are gently ruffled, and the flaring falls curl up around the edges. The white beards are brushed with yellow, and a few brown stripes emerge from the hafts. Each flower is perfectly balanced against the next. Height: 91 cm (36½ in.). Bloom: early to midseason. Parentage: 'Pageant' × 'Pervaneh'. Dykes Medal Winner UK 1940.

Iris 'War Chief'

Iris 'Wench'

Iris 'White City'

Iris 'Whole Cloth' (P. Cook 1956)
This bicolour has ruffled pure white standards that arch towards each other. The round, soft violet falls have white beards that are heavily brushed with orange. Height: 91 cm (36½ in.). Bloom: midseason. Parentage: 'Cahokia' × ('Blue Rhythm' × ((blue seedling × progenitor) × 'Distance' × blue seedling)). Dykes Medal Winner USA 1962.

Iris 'Wild Jasmine' (B. Hamner 1983)
The round, flaring, golden yellow falls are heavily speckled with dark caramel. Around the edges is a yellow band, and in front of the golden beards is a patch of white. The petals are ruffled. Height: 81–86 cm (32–34½ in.). Bloom: midseason. Parentage: 'Sketch Me' × 'Shaft of Gold'.

Iris 'Wild Wings' (K. Keppel 1998)
The neatly ruffled, velvety, very dark purple-black falls sit horizontally below the silky, dark violet standards. On these sit flat, bushy deep russet beards. The flower has a scent that is sweet and spicy. Height: 86 cm (34½ in.). Bloom: early to midseason. Parentage: 'Night Game' sibling × 'Romantic Evening'.

Iris 'Winter Olympics' (O. Brown 1961)
This pure white flower has silky, arching standards and waxy falls. The edge of the petals is gently ruffled and mildly laced. The white beards are touched with orange in the throat. Height: 98 cm (39 in.). Bloom: early to midseason. Parentage: 'Poet's Dream' × 'Eleanor's Pride'. Dykes Medal Winner USA 1967.

Iris 'World Beyond' (B. Blyth 1981)
This neatly ruffled variety has white standards that are serrated around the edges. The round, white falls are heavily speckled with very pale violet and have edges of a softer colour.

Iris 'Whole Cloth'

Iris 'Winter Olympics'

Iris 'Wild Jasmine'

Iris 'World Beyond'

Iris 'Wild Wings'

Iris 'World Premier'

Iris 'Yaquina Blue'

Iris 'Yes'

Iris 'Zandria'

Broken purple veins emerge from the hafts. The white beards are tipped with yellow. The flower is sweetly scented. Height: 86–91 cm (34–36½ in.). Bloom: early to midseason. Parentage: 'Sapharine' × 'Caramba'.

Iris 'World Premier' (Schreiner 1998)
The deep blue falls are lighter around the edges, and the fluted standards are pale blue. White stripes surround the short blue beards. The flower is scented. Height: 94 cm (37 in.). Bloom: mid to late season. Parentage: 'Yaquina Blue' × unknown.

Iris 'Yaquina Blue' (Schreiner 1992)
The flowers of this very ruffled variety are mid violet-blue in colour. The short blue beards are tipped with yellow. The flowers are borne on strong stems and are heavily scented. Height: 94 cm (37 in.). Bloom: midseason. Parentage: includes 'Sapphire Hills', 'Cup Race', 'Violet Harmony', 'Blue Rhythm', Chivalry', 'Harbor Blue', and 'Blue Sapphire'. Dykes Medal Winner USA 2001.

Iris 'Yes' (B. Blyth 1995)
This amoena has white standards that are ruffled and serrated around the edges. The large, flaring falls are rich orange-yellow, while the white beards are heavily painted with tangerine. Height: 91 cm (36½ in.). Bloom: very early to midseason. Parentage: 'Road Song' × 'Electrique'.

Iris 'Zandria' (D. Nebeker 1995)
The flaring, rich purple falls are decorated with a large white patch at the top on which sit bright rich orange beards and purple veins. The ruffled standards are soft peach-pink. The flower is lightly scented. Height: 97 cm (38¾ in.). Bloom: midseason. Parentage: 'Fancy Tales' × 'Planned Treasure'.

CHAPTER 2

Border Bearded Irises

BECAUSE OF THEIR HEIGHT, Border Bearded irises were once thrown on the compost heap, but more than 50 years ago it was decided that these vigorous, short-growing types of Tall Bearded irises were too good to ignore and that they should be given a category of their own. As a group they are simply shorter seedlings selected from a row of Tall Bearded seedlings. The goal of hybridizers is to introduce a plant with flowers that are in perfect proportion to the flower stem, but they also look for plants with a good bud count.

New varieties of Border Bearded irises are created by crossing two Border Bearded varieties, or a Tall Bearded iris with a bearded species such as *Iris aphylla*. These crosses do not produce great quantities of seed. Therefore, the number of varieties available to gardeners is limited. The flowers range from 10 to 12 cm (4–5 in.) across, and the flower stalks grow to between 38 and 71 cm (16–28½ in.) tall. Border Bearded irises bloom at the same time as Tall Bearded irises. Because of their vigour, they are perfect for mixing in a border with other plants. Most varieties, however, are shorter, only reaching 60–69 cm (24–27½ in.) tall.

Knowlton Medal

First given in 1966, the Knowlton Medal is awarded in the United States by the Median Iris Society to the best Border Bearded iris. It was named after Harold Knowlton, who was one of the first hybridizers to appreciate this type of bearded iris. He was also a president of the American Iris Society.

BORDER BEARDED IRIS SPECIES & THEIR COLLECTED FORMS

Iris albertii Regel 1877

Turkey

The long falls of this violet-coloured species hang sharply downwards. The hafts are white and covered with red-brown veins, while the bluish-white beards are tipped with yellow. The leaves are purple at the base. Height: 60 cm (24 in.).

Iris belouini Bois & Cornuault 1915

North central Morocco, Andalusia, Spain
This tetraploid, unlike any other bearded iris, loses its foliage once the bright violet flowers have finished. The white beards are tipped with yellow. The hafts are white and veined with brown. Height: 79 cm (31½ in.).

Iris imbricata Lindley 1845

Transcaucasia
This pale yellow species has falls that are veined with brownish purple and white beards that are tipped with yellow. The falls usually curl under. Height: 30–50 cm (12–20 in.).

Iris albertii

Iris imbricata

Iris 'Am I Blue'

Iris junonia Schott & Kotschy 1854
Sicilian Taurus
This species has been much debated. According to the Species Group of the British Iris Society, the leaves grow taller than the stems. The flowers are blue-purple, the hafts white and then veined with brown. The white beards are tipped with orange. Height: less than 30 cm (12 in.).

BORDER BEARDED IRIS HYBRIDS

Iris 'Am I Blue' (D. Denney 1977)
This soft blue variety has ruffled standards that are suffused with deep blue from the base of the petals. The beards are blue and tipped with white. Height: 51 cm (20½ in.). Bloom: early season. Parentage: 'Strange Magic' × 'Sapphire Hills'. Knowlton Medal Winner 1983.

Iris 'Apricot Frosty' (D. Niswonger 1992)
This ruffled variety has white standards with a light flush of apricot to the base of the petals. The flaring apricot falls have self-coloured beards. Height: 58 cm (23 in.). Bloom: midseason. Parentage: 'Beachgirl' × 'Champagne Elegance'. Knowlton Medal 2000.

Iris 'Apricot Frosty'

Iris 'Apricot Topping'

Iris 'Apricot Topping' (P. Black 1997)
This bitone has deep apricot standards and rich burgundy falls. The petals are laced and gently ruffled, and white veins surround the orange beards. Well-branched stems carry a profusion of lightly scented flowers. Height: 64 cm (25½ in.). Bloom: midseason. Parentage: 'Spiced Cider' × 'Glitz 'n Glitter'.

Iris 'Baboon Bottom' (B. Kasperek 1993)
The pale pink flowers are delicately speckled with pale purple and rivers of white. The beards are soft orange, and the edges of the petals are gently ruffled. The flower is lightly scented. Height: 66 cm (26½ in.). Bloom: midseason. Parentage: 'Date Bait' × 'Maria Tormena'. Knowlton Medal Winner 2002.

Iris 'Batik' (A. Ensminger 1985)
This broken (unstable) coloured flower has blue-purple petals that are streaked with white. The white streaks are very unstable and vary both in quantity and width from flower to flower. Height: 66 cm (26½ in.). Bloom: midseason. Parentage: 'Aegean Star' × 'Purple Streaker'. Knowlton Medal 1992.

Iris 'Bengal Tiger' (G. Sutton 1989)
This yellow variegata has falls that are strongly veined with maroon-brown and short round standards that are deep golden yellow. The fat beards are dark yellow, and the flowers are borne on well-branched stems. Height: 61 cm (24½ in.). Bloom: early to midseason. Parentage: 'Gypsy Wings' × 'Heat Flare'.

Iris 'Blackbeard' (J. Weiler 1988)
The smoothly shaped, neatly formed soft sky-blue flower has slightly wavy petals and dark ink-blue beards. In my experience it makes a good border iris, combining perfectly with soft pink perennials, such as hardy geraniums. Height: 64 cm (25½ in.). Bloom: mid to very late season. Parentage: (('Goodnight Irene' × 'Blue Luster') × ('Matinata' × 'Style Master')) × (('Matinata' × 'Style Master') × ('Regalaire' × 'Nobleman')).

Iris 'Baboon Bottom'

Iris 'Blackbeard'

Iris 'Batik'

Iris 'Calico Cat'

Iris 'Bengal Tiger'

Iris 'Copy Cat'

Iris 'Brown Lasso'

Iris 'Cotton Charmer'

Iris 'Brown Lasso' (E. Buckles & D. Niswonger 1972)
This is the only Border Bearded iris to be awarded an American Dykes Medal. Unique in colour, it has ruffled, butterscotch standards and flaring pale violet falls that are banded with tan-brown. The beards are yellow. Height: 56 cm (22½ in.). Bloom: early to midseason. Parentage: 'Punchline' × ('Wild Mustang' × 'Milestone'). Knowlton Medal Winner 1980; Dykes Medal Winner USA 1981.

Iris 'Calico Cat' (C. Lankow 1988)
This small-flowered variety has straw yellow standards and soft violet falls with yellow edges. The violet is washed across a yellow background. The hafts are highlighted with tints of violet and maroon, and the large beards are orange. The flower has a spicy, curry-like scent. Height: 51 cm (20½ in.). Bloom: mid to late season. Parentage: ('Andi' × (pink TB seedling × 'Yellow Dresden')) × 'Miss Nellie'. Knowlton Medal Winner 1995.

Iris 'Copy Cat' (J. Ghio 1973)
This bicolour has soft blue standards that are flushed with deeper blue from the base and flaring deep blue falls that are paler around the edges. The beards are deep blue. Height: 61 cm (24½ in.). Bloom: early to midseason. Parentage: 'Oracle' sibling × 'Skylab'.

Iris 'Cotton Charmer' (C. Lankow by T. Aitken 1998)
The white beards of this ruffled pure white self are brushed yellow towards the back. Height: 64 cm (25½ in.). Bloom: mid to very late season. Parentage: unknown.

Iris 'Cranapple' (T. Aitken 1995)
The red-brown flower has velvety falls and silky standards that are lighter in colour. The thick, finely shaped beards are ginger coloured. The flower is carried on a well-branched stem above blue-green foliage and is sharply scent. Height: 61 cm (24½ in.). Bloom: early to mid-season. Parentage: ('Gyro' × 'Warrior King') × 'Maid of Orange'. Knowlton Medal Winner 2001.

Iris 'Dresden Candleglow' (Reath 1964)
The pure clear yellow flowers have flaring falls with white patches in the centre and with curled up edges. The long, thin, white beards are tipped at the back with orange. The flower is sweetly scented. Height: 51 cm (20½ in.). Bloom: early season. Parentage: 'Baria' × 'Yellow Dresden'.

Iris 'Hasta la Vista' (T. Aitken 2004)
This lacy, lightly ruffled variety has white standards that flare open and horizontal peach-coloured falls. The white beards are painted with orange. The flower is said to rebloom sporadically. Parentage: 'Flambe' × ('Smitten Kitten' × 'Champagne Elegance').

Iris 'Indigo Doll' (C. Lankow by T. Aitken 1997)
This ruffled flower has soft blue standards with a wash of deep blue emanating from the base. The flaring falls are dark violet-blue, and the bushy beards are orange-red. Height: 66 cm (26½ in.). Bloom: mid to late season. Parentage: 'American Beauty' × 'Cool Treat'.

Iris 'Jungle Shadows' (Sass 1959)
The standards are a mixture of grey and brown. These colours are flecked and stained throughout the petals, which are further washed with a tint of dull violet-brown. Inside the petals is a flush of purple. The ginger-col-

Iris 'Cranapple'

Iris 'Indigo Doll'

Iris 'Dresden Candleglow'

Iris 'Jungle Shadows'

Iris 'Hasta la Vista'

oured beards are tipped with grey. This hybrid was introduced after the death of its hybridizer. Height: 99 cm (39½ in.). Bloom midseason. Parentage: unknown.

Iris 'Just Jennifer' (J. D. Taylor 1983) The pure white, perfectly proportioned flowers have gently ruffled petals. Genetically this hybrid should be listed as an Intermediate Bearded because it is the result of a cross between a Standard Dwarf Bearded iris and a Tall Bearded iris. In Britain, however, it flowers along with Border Bearded irises and was therefore registered in that group. Height: 64 cm (25½ in.). Bloom: early season. Parentage: 'Bibury' × 'Wedding Vow'.

Iris 'Lenora Pearl' (H. Nicholls 1988) This gently ruffled flower is salmon-pink in colour with bright orange beards. It is said to be reblooming. Height: 69 cm (27½ in.). Bloom: early to late season. Parentage: 'Ann Glitsch' × 'Elizabeth Marrison'. Knowlton Medal Winner 1996.

Iris 'Let's Elope' (B. Blyth 1993) The peachy orange falls are overlaid with soft brown veins, and the pink standards open out to show off a violet wash that stains the base of the inner petals. The beards are tan coloured, and the edges of the petals are laced. The flowers, which are heavily scented, are lightly bunched at the top of the stem. Height: 61 cm (24½ in.). Bloom: early to midseason. Parentage: 'Shiralee' × 'Chanted'.

Iris 'Little Sir Echo' (C. Tompkins 1962) The smoothly shaped, tailored, dark red-purple flower has velvety falls, silky standards, and self-coloured beards. Height: 99 cm (39½ in.). Bloom: early to late season. Parentage: (('Ebony Echo' × 'Great Day') × ('Great Day' × 'Ebony Echo')) × ('Orange Glint' × 'Defiance').

Iris 'Just Jennifer'

Iris 'Lenora Pearl'

Iris 'Let's Elope'

Iris 'Little Sir Echo'

Iris 'Lyrique' (B. Blyth 1996)
The ruffled flowers are soft lilac-blue, and the falls carry a large burgundy signal in the centre of the petals. Broad white stripes surround the bronze beards. Height: 51 cm (20½ in.). Bloom: mid to late season. Parentage: 'Zing Me' × 'Divine'.

Iris 'Maid of Orange' (T. Aitken 1989)
This gently ruffled orange flower has vivid orange beards, which are surrounded by a few short brown veins. The scent is light and fruity. Height: 64 cm (25½ in.). Bloom: early to late season. Parentage: 'Apricota' × Shoop orange Border Bearded seedling.

Iris 'Marmalade Skies' (D. Niswonger 1978)
The flowers of this prolific-blooming variety are soft orange with falls that are slightly deeper in colour. The white beards are brushed with orange, and the flower is scented. Height: 69 cm (27½ in.). Bloom: early season. Parentage: ('Java Dove' × (('Happy Birthday' × 'Glittering Amber') × 'Marilyn C')) × 'Sunset Snows'. Knowlton Medal Winner 1984.

Iris 'Orinoco Flow' (C. Bartlett 1989)
This white-and-violet plicata is the only Border Bearded iris to have been awarded the Dykes Medal by the British Iris Society. The flowers are very ruffled, although the ruffling is lighter on the falls. The beards are blue, and the flower is heavily scented. Height: 64 cm (25½ in.). Bloom: early to late season. Parentage: 'Blue Staccato' × 'Raziza'. Dykes Medal Winner UK 1994.

Iris 'Pink Bubbles' (B. Hager 1979)
Soft pink in colour, the petals are gently ruffled and very laced around the edges. The beards are a similar colour to the standards, which are

Iris 'Lyrique'

Iris 'Marmalade Skies'

Iris 'Maid of Orange'

Iris 'Orinoco Flow'

Iris 'Pink Bubbles'

Iris 'Preppy'

deeper in tone than the falls. Height: 51 cm (20½ in.). Bloom: early to mid-season. Parentage: 'Pink Piroutette' × 'Vanity'. Knowlton Medal Winner 1986.

***Iris* 'Preppy'** (K. Vaughn 1999)
The petals of this ruffled, white flower are lightly stippled around the edges. The white beards are brushed with yellow. The flower is said to re-bloom and is heavily scented. Height: 61 cm (24½ in.). Bloom: early to late season and reblooming. Parentage: 'Stanza' × 'Miss Nellie'.

***Iris* 'Quinalt'** (J. & V. Craig 1999)
The buff standards are gently ruffled, and the magenta falls are marked with white on the hafts. The beards are deep yellow. The flower has a spicy scent. Height: 68 cm (27 in.). Bloom: early season. Parentage: (('Little Sunrise' sibling × ('Starchild' × ('Sacred Mountain' × *I. aphylla* "Werckmeister"))) × (('Odyssey' × *I. aphylla* "Werckmeister") × ('Chapeau' × seedling))) × 'Sailing Free' sibling.

***Iris* 'Shenanigan'** (K. Keppel 1983)
The standards are peach with an occasional speckle of magenta. The falls are magenta, deepening to purple in the ruffles. Peach speckles surround the orange beards. The flower is lightly scented. Height: 64 cm (25½ in.). Bloom: early to midseason. Parentage: ('Flamenco' sibling × ('Roundup' sibling × 'April Melody')) × 'Peccadillo' sibling. Knowlton Medal Winner 1991.

***Iris* 'Sonja's Selah'** (A. Ensminger 1988)
This ruffled flower has white standards that are flushed up the midribs with tan-peach and tan-peach falls that are rimmed unevenly with white. The beards are a bright tangerine, and the flower is slightly scented. Height: 61 cm (24½ in.). Bloom: mid to late season. Parentage: ('Almost Gladys' × 'Foolish Pleasure') × 'Almost Gladys'. Knowlton Medal Winner 1997.

***Iris* 'Spy'** (J. & V. Craig 1999)
The small white flower has falls that are washed and veined with violet. The white beards are brushed with yellow. If not for its height, this hybrid could be mistaken for a Miniature Tall Bearded iris as the blooms are borne on slender, well-branched stems. Height: 60 cm (24 in.). Bloom: midseason. Parentage: sibling to 'Saucy'.

Iris 'Quinalt'

Iris 'Sonja's Selah'

Iris 'Shenanigan'

Iris 'Spy'

Iris 'Teapot Tempest' (L. Markham 1998)

The small, ruffled, rose-violet flowers have short standards that are held wide open and falls that flare out horizontally. The white beards are also short and touched with coral. The flower is strongly scented. Height: 69 cm (27½ in.). Bloom: mid to late season. Parentage: 'Angel Feathers' × 'Pops Concert'.

Iris 'Zinc Pink' (A. Ensminger 1986)

This pale pink is nearer in colour tone to peach than pink. The falls are softer in colour than the standards, and the very ruffled petals are laced around the edges. The flower has coral beards and is scented. Height: 60 cm (24 in.). Bloom: mid to late season. Parentage: 'Pink Bubbles' × 'Bohnsack'. Knowlton Medal Winner 1993.

Iris 'Teapot Tempest'

Iris 'Zinc Pink'

CHAPTER 3

Miniature Tall Bearded Irises

THIS DELIGHTFUL SECTION of bearded irises is limited to approximately 350 registered varieties and for that reason the hybrids can be difficult to find. Thankfully they are gaining in popularity due to the efforts of hybridizers. One of the difficulties lies in the rather potted history of this horticultural section. Its definition has changed with every decade. Today the Miniature Tall Bearded iris should grow to between 38 and 70 cm (15–28 in.) in height and have small flowers that are no more than 15 cm (6 in.) across; however, they are usually much smaller and the only things they have in common with Tall Bearded irises are the flowering time and form. Being diploid, Miniature Tall Bearded irises are dainty in size, delicate in structure, and carry blooms on slender, flexible, well-branched stems. As a consequence, these irises are delicate enough to place in the front of a mixed border and to cut for table decorations. For this reason the American Iris Society also knows these by the name of Table irises. Like many bearded irises with smaller rhizomes, the Miniature Tall Bearded irises may take a little longer to establish. Therefore, it is important to make sure that they are initially planted in an area where there is very little competition from other plants.

Williamson-White Medal

First awarded in 1968, this medal was named to honour E. B. Williamson and Alice White, both great supporters of miniature tall irises. Williamson's daughter Mary was the first hybridizer to introduce Miniature Tall Bearded irises.

MINIATURE TALL BEARDED IRIS SPECIES

Iris illyrica Tommasini 1875
Dalmatian coast
This species is considered to be a smaller form of *Iris pallida*. The large flowers are rich blue, and the beards are yellow and touched with deep yellow at the back. Height: 45 cm (18 in.).

Iris plicata Lambert
Listed by Köhlein (1987) as *Iris sweertii* (sometimes spelled *I. swertii*), this species was originally named after Dutch businessman and author Emmanuel Sweert, who mentioned it as a form of *I. pallida* in his *Florilegium* of 1612. I received this plant from the Royal Botanic Gardens Kew over 20

Iris illyrica

Iris plicata

years ago under the name *I. plicata* and, as I am unable to trace the name *I. swertii* in books on species irises, I shall continue to list it under *I. plicata*. This delightful plant has slender, well-branched stems that grow to 75 cm (30 in.). It produces white flowers that are very precisely stitched around the edges with violet. The flower is distinctive because the falls droop down, then curl up into a V shape, and the standards collapse into themselves. The white beards are touched with yellow at the back, and the style arms are violet. Height: 60 cm (24 in.).

Iris variegata Linnaeus 1753
Balkan states, Austria

Much used as a parent of the Tall Bearded iris, this delicate-looking species has yellow standards that can vary from lemon to almost gold and falls that can be nearly white to yellow. The falls are more or less heavily veined with red-brown. The beards are a bright yellow. In the wild this species grows in stony areas. Height: 45 cm (18 in.).

FORMS OF *IRIS VARIEGATA*

Iris reginae I. Horvat & M. D. Horvat 1947
Macedonia

Once considered a species in its own right, *Iris reginae* is now included with *I. rudskyi* under *I. variegata* (Mathew 1981). A charming plant, it has narrow, white standards and falls. The falls are beautifully lined with purple. The same colour is speckled and lined over the standards, which flare open. The beards are white and just touched with cream at the back. The flowers are borne on delicate, well-branched stems above light green, curved foliage. Height: 60 cm (24 in.).

Iris variegata

Iris reginae

Iris rudskyi I. Horvat & M. D. Horvat 1947
Macedonia

This species is similar to *Iris variegata* but has flowers that are deeper in colour. The standards are caramel and, on close inspection, flecked with a deeper tone. The very narrow white falls are heavily lined with purple. The beards, though small, are white and tipped with yellow at the back. Height: 30 cm (12 in.).

Iris 'Petit Lion' (L. Baumunk 2001)
Introduced as a species, this plant was raised from *Iris variegata* seed acquired through the Species Iris Group of North America (SIGNA). It has dark yellow standards that sit wide apart and white falls that are evenly veined with burgundy. The beards are white and tipped with yellow towards the back. Height: 30 cm (12 in.).

Iris rudskyi

Iris 'Petit Lion'

HYBRIDS OF *IRIS VARIEGATA* & *I. PALLIDA*

Iris lurida Ker-Gawler 1789

As far as I can ascertain, *Iris lurida* is the correct name for the plant described by W. R. Dykes in his book *The Genus* Iris. Received from the Royal Botanic Gardens Kew, this plant is considered a hybrid by Brian Mathew (1981). The flowers are not large; they have maroon-red falls with white patches on the hafts that are veined with the same colour. The standards are a rosy brown-purple and slightly ruffled around the edges. The beards are deep yellow, and the flowers are carried on well-branched slender stems. Height: 70 cm (28 in.).

Iris sambucina Linnaeus

Germany

Dykes gives two descriptions for these plants and I imagine that is why they survived at the Royal Botanic Gardens Kew for so long. In his book *The Genus* Iris, Dykes describes *Iris squalens* as having falls that are 'much veined with deep bluish-purple'. In fact the veins are brown-purple and sit on a yellow-white background. The standards are dingy yellowish purple, while the beards are orange. Dykes adds that this description applies equally to *I. squalens*. For the purposes of this book, this hybrid between *I. variegata* and *I. pallida* is *I. sambucina*. Height: 70 cm (28 in.).

Iris squalens Linnaeus

Germany

Dykes says that the original description of *Iris squalens* is similar to that of *I. sambucina*, except that *I. squalens* has yellow or murky yellow standards and the falls are veined with claret-red. The identification of this seems to be in some confusion. Height: 60 cm (24 in.).

Iris lurida

Iris squalens

Iris sambucina

Iris 'Ace'

MINIATURE TALL BEARDED IRIS HYBRIDS

Iris 'Ace' (L. Miller 1999)

This plicata has white falls speckled with violet around the edges. A purple line extends from the pale violet beard down the falls, which are tipped with bronze. The standards are more heavily marked with violet. The flower is lightly scented. Height: 56 cm (22½ in.). Bloom: midseason. Parentage: 'Cherry' × 'Manisses'.

Iris 'Apricot Drops' (T. Aitken 1995)
This wonderfully prolific variety produces lots of stems with small, soft orange flowers. The colour is slightly deeper around the orange beards, and the petals have a metallic sheen. Height: 46 cm (18½ in.). Bloom: very early to midseason. Parentage: 'Abridged Version' × 'Pele'. Williamson-White Medal Winner 2003.

Iris 'Bangles' (L. Miller 1993)
This small flower has soft rosy lavender standards and lavender-blue falls that are veined with deeper violet. The hafts are white, and the white beards are brushed with yellow. Height: 53 cm (21 in.). Bloom: early to midseason. Parentage: 'Lucky Mistake' × 'Rosemary's Dream'. Williamson-White Medal Winner 2001

Iris 'Bumblebee Deelite' (J. & G. Norrick 1985)
This neat flower has flaring, black-maroon falls that are finely edged with yellow and standards that are yellow. It produces many buds on delicate stems. The foliage is bright green, unlike the foliage of most bearded irises. Height: 46 cm (18½ in.). Bloom: early to midseason. Parentage: 'Peewee' × 'Ornate Pageant'. Williamson-White Medal Winner 1990 and 1993.

Iris 'Carolyn Rose' (M. Dunderman 1970)
This variety produces white flowers with pink-violet plicata markings. The pink-violet colouring is neatly stitched around the edges of the falls and heavily peppers the laced standards. The beards are white and tipped with yellow. Height: 58 cm (23 in.). Bloom: midseason. Parentage: from a line of pink plicata Miniature Tall Bearded iris seedlings involving 'Widget', 'Noweta', 'Pink Ruffles', 'Clare Louise', and 'Little Lucy'.

Iris 'Apricot Drops'

Iris 'Bumblebee Deelite'

Iris 'Bangles'

Iris 'Chartres' (J. & V. Craig 1997)
The rosy purple falls have lightly bleached, ruffled edges, and the standards are palest rosy-blue, almost white, and suffused at the base with rosy purple. The violet beards are brushed with gold. The flowers are carried on long stems and have a sweet scent. Height: 64 cm (25½ in.). Bloom: early season. Parentage: (('Payoff' × 'Reformation' sibling) × (('En Route' × 'Maroon Caper') × ('Chapeau' × ('Sacred Mountain' × *I. aphylla* "Werckmeister")))) × 'Bouquet Magic'.

Iris 'Frosted Velvet' (K. Fisher 1988)
The standards are pure white, and the flaring, purple falls are rimmed with white. The hafts are marked with white veins and on these sit whiskery, yellow beards. The lightly scented flowers have laced petals. The leaves are bright green and relaxed. Height: 56 cm (22½ in.). Bloom: midseason. Parentage: 'Consummation' × 'White Canary'. Williamson-White Medal Winner 1995.

Iris 'Honorabile' (Lémon ca. 1840)
This is one of the oldest surviving hybrids. It produces yellow flowers with falls that are heavily veined with maroon. The beards are also yellow. The flowers are carried gracefully on slender stems and produced in profusion. Height: 60 cm (24 in.). Bloom: midseason. Parentage: unrecorded.

Iris 'Joseph's Coat' (Katkamier 1930)
A mutant of *Iris* 'Honorabile', *I.* 'Joseph's Coat' is similar in all respects except that the colours are unstable. The standards often exhibit large white flashes, while the falls have additional yellow streaks. Height: 60 cm (24 in.). Bloom: midseason.

Iris 'Carolyn Rose'

Iris 'Frosted Velvet'

Iris 'Honorabile'

Iris 'Chartres'

Iris 'Joseph's Coat'

Iris 'Larry's Girl' (S. Markham 2002)
This petite flower has white standards that are heavily dotted with violet. The falls are white and gently edged with violet dots. Parentage: 'Astra Girl' × 'Rosemary's Dream'.

Iris 'Medway Valley' (O. Wells 2001)
This floriferous variety has dark caramel-coloured standards and white falls that are heavily washed with burgundy. The falls are further highlighted with a flush of violet. The beards are yellow. In England, this hybrid will rebloom in the autumn. Height: 51 cm (20½ in.). Bloom: mid to late season and reblooming. Parentage: 'Lady of Marietta' × unknown.

Iris 'Merit' (K. Fisher 1996)
The yellow standards are heavily veined with dark caramel. The white falls are spotted with violet and overlaid at the edges with brown. The small flowers have little ruffles along the edges. I have grown this for two seasons and it has rebloomed both autumns. Height: 51 cm (20½ in.). Bloom: early season. Parentage: ('Ozark Sky' × ('Slim Jim' × 'Dainty Damsel')) × (('Spanish Coins' × 'White Canary') × ('White Canary' seedling × 'Spanish Coins')). Williamson-White Medal Winner 2004.

Iris 'My Souvenir' (J. & V. Craig 1998)
The lightly scented white flowers are flushed with lilac and have bright yellow beards. Height: 56 cm (22 in.). Bloom: early season. Parentage: includes 'Payoff', 'Puppylove', 'Little Sunrise', 'Abridged Edition'.

Iris 'New Idea' (B. Hager 1970)
Described as rosy mulberry, the falls are flushed with a smear of violet that enhances their smooth form. The beards are yellow, and the blooms are

Iris 'Larry's Girl'

Iris 'Medway Valley'

Iris 'Merit'

Iris 'My Souvenir'

Iris 'Smash'

Iris 'New Idea'

Iris 'Somewhat Quirky'

Iris 'Robin Goodfellow'

Iris 'That's Red'

borne in spires. After damp summers, this hybrid will rebloom in autumn. Height: 66 cm (26½ in.). Bloom: early to midseason. Parentage: ('June Bride' × 'Thisbe') × ('Frenchi' × 'Pagoda'). Williamson-White Medal Winner.

Iris 'Robin Goodfellow' (C. Mahan 1993)

The petals of this pure white variety are smooth and round, while the large white beards are tipped with yellow. Height: 48 cm (19 in.). Bloom: mid to late season. Parentage: 'White Canary' × 'Table Queen'.

Iris 'Smash' (J. & V. Craig 2001)

The flowers have pale tan standards and rose violet falls that are round. On these sits a flash of bright violet and short yellow beards that are surrounded by short brown veins. Height: 56 cm (22 in.). Bloom: early and reblooming. Parentage: 'Payoff' × 'Rave Review'.

Iris 'Somewhat Quirky' (R. Probst 1997)

This variety has lemon standards and flaring, gently ruffled white falls with lilac veins. Height: 53 cm (21 in.). Bloom: midseason. Parentage: 'Pretty Quirky' × 'Real Jazzy'.

Iris 'That's Red' (Fisher 1999)

The rich red-brown flowers are not dissimilar to those of one of this hybrid's parents, Iris 'New Idea'. The falls each have a violet flash, but the beards are bronze. Height: 53 cm (21 in.). Bloom: early to midseason. Parentage: ('New Idea' × 'New Wave') × (('Puppy Love' × 'Pink Kewpie') × 'New Idea').

Iris 'Tom Tit' (A. Bliss 1919)
This old variety produces unruffled violet-blue flowers with round, open standards and yellow beards. The flowers are carried on well-branched, slender stems above a clump of curling leaves. Height: 67 cm (26¾ in.). Bloom: early season. Parentage: unrecorded.

Iris 'Virginia Lyle' (A. & D. Willott 1994)
This plant produces petite, pale blue-violet flowers with yellow beards. Height: 61 cm (24½ in.). Bloom: mid-season. Parentage: 'White Canary' × 'Surprise Blue'.

Iris 'Welch's Reward' (W. Welch by E. Hall 1987)
A profuse bloomer, this hybrid produces flowers with yellow standards and maroon falls. The falls are finely edged with yellow and veined half-way from the hafts with white. The beards are dark yellow. Height: 56 cm (22½ in.). Bloom: midseason. Parentage: (Welch seedling × pale amoena) × seedling. Williamson-White Medal Winner 1992.

Iris 'White Wine' (J. & V. Craig 1998)
As the flowers open they are grey-lilac in colour, fading to palest lilac-white, but the standards retain a flush of lilac. Short yellow beards and brown veins mark the falls. The flowers are no more than 5 cm (2 in.) in height, lightly scented, and carried on wide branches. Height: 53 cm (21 in.). Bloom: midseason. Parentage: includes 'Light Fantastic', *I. aphylla* "Van Nes", 'Starchild', 'Sacred Mountain', *I. aphylla* "Werckmeister", 'Abridged Version', 'Puppy Love', 'En Route', 'Pink Taffeta', and 'New Moon'.

Iris 'Tom Tit'

Iris 'Welch's Reward'

Iris 'Virginia Lyle'

Iris 'White Wine'

Iris 'Wistful Wisteria' (O. Wulff 1997)
The blue-violet flower has round standards and falls, golden yellow beards, and a sweet scent. Height: 41 cm (16½ in.). Bloom: late season. Parentage: 'Lisette' × 'Snickerdoodle'.

Iris 'Wistful Wisteria'

CHAPTER 4

Intermediate Bearded Irises

INTERMEDIATE BEARDED IRISES produce a prolific number of flower stems with blooms that open just above the foliage to form a dome of colour. These irises grow to between 40 and 68 cm (16–27 in.) tall with flowers 10–13 cm (4–5 in.) across. Intermediate Bearded irises start to bloom halfway through the Standard Dwarf Bearded iris flowering season, which is late May in Britain, and last around two weeks, fading as the Tall Bearded irises begin to bloom. They are ideal border plants, provided, like all bearded irises, they are not crowded by other more vigorous perennials and shrubs. Because of their Standard Dwarf Bearded heritage, the intermediates tend to expand rapidly. Spacing them 45 cm (18 in.) apart should allow sufficient room for future growth.

Intermediate by name and nature, this group of bearded irises is usually the result of crossing Standard Dwarf Bearded irises and Tall Bearded irises. Because the two groups have different numbers of chromosomes, the resultant offspring are often sterile. Intermediate irises can also be achieved by crossing Border Bearded irises with Standard Dwarf Bearded irises, or with any other type of bearded iris except for the delicate Miniature Tall and Miniature Dwarf Bearded groups.

The shape of the older Intermediate Bearded irises closely resembles that of their tall parents. They tend also to have closed standards and long, downward-hanging falls. Over the years the flowers have gained shorter, more rounded petals, while the standards splay outwards, allowing the style arms to be seen. Because the flower stems are not tall, the flowers can be seen from above.

Another change over the years has taken place in the substance of the petals. Older varieties often had translucent petals, while the newer ones have thicker petals, resembling the skin that forms on top of cream.

As a group the Intermediate Bearded irises are the most recent, but much work has been done to increase the numbers available. Consequently, not only have the flowers changed, but also the flowering period has lengthened.

Hans and Jacob Sass Medal

The Hans and Jacob Sass medal was first awarded by the American Iris Society in 1966. It was given to honour the two most important breeders of early Intermediate Bearded irises.

INTERMEDIATE BEARDED IRIS SPECIES & THEIR COLLECTED FORMS

Iris albicans Lange 1860
Yemen, southern Arabia
This species has long been cultivated due to the custom of placing it on Muslem graves in the East. It produces white flowers with white beards that are tipped with yellow. Short olive green veins surround the beards. In harsh winters the foliage may become damaged. Height: 45 cm (18 in.).

Iris albicans

Iris germanica Linnaeus 1753
Not found in the wild, this plant has been cultivated in gardens for centuries and is sometimes known as common flag or German iris. If it ever was a species, what we now know as *Iris germanica* is likely to be a hybrid of many wild irises. One indication of this is the lack of seed production and, when it does produce seeds, the resultant seedlings do not usually turn out like their parents. Nonetheless, this vigorous plant often produces a second flush of blooms later in the year. The flowers have purple-violet falls and paler-coloured blue falls. The white beards are tipped with yellow. Height: 60 cm (24 in.).

FORMS OF *IRIS GERMANICA*

Iris 'Florentina' Linnaeus 1762
Italy and Mediterranean Islands
Historically, the plant we know as *Iris* 'Florentina' is one of the most important irises to be grown commercially in Europe. Cultivated in Italy for centuries, it has be used to make orris root, a powder that can add fragrance to perfume or flavour to Chianti wine. The blooms are white with a tinge of blue, and white beards can also be found on the low parts of the standards. Height: 45 cm (18 in.).

Iris germanica 'Kharput'
The flowers have deep red-purple falls with softer edges and brownish-purple veins sitting over a ground of white on the hafts. The beards are white and tipped with yellow, while the standards are soft violet in colour. This plant gains its name from the village of Harput, in Turkey, where it was first discovered growing. Height: 60 cm (24 in.). Bloom: early season.

Iris germanica 'Nepalensis'
The reddish-purple flowers have falls that are slightly darker in tone. On the hafts sit veins of brown-purple

and white beards that are tipped with yellow. This iris, also known as *Iris* 'Purple King', was introduced from Kathmandu, in Nepal. Height: 60 cm (24 in.). Bloom: early season.

Iris kochii A. Kern 1887
Italy
The purple-violet flowers have white patches on the hafts that are lined with brown veins. The beards are white and tipped with yellow. Height: 45 cm (18 in.). Bloom: early season.

Iris marsica I. Ricci & Colasante
Italy
A more recently described specie, *Iris marsica* is similar in appearance to *I. germanica*. It has royal purple falls that curl under and deep blue-violet standards. The beards are white, and the flower has a light scent. Height: 60 cm (24 in.). Bloom: early season.

INTERMEDIATE BEARDED IRIS HYBRIDS

Iris 'Agatha Christie' (G. Sutton 1996)
This profuse bloomer with evenly proportioned, ruffled flowers has small, round grey-purple standards that are washed with soft blue. The cream-coloured falls are edged with purple, while the bushy white beards are tipped with yellow. Height: 61 cm (24½ in.). Bloom: very early to mid-season. Parentage: ('Momentum' × (('Heavenly Harmony' × 'Petite Posy') × 'French Gown')) × 'Le Flirt'.

Iris 'American Patriot' (C. Bartlett 1996)
This white variety has gently ruffled and laced petals. The falls are severely marked with a stain of purple and eaten into by white veins. The white beards are heavily painted with orange. Height: 53 cm (21 in.). Bloom: midseason. Parentage: 'Fierce Fire' sibling × ('Wychwood' × 'Battle Fury').

Iris 'Florentina'

Iris germanica 'Kharput'

Iris marsica

Iris 'Agatha Christie'

Iris 'American Patriot'

Iris 'Arctic Fancy'

Iris 'Arctic Fancy' (A. Brown 1964)
This Intermediate Bearded iris has a perfect pedigree: one of its parents is the first Standard Dwarf bearded plicata, the other a popular, well-branched plicata raised by Schreiner's and introduced in 1960. The white flowers are heavily marked with violet, and the beards are soft lilac-blue. Height: 51 cm (20½ in.). Bloom: early season. Parentage: 'Dale Dennis' × 'Rococo'.

Iris 'Ask Alma' (C. Lankow 1986)
This peachy pink variety has petals that are very gently ruffled around the edges and white beards that are tipped with orange. Height: 53 cm (21 in.). Bloom: midseason. Parentage: ('Pink Pirouette' × ((('Pink Cushion' × 'Lenna M') × 'Amber Shadow') × 'Cotton Blossom'). Hans and Jacob Sass Medal Winner 1994.

Iris 'Ask Alma'

Iris 'Az Ap' (A. Ensminger 1979)
This variety blooms for many weeks,
producing sky-blue flowers that are
very slightly veined with purple
around the edges of its petals. The
bushy beards are bright blue. Height:
56 cm (22½ in.). Bloom: early to late
season. Parentage: includes
'Charmed Circle', 'Spring Salute', 'Patience', 'Jungle Shadows', and *I.
pumila*. Hans and Jacob Sass Medal
Winner 1987.

Iris 'Bistro' (J. Gatty 1998)
Golden yellow in colour, this flower
has flaring falls that are ruffled along
the edges and heavily peppered with
mid red-brown. The beards are mustard coloured, and the flower is
sweetly scented. Height: 69 cm (27½
in.). Bloom: early to late season.
Parentage: 'Quote' × ('Foreign Accent' sibling × (('Morocco' × 'Santana') × 'Phoenix')).

Iris 'Blackcurrant' (M. Smith 1998)
This luminata has plum-purple flowers with petals that are very ruffled
around the edges and finely edged
with yellow. The standards open wide
to reveal a soft yellow inside. The
flower is scented. Height: 64 cm
(25½ in.). Bloom: early to midseason.
Parentage: 'Fancy Woman' × 'Gemstar'.

Iris 'Bold Print' (J. Gatty 1981)
This neatly shaped plicata has white
petals that are stitched with purple
and standards that are also washed
with purple. The beards are soft violet. This free-flowering variety carries
the blooms on strong upright, well-
branched stems to form an excellent
robust border plant. Height: 56 cm
(22½ in.). Bloom: midseason. Parentage: (('Dainty Royal' × 'Golden Fair')
× 'Zip') × ('Bonifay' sibling ×
('Dancer's Veil' × 'Tea Apron')).

Iris 'Az Ap'

Iris 'Blackcurrant'

Iris 'Bistro'

Iris 'Bold Print'

Iris 'Bronzaire' (C. Bartlett 1991)
The bronze-yellow flowers have ruffled standards and velvety falls with wavy edges. The beards are thick and bushy. Height: 51 cm (20½ in.). Bloom: early to midseason. Parentage: 'Diligence' × 'Warm and Toasty'.

Iris 'Butter Pecan' (B. Hager 1983)
This small-flowered variety has rich yellow falls that are held horizontally and are speckled around the edges with russet-brown. The standards have a yellow background over which is smeared bronze. The beards also are bronze coloured. Height: 56 cm (22½ in.). Bloom: midseason. Parentage: 'Picayune' × 'Pepper Mill'.

Iris 'Candy Rock' (G. Sutton 1999)
The bright violet flowers have standards that are pinker than the falls. The petals are ruffled, and the long, horned beards are violet. The plant is said to be reblooming. Height: 66 cm (26½ in.). Bloom: early to midseason. Parentage: 'Aaron's Dagger' × 'Chanted'.

Iris 'Cee Jay' (C. Lankow by T. Aitken 1992)
This dusky, deep violet plicata has flaring falls. The violet markings form a broad band on the falls and cover most of the ruffled standards. Because the standards and falls are of equal size, they form a rather flat flower. The violet beards are tinged with bronze. Height: 61 cm (24½ in.). Bloom: early season. Parentage: 'Chubby Cheeks' × 'Jesse's Song'. Hans and Jacob Sass Medal Winner 1998.

Iris 'Citizens Band' (K. Keppel 2001)
The flower has soft blue standards and white falls that are stitched along the edges with violet. This hybrid has the same parents as *Iris* 'Starwoman'; however, with this variety the pollen

Iris 'Bronzaire'

Iris 'Butter Pecan'

Iris 'Cee Jay'

Iris 'Candy Rock'

Iris 'Citizens Band'

parent has become the pod parent. What a difference a parent can make! Height: 64 cm (25½ in.). Bloom: early season. Parentage: ('Snowbrook' × sibling) × 'Chubby Cheeks'.

Iris 'Concertina' (G. Sutton 1999)
This ruffled flower is a soft pink on the side of violet rather than yellow. The beards are a contrasting violet-blue, a colour that extends into the long horns. The plant is said to be re-blooming. Height: 69 cm (27½ in.). Bloom: early to midseason. Parentage: 'Aaron's Dagger' × 'Chanted'.

Iris 'Country Dance' (E. Jones 1996)
The soft pink flowers have a mauve flush on the falls and big, bushy tangerine beards with lilac ends. The petals are ruffled, and the flower is scented. Height: 61 cm (24½ in.). Bloom: midseason. Parentage: 'Champagne Elegance' × 'Chanted'.

Iris 'Curlew' (J. Taylor 1967)
A good plant, Iris 'Curlew' produces clear yellow flowers with white flashes extending down the falls from the bright yellow beards. The petals are very gently ruffled, and the flower is heavily scented. Height: 48 cm (19 in.). Bloom: midseason. Parentage: (('Langdale' × 'Pogo') × tall seedling) × 'Atomic Blue'.

Iris 'Cutie' (Schreiner 1962)
The pure white flowers have pale blue lashes washed into the falls. The blooms are large and heavily scented but not produced prolifically. Height: 60 cm (23 in.). Bloom: early season. Parentage: ('Jane Phillips' × blue pumila) × 'Mrs Douglas Pattison'. Hans and Jacob Sass Medal Winner 1965.

Iris 'Delirium' (M. Smith 1999)
Much admired by iris breeders, this hybrid produces soft golden orange

Iris 'Concertina'

Iris 'Delirium'

Iris 'Country Dance'

Iris 'Curlew'

Iris 'Cutie'

Iris 'Dream Indigo'

Iris 'Finsterwald'

Iris 'Dumbledore'

Iris 'Fresh Image'

flowers that are heavily stippled with maroon on the falls. This colour is matt in tone and does not reach to the edges of the petal. The beards are vermilion, and the flower has a strong scent. Height: 69 cm (27½ in.). Bloom: early to midseason. Parentage: 'Flights of Fancy' × 'Brash'.

Iris 'Dream Indigo' (C. Bartlett 1994) The falls are dark violet and flare out below ruffled, soft grey-blue standards. The lightly scented flowers have grey beards that are tipped with yellow. Height: 58 cm (23 in.). Bloom: midseason. Parentage: 'Gossip' × 'Wensleydale'.

Iris 'Dumbledore' (S. Innerst 1999) The bluish-white flowers have falls that are stained with a red spot. A ray-like pattern of white veins surrounds the yellow beards. The flower has a spicy scent. Height: 48 cm (19 in.). Bloom: mid to late season. Parentage: ((('Appalachian Spring' × 'Navy Strut') × (('Captain Jack' × 'Warm Laughter') × seedling)) × 'Twice Delightful') × 'Smart'.

Iris 'Finsterwald' (S. Innerst 1993) The richly scented yellow flower has falls that are washed with large maroon spots. The beards are soft orange. Height: 41 cm (16½ in.). Bloom: midseason. Parentage: ('Glazed Gold' × 'Catalyst') × ('Dash' sibling × 'Comma').

Iris 'Fresh Image' (J. & V. Craig 2000) This bicolour has soft lemon yellow standards and rose-violet falls. In the centre, just in front of the yellow beards, sits a wash of pale blue. The edges of the petals are wavy. Height: 60 cm (24 in.). Bloom: midseason. Parentage: 'Payoff' × 'Rave Review'.

Iris 'Glam' (B. Blyth 1999)
This ruffled plicata has standards so
heavily speckled that the colour is
solid rosy lilac. The white beards are
brushed with orange. The flower is
sweetly scented. Height: 61 cm (24½
in.). Bloom: mid to late season.
Parentage: 'Proton' sibling × ('Surfie
Girl' × 'Legato').

Iris 'Gnuz Rayz' (B. Kasperek 1996)
The round, soft yellow petals are
strikingly marked with violet, and the
standards are almost entirely violet in
colour. The white beards are tipped
with bronze. Height: 66 cm (26½
in.). Bloom: early to midseason.
Parentage: 'Tiger Honey' × 'Flea Circus'. Hans and Jacob Sass Medal Winner 2004.

Iris 'Happy Mood' (A. Brown 1967)
The lightly ruffled, traditionally
shaped flower is white and gently
spotted with soft lilac. The petals
shimmer and are lightly ruffled. The
white beards are brushed with yellow.
Height: 56 cm (22½ in.). Bloom:
early season. Parentage: 'Knotty Pine'
× 'Rococo'.

Iris 'Helen Proctor' (H. Briscoe 1977)
This shiny, purple-black variety has
matching black beards and very gently ruffled petals. Height: 56 cm (22½
in.). Bloom: early to midseason.
Parentage: 'Lou Brock' × 'Sable Robe'.

Iris 'Hellcat' (T. Aitken 1981)
This bitone has soft lavender-blue
standards and rich blue-purple, velvety falls that flare outwards. The
beards are dark blue. Height: 41 cm
(16½ in.). Bloom: mid to late season.
Parentage: 'Hocus Pocus' × 'Mystique'. Hans and Jacob Sass Medal
Winner 1990

Iris 'Glam'

Iris 'Helen Proctor'

Iris 'Gnuz Rayz'

Iris 'Hellcat'

Iris 'Happy Mood'

Iris 'Honey Glazed'

Iris 'Honey Glazed' (D. Niswonger 1982)

The lightly scented flower produces cream standards and caramel falls streaked with maroon. The white beards are heavily tipped with yellow. The petals are very gently ruffled and laced. Height: 61 cm (24½ in.). Bloom: midseason. Parentage: ('Beau' × 'Celestial Doll') × 'Turtle Dove'. Hans and Jacob Sass Medal Winner 1989.

Iris 'Hot Fudge' (B. Hager 1982)

The standards are the colour of dark chocolate with a yellow undertone.

Below them sit creamy yellow, flaring falls that are heavily speckled and edged with the same brown colour. The beards are white. Height: 58 cm (23 in.). Bloom: midseason. Parentage: 'Picaynue' × 'Pepper Mill'. Hans and Jacob Sass Medal Winner 1992.

Iris 'Hot Spice' (T. Aitken 1989)

A kaleidoscope of colour covers this flower. The background of the short falls is yellow. The edges have a speckling of dark brown, then an inner ring of bright yellow, and finally they have a flash of white. The caramel standards are flecked with

mahogany-brown. The beards and style arms are yellow, but the style arms are also streaked with caramel. Height: 51 cm (20½ in.). Bloom: midseason. Parentage: 'Pepper Mill' × 'Flamenco'. Hans and Jacob Sass Medal Winner 1997

Iris 'Lemon Pop' (L. Lauer 1989)

The neatly ruffled, soft yellow flower has white patches on the falls that sit around the thick, white beards which are tipped with yellow towards the back. The flower is scented. Height: 41 cm (16½ in.). Bloom: early season. Parentage: 'Lemon Custard' × 'Highborn Kinsman'. Hans and Jacob Sass Medal Winner 1996.

Iris 'Local Hero' (B. Blyth 2000)

This frilly flower has standards that are mustard coloured, falls that are white with a broad band of mustard, and beards that are bronze. Height: 56 cm (22½ in.). Bloom: mid to late season. Parentage: ('Bee's Knees' × ('Imbue' sibling × 'Toff' sibling)) × 'Epicenter'.

Iris 'Hot Fudge'

Iris 'Hot Spice'

Iris 'Lemon Pop'

Iris 'Local Hero'

Iris 'Logo' (K. Keppel 1984)
This orange-beige flower has silky falls coated with corn beige and speckled in a heart shape with purple around the bright orange beards. The flower is scented. Height: 46 cm (18½ in.). Bloom: midseason. Parentage: 'Gigolo' sibling × 'Nazette'.

Iris 'Londonderry' (K. Keppel 1996)
This delicate soft blue flower has petals suffused with palest pink. The beards are pale blue. Height: 61 cm (24½ in.). Bloom: early to midseason. Parentage: (('Nefertiti' × 'Playgirl') × 'Presence') × 'Chanted'.

Iris 'Low Ho Silver' (M. Byers 1988)
The lightly ruffled, greenish-white flowers have bright white beards. The flower is scented, and the plant continues to bloom for many weeks. Height: 48 cm (19 in.). Bloom: early to late season. Parentage: 'Howdy Do' × 'Baby Blessed'.

Iris 'Lunar Frost' (K. Keppel 1995)
The ruffled, white flowers have flaring standards that are stained with yellow. The white beards are touched with yellow in the throat. The flowers have a sweet scent. Height: 58 cm (23 in.). Bloom: midseason. Parentage: 'Over Easy' × 'Overjoyed'.

Iris 'Magic Bubbles' (A. & D. Willott 1994)
This frilly edged, pink flower has soft petals that are tinged with yellow. On the falls sit sparsely formed coral beards. The flower is scented. Height: 61 cm (24½ in.). Bloom: midseason. Parentage: 'Pink Bubbles' × ('Coral Wings' × 'Magic').

Iris 'Masked Bandit' (K. Keppel 1997)
This very ruffled variety has caramel standards heavily flushed with purple. The velvety falls are yellow, and the beards are deep copper. The scent is like that of hyacinths. Height: 66

Iris 'Logo'

Iris 'Londonderry'

Iris 'Lunar Frost'

Iris 'Low Ho Silver'

Iris 'Magic Bubbles'

cm (26½ in.). Bloom: early to mid-season. Parentage: ('Jitterbug' × 'Hot Streak') × 'Quote' sibling.

Iris 'Maui Moonlight' (T. Aitken 1986) Every thing about this lightly ruffled flower is lemon: the petals, the beards, and the scent. Height: 58 cm (23 in.). Bloom: midseason. Parentage: 'Lemon Rings' × 'Dream Affair'. Hans and Jacob Sass Medal Winner 1993.

Iris 'Ming' (M. Smith 1997) The blue-tinged buds open into flowers with soft lemon standards and cream falls that are edged with lemon. The white beards are tipped with yellow at the back. The flower is fragrant. Height: 64 cm (25½ in.). Bloom: midseason. Parentage: 'Violet Lulu' × Keppel seedling.

Iris 'Orangeux' (R. Cayeux 1995) This richly coloured variety has copper-yellow standards, red-black falls, and copper beards. Height: 55 cm (22 in.). Bloom: midseason. Parentage: 'Rabbit's Foot' × 'Broadway'.

Iris 'Perfume Shop' (K. Keppel 1997) This deep violet plicata has distinctive white patches etched around the

Iris 'Masked Bandit'

Iris 'Ming'

Iris 'Maui Moonlight'

Iris 'Orangeux'

Iris 'Perfume Shop'

big blue beards. The falls are small, and the flower is sharply yet sweetly scented. Height: 66 cm (26½ in.). Bloom: early to midseason. Parentage: 'Faux Pas' × 'Quote' sibling.

Iris 'Pink Kitten' (V. Wood 1976)
This very pale pink variety has tangerine tipped beards and a sweet scent. The flowers are produced in heavy abundance over many weeks. Height: 51 cm (20½ in.). Bloom: early season. Parentage: ('New Frontier' × 'Signature') × 'Dove Wings'. Hans and Jacob Sass Medal Winner 1982.

Iris 'Pink Pele' (T. Aitken 1996)
The apricot-pink flowers have falls marked with large rose-purple spots. The beards are coral coloured. This hybrid looks like a smaller, more ruffled version of *Iris* 'Carnaby', a Tall Bearded iris. Height: 64 cm (25½ in.). Bloom: mid to late season. Parentage: 'Pele' × 'Marmalade Skies'.

Iris 'Prince of Burgundy' (D. Niswonger 1992)
This purple plicata is more brown-purple than blue-purple. The colour is speckled over a white background and is further enhanced with a peppering of yellow. The open standards are almost entirely purple, and the flaring falls tip down at the ends of the petals. The soft blue beards are tipped with yellow. The flower is scented. Height: 56 cm (22½ in.). Parentage: 'Goddess' × 'Chubby Cheeks'. Hans and Jacob Sass Medal Winner 1999.

Iris 'Protocol' (K. Keppel 1994)
The frilly flowers have white standards that are flushed from the base with yellow, making them appear lemon. The deep golden yellow falls flare outwards, while the white beards are tipped with yellow at the back. The flower is slightly scented. Height: 58 cm (23 in.). Bloom: early

Iris 'Pink Kitten'

Iris 'Protocol'

Iris 'Pink Pele'

Iris 'Rare Edition'

Iris 'Prince of Burgundy'

Iris 'Romp'

to midseason. Parentage: 'Over Easy' × 'Amber Snow'. Hans and Jacob Sass Medal Winner 2002.

Iris 'Rare Edition' (J. Gatty 1980)

The colour of this rich violet plicata is thinly speckled around the edges of the bright white falls and more thickly laid over the standards. The white beards are tipped with bronze. Height: 61 cm (24½ in.). Bloom: early to midseason. Parentage: (('Dainty Royal' × 'Golden Fair') × 'Zip') × ('Bonifay' sibling × ('Dancer's Veil' × 'Tea Apron')). Hans and Jacob Sass Medal Winner 1986.

Iris 'Raspberry Blush' (M. Hamblen 1975)

The main colour of this flower is blue-pink. The falls flare out and are covered with large spots of raspberry-pink. The beards are dark tangerine. Height: 51 cm (20½ in.). Bloom: mid to late season. Parentage: 'Pretty Karen' sibling × 'Dove Wings'. Hans and Jacob Sass Medal Winner 1981.

Iris 'Romp' (B. Blyth 1988)

The standards are soft creamy orange, and the flaring falls are apricot-orange. The beards are bright orange, and the hafts exhibit a few brown veins. Height: 46–51 cm (18–20½ in.). Bloom: mid to late season. Parentage: 'Marmalade Skies' × (('Catani' × 'Tiger Rouge') × ('Inscription' × 'Centricity')).

Iris 'Ruby Chimes' (A. Brown 1971)

The smoothly shaped, velvety, purple-maroon flowers have sparsely whiskered, purple beards and a spicy scent. Height: 53 cm (21 in.). Bloom: midseason. Parentage: 'Jewel Tone' × 'Cherry Garden'.

Iris 'Sangria' (K. Keppel 2003)

The ruffled, velvety dark wine-burgundy flower has falls that are darker in colour and held out horizontally. The beards are burnt orange. Height: 56 cm (22½ in.). Bloom: early to midseason. Parentage: (('Candy Floss' sibling × 'Orange Tiger') × ('Orange Tiger' × 'Chanted')) × 'Game Plan' pod parent.

Iris 'Shampoo' (V. Messick 1975)

The flowers are a colour that is difficult to describe, a rather strange greenish brown, or a yellow-bronze overlaid with smears of green and grey. The petals are crystalline, and a purple-maroon flush surrounds the hafts. The flower is scented. Height:

Iris 'Raspberry Blush'

Iris 'Ruby Chimes'

Iris 'Sangria'

Iris 'Shampoo'

46 cm (18½ in.). Bloom: early season. Parentage: 'Cambodia' × 'Gingerbread Man'. Hans and Jacob Sass Medal Winner 1984.

Iris 'Sherbet Lemon' (C. Bartlett 1991) Profuse in its flower production, this hybrid has translucent, clear yellow ruffled petals and slightly lighter-coloured standards. The beards are lemon coloured. Height: 51 cm (20½ in.). Bloom: early season. Parentage: 'Mrs Nate Rudolph' × 'Sunny and Warm'.

Iris 'Sinister Desire' (P. Black 1998) The flowers are very dark maroon-black with velvety falls and black beards that are tipped with bronze. The flower has a spicy scent. Height: 63 cm (25 in.). Bloom: late season. Parentage: 'Red Zinger' × 'Tom Johnson'.

Iris 'Sonoran Sands' (R. Tasco 1995) The golden yellow flower has short standards and flaring falls. The falls are sanded with toffee; the dots sit in rivers across the lightly ruffled petals. The beards are thin, bushy, and copper in colour. The flower is very scented. Height: 61 cm (24½ in.). Bloom: midseason. Parentage: 'Panocha' × 'Sam'.

Iris 'Starwoman' (M. Smith 1998) The blue-purple colour of this scented, free-flowering, ruffled plicata is so heavily laid over the falls that only a white spot remains of the underlying background. Long smears of purple extend from the blue-white beards. The edges of the falls flare upwards to form a lip. The petals are of a thick substance, and the stem is excellently branched. Height: 64 cm (25½ in.). Bloom: midseason. Parentage: 'Chubby Cheeks' × ('Snowbrook' × sibling).

Iris 'Sherbet Lemon'

Iris 'Sinister Desire'

Iris 'Starwoman'

Iris 'Sonoran Sands'

Iris 'Strawberry Love'

Iris 'Sugar'

Iris 'Tantrum'

Iris 'Strawberry Love' (B. Blyth 1985)
The rose-pink flower has gently ruffled, flaring falls that are washed with deeper rose-pink. The beards are vivid orange. Height: 51 cm (20½ in.). Bloom: early to midseason. Parentage: (('Guinea Gold' × 'Pulse Rate') × 'Catani' sibling) × ('Tomorrow's Child' × ('Love Chant' × 'Festive Skirt')).

Iris 'Sugar' (B. Warburton 1961)
This old but prolific variety has pale lemon standards and cream-coloured falls. The edges of the petals curl very slightly upwards. Deep yellow veins surround the white beards. The flower is lightly scented. Height: 51 cm (20½ in.). Bloom: early to midseason. Parentage: ('Great Lakes' × AM-5 blue pumila) × 'Pinnacle'.

Iris 'Tantrum' (K. Keppel 1996)
The round, golden falls are heavily dotted around the edges with mahogany. The standards are soft toffee in colour, the whiskery beards yellow. The flower is scented. Height: 61 cm (24½ in.). Bloom: early to midseason. Parentage: ('Jitterbug' × 'Hot Streak') × 'Quote' sibling.

CHAPTER 5

Standard Dwarf Bearded Irises

A DISTINCTIVE GROUP of little plants, the Standard Dwarf Bearded irises are more robust than the smaller Miniature Dwarf Bearded irises. They are easier to grow and considerably more disease resistant than Tall Bearded hybrids. Standard Dwarf Bearded irises are wonderful for planting along the edges of borders, while many of the smallest varieties thrive in a rock garden.

The flowers start to emerge in mid-spring, after the Miniature Dwarf Bearded irises and before the Intermediate Bearded irises. In Britain they bloom when the weather is not at its best, at a time when it is less enticing to go into the garden. Therefore, they should be planted in a prominent spot near the house.

A particular hybrid might bloom for only two weeks, but by growing a few hybrids with different blooming periods, something will be in flower for up to a month. Some Standard Dwarf Bearded irises will also re-bloom during midsummer. Each flower is usually between 7 and 9 cm (2–3½ in.) across, and most are scented. Plants grow 21–40 cm (8–16 in.) tall, and a mound may spread to 45 cm (18 in.).

Development

The earliest named dwarf irises were selected clones of *Iris pumila* and *I. lutescens* subsp. *chamaeiris* (the latter was known at the time as *I. chamaeiris*). These hybrids were chosen for their large and colourful flowers. During the early twentieth century, William R. Dykes, Sir Michael Foster, and William J. Caparne in England attempted to produce smaller hybrid irises by crossing Tall and Dwarf Bearded irises. However, it was not until the 1950s that Standard Dwarf Bearded irises appeared.

Americans Paul Cook and Geddes Douglas were the first hybridizers to be recognized for developing these little beauties. The two men live some 800 kilometres (500 miles) apart, Douglas in Tennessee and Cook in Indiana. Because Douglas's plants bloomed several weeks ahead of Cook's, Douglas could send pollen from his Tall Bearded irises north to Cook to use on clones of *Iris pumila*. In return Cook sent pollen from his dwarf irises south to be pollinated onto Douglas's Tall Bearded irises. The results came to be known as 'Lilliputs', a term coined by Douglas and one still used today by Schreiner's nurseries to describe Miniature Dwarf Bearded and Standard Dwarf Bearded iris hybrids.

These new irises were greeted with immense enthusiasm throughout the iris world. They became so popular that some years later the Median Iris Society was formed in the United States, largely by hybridizers, who renamed the group 'Standard Dwarf Bearded irises'. The early hybrids had large flowers, downward-hanging petals, and a greater colour range than the taller bearded irises.

Over the years hybridizers such as Bennett Jones and Terry Aitken in the United States and John Taylor in Britain have done much to develop the blooms of Standard Dwarf Bearded irises. Today these hybrids have shorter falls, which flare outwards, allowing the colour and beards to be seen from above. Recent advances by Barry Blyth in Australia and Paul Black and Marky Smith in the United States have taken this group of hybrids to a more advanced level, producing flowers in colours and combinations of colour not previously available.

Standard Dwarf Bearded irises should be grown in the same ways as bearded, or pogon, irises in a well-drained, sunny spot not crowded by other plants. When planted in a group, space these irises about 30 cm (12 in.) apart. They do not require deadheading. The dwarf bearded irises take a little longer to establish than do the taller bearded irises. Therefore, do not expect a great flush of blooms until the second year. The plants must be divided at least every fourth year or they will stop flowering.

Cook-Douglas Medal

The Cook-Douglas Medal is the highest award given by the American Iris Society to Standard Dwarf Bearded irises. It honors Paul Cook and Geddes Douglas, the first hybridizers to be recognized for developing these shorter irises.

STANDARD DWARF BEARDED IRIS SPECIES & THEIR COLLECTED FORMS

Iris aphylla Linnaeus 1753
Southern and central Germany to European Russia
The falls of this dark violet species are twice as long as they are wide. They are veined with a darker colour around the hafts and have white beards tipped with yellow at the back. Sometimes this species will rebloom in the autumn. The leaves, which die back during the winter, are often flushed with purple at the base, and the green spathes are also sometimes flushed with purple. The flower stems are slender, producing one or two branches. Height: variable, to 25 cm (10 in.).

Iris lutescens Lambert 1789
Eastern Spain, along the Mediterranean to northwest Italy.
This diploid species has many subspecies. One of them, *Iris lutescens*

subsp. *chamaeiris*, is familiar to those who grew these dwarf irises more than 20 years ago. It is the last dwarf iris to bloom and the tallest. The flowers are carried on long stems and can be found in tones of purple or pale yellow. The beards can be blue, violet, or white but are usually soft yellow. Height: to 30 cm (12 in.).

Iris schachtii Markgraf 1957
Turkey, south of Ankara
This violet- to purple-flowered species has white beards tipped with yellow, long narrow standards, and wide falls. The plant needs a well-drained sunny spot and is probably best grown in a bulb frame. Height: 20 cm (8 in.).

Iris subbiflora Brotero 1834
Portugal and the Andalusia region of Spain
This evergreen species has falls up to twice as wide as the standards. The flowers are violet, deep blue-black, dull reddish-purple, or dark purple with white hafts that are covered by brown-purple veins. The falls are

paler in colour. The beards are blue-white and dark yellow at the back. This species is not a reliable grower in the damper climates of Britain and may not produce flowers in climates with very damp springs. Height: to 30 cm (12 in.).

Iris aphylla

Iris lutescens. Photo by Sydney Linnegar.

STANDARD DWARF BEARDED IRIS HYBRIDS

Iris 'Add it Up' (D. Niswonger 1996)
The ruffled, soft peachy orange flowers have hints of blue and coffee infused into the petals. The short beards are soft violet in colour. Height: 31 cm (12½ in.). Bloom: midseason. Parentage: 'Candy Queen' × 'That's Pink'.

Iris 'Alene's Other Love' (W. Dean 1993)
This soft dusky pink variety has standards flushed with violet, which extends from its bushy soft violet beards. To either side of these sit veins of soft brown. Height: 25–28 cm (10–11 in.). Bloom: midseason. Parentage: 'Triplicate' × 'Third Charm'.

Iris 'Baby Blessed' (L. Zurbrigg 1979)
The soft yellow flowers have rounded standards and falls that are striped with white around the pale lemon beards. In my garden this rebloomer sends up only a few flower stems in autumn. Height: 25 cm (10 in.). Bloom: early season and reblooming. Parentage: 'Baby Snowflake' × 'Twice Blessed'. Cook-Douglas Medal Winner 1989.

Iris 'Alene's Other Love'

Iris 'Baby Blessed'

Iris 'Add it Up'

Iris 'Ballet Lesson'

Iris 'Ballet Slippers'

Iris 'Betsy Boo'

Iris 'Banbury Ruffles'

Iris 'Bedford Lilac'

Iris **'Ballet Lesson'** (D. Niswonger 1992) This very ruffled soft peach-orange variety has falls that are pinched into pleats around the edges. The standards are also ruffled and splay outwards, and the bright orange beards are white at the front. Height: 30 cm (12 in.). Bloom: midseason. Parentage: 'Straw Hat' × 'Ballet Slippers'.

Iris **'Ballet Slippers'** (A. & D. Willott 1986) The flowers are soft peach and have flaring falls that are very gently ruffled around the edges. The white beards are tipped with orange towards the back, and short tan veins surround them. Height: 30 cm (12 in.). Bloom: midseason. Parentage: 'Pink Crystal' × 'Coral Wings'.

Iris **'Banbury Ruffles'** (D. Reath 1970) The rich violet flowers have white beards tipped with violet and surrounded by large maroon-purple patches. The petals are serrated around the edges and gently curl outwards. Height: 38 cm (15 in.). Bloom: very early season. Parentage: seedling × 'Navy Ruffles'.

Iris **'Bedford Lilac'** (B. Jones 1990) The falls of this sparkling sky-blue variety are washed with a large but feint spot. The bushy beards are soft blue. Height: 28 cm (11 in.). Bloom: midseason. Parentage: includes 'Sapphire Jewel', 'Blithe Blue', 'Meadow Moss', 'Gingerbread Man', and 'Kentucky Bluegrass'. Cook-Douglas Medal Winner 1997.

Iris **'Betsy Boo'** (B. Warburton 1974) The soft pink flower has crumpled standards that touch at the top and falls with soft brown veins. The whiskery beards are soft coral-red. Height: 37 cm (14¾ in.). Bloom: early to late season. Parentage: 'Sweetie' × 'Lenna M' sibling.

Iris 'Bibury' (J. D. Taylor 1975)
This cultivar is the only Standard Dwarf Bearded iris to be awarded the Dykes Medal in Britain. The creamy flowers are washed with mustard-yellow and have bushy white beards heavily tipped with deep yellow towards the back. Height: 30 cm (12 in.). Bloom: early season. Parentage: 'Saltwood' × seedling. Dykes Medal Winner UK 1982.

Iris 'Blue Denim' (B. Warburton 1958)
One of the early Lilliputs, this variety produces soft blue flowers with large violet-blue patches on the falls and white beards that are surrounded by large veins of white. The falls flare out, the standards sit slightly apart, and all the petals are crumpled around the edges. Height: 36 cm (14½ in.). Bloom: midseason. Parentage: unknown. Cook-Douglas Medal 1966.

Iris 'Blue Line' (B. Jones 1987)
This dainty, creamy white flower has small bushy blue beards. Height: 25 cm (10 in.). Bloom: midseason. Parentage: ('Kentucky Bluegrass' × 'Cotton Blossom') × (('Gingerbread Man' × 'Meadow Moss') × ('Meadow Moss' × Kentucky Bluegrass')).

Iris 'Boo' (L. Markham 1971)
This large flower has white standards and slender, purple falls that are edged with white. The white edges are sometimes stained with purple. The short beards are also white. Height: 30 cm (12 in.). Bloom: midseason. Parentage: 'Elisa Bee' × (('Fairy Flax' × 'Blue Denim') × sibling).

Iris 'Bibury'

Iris 'Boo'

Iris 'Blue Denim'

Iris 'Blue Line'

Iris 'Brannigan'

Iris 'Brass Tacks'

Iris 'Brannigan' (J. D. Taylor 1966)
The velvety rich-purple flower has darker-coloured falls and whiskery, violet beards. Height: 33 cm (13 in.). Bloom: early season. Parentage: (('Clear Sailing' × 'Sulina') × sibling) × (('Sylvia Murray' × 'Sky Song') × Welch H.503) × 'Green Spot'.

Iris 'Brass Tacks' (K. Keppel 1977)
The bright yellow flowers have deeper-coloured, long, slender falls and short round standards that touch at the top. The whiskery beards are rich yellow. Height: 30 cm (12 in.). Bloom: mid to late season. Parentage: 'Moonblaze' × 'Gingerbread Man'.

Iris 'Bright Button' (Schreiner 1981)
The short standards are soft brown, a sort of drinking-chocolate brown. The falls have rich maroon-brown edges and large bushy white beards tipped with violet. The flower is gently ruffled. Height: 36 cm (14½ in.). Bloom: midseason. Parentage: a complicated mixture of seedlings.

Iris 'Cat's Eyes' (P. Black 2002)
The soft rosy mauve flowers have large, deep maroon spots on the falls and short, whiskery, soft violet beards. Short white veins emerge from the hafts. The cream style arms are ribbed with violet and so large that they push the short, ruffled standards outwards. Height: 38 cm (15 in.). Bloom: early season. Parentage: 'Snugglebug' × 'Buddy Boy'.

Iris 'Bright Button'

Iris 'Cat's Eyes'

Iris 'Chanted' (B. Blyth 1991)
This variety has been used extensively to raise pink-toned flowers. The plant itself has dusky apricot-pink flowers with pale blue beards. It is lightly ruffled around the edges, has short brown veins emerging from the hafts, and is heavily scented. Height: 31–36 cm (12–14½ in.). Bloom: midseason. Parentage: 'Oladi' × ('Peach Eyes' × 'Kandi Moon').

Iris 'Cherry Tart' (T. Aitkin 1985)
The sparkling flowers have soft bronze standards and falls. The falls are heavily washed with maroon-brown. The violet beards are tipped with brown and edged with caramel. This cultivar is said to rebloom. Height: 30 cm (12 in.). Bloom: midseason. Parentage: 'Pet Set' × unknown.

Iris 'Chubby Cheeks' (P. Black 1984)
This plicata has small, white flowers with wavy, round petals edged with very pale violet speckles, which extend into the falls. The standards are mainly pale violet, have a crumpled feel, and are edged with green. The soft violet beards are tipped with bronze. The flower is scented. Height: 30 cm (12 in.). Bloom: early season. Parentage: ('Concord Touch' × 'Daisy') × 'Soft Air'. Cook-Douglas Medal Winner 1991.

Iris 'Church Stoke' (J. D. Taylor 1979)
This variety has long, narrow, rigidly flaring falls of rose violet that are heavily stained with maroon, a colour that is flushed towards the ends. The standards are also rosy violet and touch at the top. Height: 36 cm (14½ in.). Bloom: early season. Parentage: 'Double Lament' seedling × 'Double Lament'.

Iris 'Chanted'

Iris 'Cimarron Rose'

Iris 'Cherry Tart'

Iris 'Chubby Cheeks'

Iris 'Church Stoke'

Iris 'Cirrus Veil'

Iris 'Cream Pixie'

Iris **'Cimarron Rose'** (H. Nicholls 1988)
This flower has unusual colouring: ochre with a heavy wash of maroon. The standards are gently ruffled, and the falls are decorated with a large patch of maroon. The violet beards are tipped with copper, the same colour as the style arms. The flower has a spicy scent and is said to rebloom. Height: 36 cm (14½ in.). Bloom: mid to late season. Parentage: 'Bright Buttons' × 'Cheery Cherry'.

Iris **'Cirrus Veil'** (R. Watkins 1988)
This large-flowered plicata has soft violet standards and white falls that are edged with a broad band of violet, a colour that is etched into the falls in the form of small dots. Height: 23 cm (9 in.). Bloom: early season. Parentage: 'Dancer's Veil' × (*I. pumila* × 'Cute Capers').

Iris **'Cream Pixie'** (C. Chapman 1996)
The very short, flaring standards are lemon coloured, and the short ruffled falls are deeper coloured, except for the edges which are paler. The large, tufted white beards are tipped with yellow at the back, and the flower is scented. Height: 28 cm (11 in.). Bloom: late season. Parentage: 'Mary's Lamb' × 'Tender Tears'.

Iris 'Cute or What' (D. Niswonger 1996)
The flower has peachy standards that are lightly ruffled and long, large flaring standards that are white and edged with soft orange. Short dark brown veins sit behind the thin, lavender-pink beards. Height: 36 cm (14½ in.). Bloom: midseason. Parentage: (('Oriental Blush' × unknown) × 'Tillie') × 'Chanted'.

Iris 'Cute Stuff' (C. Boswell 1985)
The gently ruffled soft violet flowers have falls that are heavily veined with maroon, a colour that seeps into the petals forming a large spot but stopping short of the violet rims. White veins surround the white beards. Height: 30 cm (12 in.). Bloom: midseason. Parentage: 'Plum Spot' sport.

Iris 'Dale Dennis' (D. Dennis 1955)
Introduced by Dorothy Dennis, this cultivar is the first Standard Dwarf Bearded plicata. The lightly ruffled white flowers have long, hanging falls and large standards that touch at the top. The petals are broadly banded with violet, a colour that is speckled over other parts of the petals. The white beards are lightly tipped with violet. Height: 30 cm (12 in.). Bloom: early season. Parentage: unknown.

Iris 'Dark Spark' (D. Sindt 1967)
This deep red-purple flower has a large patch of deeper purple on the falls and soft blue beards. The falls sit horizontally to the large standards, which touch at the top. Height: 28 cm (11 in.). Bloom: early season. Parentage: 'Black Forest' × 'Sulina'.

Iris 'Dark Vader' (R. & L. Miller 1987)
This purple variety has evenly proportioned, ruffled petals with velvety, dark purple falls and softer-coloured standards. The standards open out-

Iris 'Cute or What'

Iris 'Dale Dennis'

Iris 'Cute Stuff'

Iris 'Dark Vader'

Iris 'Dark Spark'

Iris 'Dixie Pixie'

wards to reveal large, fluted style arms. The bushy beards are tipped with copper. Height: 28 cm (11 in.). Bloom: midseason. Parentage: 'Mrs Nate Rudolph' × 'Abracadabra'. Cook-Douglas Medal Winner 1993.

Iris 'Dixie Pixie' (B. Jones 1977)

The soft white flowers have long, narrow petals that are slightly ragged around the edges. Around the hafts the falls are stained with yellow-green veins, and the white beards are tipped with yellow. Height: 30 cm (12 in.). Bloom: midseason. Parentage: ('Spring Bells' × ('Kentucky Blue-grass' × 'Meadow Moss')) × 'Canary Isle'.

Iris 'Dot Com' (B. Jones 1996)

This white variety has large pools of pale lilac-blue on the flaring falls and bushy violet-blue beards that are tipped with yellow at the back. Height: 30 cm (12 in.). Bloom: midseason. Parentage: 'Bedford Lilac' × 'Tu Tu Turquoise'. Cook-Douglas Medal Winner 2003.

Iris 'Double Lament' (J. D. Taylor 1969)

This neatly formed flower has short velvety, purple-black falls and rounded, shiny, rose-purple standards. The beards are purple. Height: 30 cm (12 in.). Bloom: midseason. Parentage: ('Green Spot' × pumila) × 'Velvet Caper'.

Iris 'Easter' (K. Keppel 1995)

The laced flowers have dark lemon standards that are infused with speckles of lavender-blue, a colour that is also dotted across the white falls. The falls are washed with pale blue and edged with a broad yellow band. The beards are soft lavender-blue at the tips, white in the middle, and strong yellow at the back. The flower is sweetly scented. Height: 38 cm (15 in.). Bloom: early to midseason. Parentage: 'Le Flirt' × Gatty seedling.

Iris 'Dot Com'

Iris 'Easter'

Iris 'Double Lament'

Iris 'Eramosa Skies' (C. Chapman 1996)
The violet-blue flower has short self-coloured beards and rounded standards that splay outwards. The large style arms are stained with soft peach. Height: 33 cm (13 in.). Bloom: midseason. Parentage: 'Rain Dance' × 'Chubby Cheeks'.

Iris 'Eye Shadow' (E. Roberts 1962)
The soft mauve flowers have long, roundly ended falls and large maroon spots. Short white veins occur at the back of the falls. The beards are violet. Height: 36 cm (14½ in.). Bloom: early season. Parentage: 'Lipstick' × red-purple 'Hanselmeyer' pumila.

Iris 'Eyebright' (J. D. Taylor 1977)
The large bright yellow flower has flaring falls and short rounded standards. The falls have long deep brown veins that look like eyelashes. Height: 30 cm (12 in.). Bloom: midseason. Parentage: (('Green Spot' × seedling) × ('Garnet Lass' × seedling)) × 'Flame Spot' seedling.

Iris 'Fairy Ring' (D. Meek 1998)
This white flower has short, round falls that are palest cream and rimmed with violet stitches. The standards have a band of violet, a colour that is splashed across the petals. The white beards are tipped with violet, and the flower is scented. Height: 28 cm (11 in.). Bloom: early season. Parentage: 'Levity' × 'Chanted'.

Iris 'Forever Blue' (C. Chapman 1996)
The soft grey-blue flowers have green patches on the falls around the bright blue V-shaped beards. The plant reblooms reliably even in the West Midlands of England. Height: 30 cm (12 in.). Bloom: early season and reblooming. Parentage: 'Shy Violet' × (('Velvet Caper' × 'Michael Paul') × 'Sigh').

Iris 'Eramosa Skies'

Iris 'Eye Shadow'

Iris 'Eyebright'

Iris 'Fairy Ring'

Iris 'Gemstar'

Iris 'Forever Blue'

Iris 'Forfun'

Iris 'Gentle Grace'

Iris **'Forfun'** (B. Blyth 1993)
This plicata has slender flared falls
that look like propellers. The soft
peach-yellow background is speckled,
lined, and edged with mauve. The
hafts are touched with bronze, and
the standards are entirely of one colour. Height: 36–38 cm (14–15 in.).
Bloom: midseason. Parentage:
'Smoky Imp' × 'Chanted'.

Iris **'Gemstar'** (M. Smith 1994)
The violet flower has short petals and
white beards that are just touched
with yellow at the back. The colour is
uneven. Sharp white flashes extend
from the beards. Height: 30 cm (12
in.). Bloom: early to midseason.
Parentage: 'Ripple Chip' × 'Coal-
bucket'.

Iris **'Gentle Grace'** (J. Boushay 1979)
The pure white flowers have round
petals and flaring falls that are
painted with short, round, violet-blue
spots. The tufted white beards are
tipped with yellow at the back and
surrounded by small, fat veins.
Height: 30 cm (12 in.). Bloom: early
to midseason. Parentage: 'Gentle
Smile' × 'Indian Jewel'.

Iris 'Irish Moss' (B. Jones 1993)
Very pale blue in colour, the flower
has soft green veins around the
whiskery, soft blue beards. Height: 30
cm (12 in.). Bloom: midseason.
Parentage: ('Sun Doll' × 'Dixie Pixie')
× 'Bedford Lilac'.

Iris 'Jazzamatazz' (H. Blyth)
This neatly ruffled variety has yellow
standards and maroon falls banded
with the same yellow. The large
lemon-coloured beards are tipped
with orange, and the flower is
scented. Height: 38 cm (15 in.).
Bloom: mid to late season. Parentage:
'Real Coquette' × 'Be Dazzled'.

Iris 'Jeremy Brian' (B. Price 1975)
The colour of this soft sky-blue flower
is uneven, and streaks of violet cross
the falls. The falls have white veins at
the back, while the small, white
beards are tipped with yellow in the
throat. Height: 25 cm (10 in.). Bloom:
early season. Parentage: 'Blue
Denim' × 'Sparkling Champagne'.

Iris 'Katy Petts' (J. D. Taylor 1978)
This large violet-blue variety has
long, flaring falls and standards that
just touch at that top. On the falls sit
large pools of purple and white
beards that are stained with yellow towards the back. Height: 36 cm (14½
in.). Bloom: midseason. Parentage:
seedling involving 'Curlew' and
'Garda'.

Iris 'Kentucky Bluegrass' (B. Jones
1970)
The green-blue flowers have narrow,
flaring falls that are heavily flushed
with ochre-green and decorated with
baby-blue beards. As a parent this
cultivar has produced many
offspring. Height: 30 cm (12 in.).
Bloom: midseason. Parentage: 'Blueberry Muffins' × 'Blue Moss'.

Iris 'Irish Moss'

Iris 'Katy Petts'

Iris 'Jazzamatazz'

Iris 'Kentucky Bluegrass'

Iris 'Jeremy Brian'

Iris 'Klingon Princess'

Iris 'Lady in Red'

Iris 'Learn'

Iris 'L'Elegance'

Iris 'Lemon Flare'

Iris 'Klingon Princess' (C. Chapman 1996)
The greenish-yellow flower has standards that flare outwards, displaying a heavy wash of violet at the base of the petals. This adds contrast to the upright, green-stained, yellow style arms. Height: 23 cm (9 in.). Bloom: midseason. Parentage: 'Chubby Cheeks' × 'Bantam'.

Iris 'Lady in Red' (A. & D. Willott 1973)
Almost red, the large flowers are bright pink-maroon. The lightly ruffled falls flare up, showing off the rich brown-red spots and copper-coloured beards. In front of the beards sit bright violet flares. The flower has a chocolate scent. Height: 30 cm (12 in.). Bloom: midseason. Parentage: ('Eye Shadow' × 'Lemon Spot') × 'Laced Lemonade'.

Iris 'Learn' (S. Innerst 1990)
This variety has small, neat, coral-pink flowers and short white beards that are tipped with orange. Height: 25 cm (10 in.). Bloom: mid to late season. Parentage: (('Betsey Boo' × 'Cherub Tears') × ('Soft Air' × 'Pink Cushion')) × 'Bright Vision'.

Iris 'L'Elegance' (B. Hager 1997)
The soft pink flowers have white beards touched with tangerine at the back. The petals are ruffled and laced around the edges. Height: 30 cm (12 in.). Bloom: early to midseason. Parentage: 'Play Pretty' × 'Pretty Cute'.

Iris 'Lemon Flare' (Muhlestein 1953)
Very pale lemon in colour, the petals of this flower are so delicate that they are almost translucent. The falls have yellow veins, and the short white beards are just touched with yellow. Height: 30 cm (12 in.). Bloom: midseason. Parentage: unknown.

Iris 'Lilli-white' (W. Welch 1957)
This white flower with white beards
has large standards and drooping
falls. It is one of the earliest Standard
Dwarf Bearded varieties. Height:
30–35 cm (12–14 in.). Bloom: midseason. Parentage: ('Blue Shimmer'
× 'Carpathia') × white form of *I.
lutescens* subsp. *chamaeiris*. Cook-
Douglas Medal 1964.

Iris 'Lime Ruffles' (W. Maryott 1995)
The sparkling white, ruffled flowers
have cream patches on the falls and
pure white, bristly beards. Height: 25
cm (10 in.). Bloom: midseason.
Parentage: 'Starlight Waltz' × 'Jazzamatazz'.

Iris 'Lime Smoothy' (T. Aitken 1997)
The large, ruffled, soft white flowers
are heavily smeared with straw yel-
low on the falls. The beards are white
and tipped with orange in the throat.
The flowers are scented. Height: 25
cm (10 in.). Bloom: midseason.
Parentage: ('Stockholm' × 'Combo') ×
(('Blue Trinket' × 'Cotton Blossom') ×
'Rain Dance').

Iris 'Little Blackfoot' (M. Reinhardt 1966)
This deep purple variety has flaring,
velvety falls that often curl up around
the edges. The silky standards are
softer in colour, and the short beards
are soft blue. Height: 30 cm (12 in.).
Bloom: early to midseason. Parentage: 'Brassie' × 'Inky'.

Iris 'Little Blue-Eyes' (J. Weiler 1993)
This cultivar has wavy, mustard-yellow flowers; the colour is paler
around the edges and on the short
falls that tip down at the ends. The
beards are deep blue. Said to be a rebloomer, this variety has so far failed
to do so at my nursery. Height: 28 cm
(11 in.). Bloom: mid to late season.
Parentage: a cross of two complicated
seedlings including 'Brighteyes',

Iris 'Lilli-white'

Iris 'Lime Ruffles'

Iris 'Little Blue-Eyes'

Iris 'Lime Smoothy'

Iris 'Little Blackfoot'

Iris 'Little Dream'

Iris 'Little Episode'

Iris 'Little Firecracker'

'Gingerbread Man', 'Stockholm', 'Ruby Contrast', and 'Little Blackfoot'. Cook-Douglas Medal Winner 2002.

Iris **'Little Dream'** (Schreiner 1970)
Rose violet is not a common colour among the Standard Dwarf Bearded irises. The flowers are old fashioned in form, with long falls and large, touching standards. The substance of the petals is thin, and the falls are stained with a large spot of rosy purple. White veins surround the sparse, soft violet beards. Height: 36 cm (14½ in.). Bloom: very early season. Parentage: 'Amethyst Flame' × collected 'Hanselmeyer' orchid pumila from Austria.

Iris **'Little Episode'** (D. Rawlins 1981)
This ruffled variety has soft violet standards and dark blue-purple falls that are banded with violet. The whiskery beards are blue-violet, as are the style arms. The plant is very scented and blooms profusely. Height: 30 cm (12 in.). Bloom: midseason. Parentage: 'Velvatine' × 'Velvet Caper'.

Iris **'Little Firecracker'** (C. Chapman 1997)
This flower has rich orange standards, rich coffee falls with bushy bright orange beards, and an unusual scent. Height: 38 cm (15 in.). Bloom: midseason. Parentage: ('Mister Roberts' × 'Solar Flight') × (('Melon Honey' × 'Pulse Rate') × 'Orange Tiger').

Iris 'Live Jazz' (C. Lankow 1986)
This bicolour has soft peachy pink standards that touch at the top and peachy orange falls. The beards are coral coloured. Height: 30 cm (12 in.). Bloom: early to midseason. Parentage: 'Spring Bonnet' × ((('Pink Cushion' × 'Lena M') × 'Amber Shadow') × 'Cotton Blossom').

Iris 'Making Eyes' (B. Blyth 1982)
The flower has pale lemon standards and violet purple falls that are edged with a fine line of the same lemon. The short bristly white beards are tipped with yellow and have broad white veins sitting in front. Height: 30–36 cm (12–14½ in.). Bloom: very early season. Parentage: 'Frost Tipped' × 'Amazon Princess'.

Iris 'Meadow Court' (L. Neel 1965)
Rich yellow in colour, this flower has falls that are stained with maroon. The yellow beards are surrounded by yellow stripes, and the petals are gently ruffled. This vigorous variety was named after a British racehorse. Height: 30 cm (12 in.). Bloom: midseason. Parentage: 'Pogo' × seedling.

Iris 'Melon Honey' (E. Roberts 1972)
A tough grower, this cultivar produces masses of small soft orange gently ruffled flowers. Each bloom has a white flash extending from the white beard. Height: 33 cm (13 in.). Bloom: early to midseason. Parentage: 'Pagan Butterfly' × ('Sky Torch' × 'Dove Wings').

Iris 'Minidragon' (M. Smith 1996)
This petite flower is rich maroon with velvety falls and silky standards. The large, bushy beards are tangerine coloured. The plant is said to rebloom. Height: 33 cm (13 in.). Bloom: midseason. Parentage: ('Mad Dash' × 'Little Annie') × ('Torchy' × 'Bright Chic'). Cook-Douglas Medal Winner 2004.

Iris 'Live Jazz'

Iris 'Making Eyes'

Iris 'Meadow Court'

Iris 'Melon Honey'

Iris 'Minidragon'

Iris 'Moocha' (P. Blyth 1988)

This plicata has yellow falls that are veined and sprinkled with dots of chocolate-brown. On the falls sit white beards that are just touched with brown, and the standards are entirely chocolate in colour. The petals are gently ruffled around the edges. Height: 25 cm (10 in.). Bloom: midseason. Parentage: (('Wishful Thought' × ('Smoky Pecan' × 'Marinka')) × (('Confederate Soldier' × (('Serenity' × 'Regards') × "Pulse Rate')) × 'Bravida')).

Iris 'Motto' (J. Gatty 1993)

The large, ruffled white flowers are etched and stitched around the edges with violet. The blue-white beards are tipped with orange, and the flower is sweetly scented. Height: 30 cm (12 in.). Bloom: early to midseason. Parentage: 'Chubby Cheeks' × 'Toy Clown' sibling.

Iris 'Mrs Nate Rudolph' (H. Briscoe 1972)

A milky coffee colour, the falls are smeared with pale blue and are lighter in colour than the standards. Stripes of deeper ochre emerge from the hafts. The white beards are tipped with yellow. Height: 38 cm (15 in.).

Iris 'Moocha'

Iris 'Motto'

Iris 'Mrs Nate Rudolph'

rimmed with a broad band of white. The petals shimmer in the light, and on the falls sit large violet-white beards that are tipped with yellow at the back and surrounded by large cream veins. Height: 33 cm (13 in.). Bloom: late season. Parentage: 'Well Suited' × 'Jazzamatazz'.

Iris 'Pumpin' Iron' (P. Black 1990)
This ruffled, rosy purple flower has falls that are almost black. Each fall is stained with a violet spot and carries a large, thick bushy violet beard. The standards open out wide to show a yellow centre. Height: 36 cm (14½ in.). Bloom: midseason. Parentage: ('Demon' × ('Cherry Garden' × 'Bloodspot') × 'Forte'). Cook-Douglas Medal Winner 1996.

Iris 'Rain Dance' (B. Jones 1978)
The soft blue flowers have short round petals and violet beards. The plant's raiser tells me that the name originates from a car polish that was new to the market at the time. Height: 25 cm (10 in.). Bloom: midseason. Parentage: (('Gingerbread Man' × 'Meadow Moss') × (('Little Shadow' × 'Zwanimir') × 'Truce')). Cook-Douglas Medal Winner 1986.

Iris 'Ringer' (K. Keppel 1996)
The petals of this yellow plicata are sprinkled with chestnut spots and neatly ruffled around the edges. The beards are mustard, and the bronze style arms can clearly be seen between the open standards. Height: 25 cm (10 in.). Bloom: early to midseason. Parentage: 'Firestorm' × 'Quote'.

Iris 'Royal Contrast' (A. Brown 1961)
This smoothly shaped flower is rose purple in colour and has white beards tipped with yellow towards the back. Height: 36 cm (14½ in.). Bloom: early season. Parentage: 'Green Spot' × 'Florinda'.

Iris 'Pumpin' Iron'

Iris 'Rain Dance'

Iris 'Royal Contrast'

Iris 'Ringer'

Iris 'Ruby Eruption'

Iris 'Ruby Contrast'

Iris 'Ruby Tuesday'

Iris 'Sapphire Gem'

Iris 'Sarah Taylor'

Iris **'Ruby Contrast'** (A. Brown 1970)
The dark brown-red flower has falls that are slightly deeper in colour towards the centre. The long, bushy beards are soft blue. Height: 33 cm (13 in.). Bloom: early season. Parentage: ('Snow Troll' × 'Lilli-Var') × 'Gingerbread Man'.

Iris **'Ruby Eruption'** (C. Chapman 1997)
This scented, ruffled plicata has deep rose-purple spots stippled across a background of yellow. The spots almost form a solid band around the edges of the falls, and the standards are almost solidly rose purple in colour. The falls tip down at the ends. Height: 30 cm (12 in.). Bloom: mid to late season. Parentage: 'Rusty Dusty' × 'Chubby Cheeks'.

Iris **'Ruby Tuesday'** (W. Maryott 1992)
The caramel flowers have gently ruffled, velvety mahogany-red falls edged with a broad rim of caramel. Thick yellow veins surround the orange beards. Height: 25 cm (10 in.). Bloom: midseason. Parentage: 'Jazzamatazz' × 'Logo'.

Iris **'Sapphire Gem'** (H. Schmelzer 1975)
This prolific bloomer produces soft blue flowers that are stained with bright blue on the falls. The beards are white. Height: 36 cm (14½ in.). Bloom: early season. Parentage: from complicated seedlings. Cook-Douglas Medal Winner 1983.

Iris **'Sarah Taylor'** (J. D. Taylor 1979)
Named after the breeder's daughter, this cultivar produces creamy yellow flowers with bright blue beards. The falls are large, and the short, ruffled standards open out as they age. Height: 23 cm (9 in.). Bloom: midseason. Parentage: seedling × 'Stockholm'.

Iris 'Serenity Prayer' (P. Dyer 1987)
The milky white flower has flaring falls and small, round standards. The beards are bright blue, and the flower is scented. Height: 33 cm (13 in.). Bloom: early to late season. Parentage: ((('Sunny Heart' × 'Blue Canary' sibling) × 'Canary Isle') × 'Tumwater') × 'Sapphire Jewel'. Cook-Douglas Medal Winner 1989.

Iris 'Smart' (S. Innerst 1990)
The rosy violet standards open out to reveal large style arms that are washed with soft purple. The round, dark purple-maroon falls are broadly edged with rose violet, and the beards are blue. Height: 33 cm (13 in.). Bloom: midseason. Parentage: 'Little Episode' × 'Pippi Longstockings'.

Iris 'Snow Troll' (Goett 1963)
This old variety has blue-white standards that just touch at the top and ochre falls that are veined with white. The petals are rather crumpled, and the white beards are tipped with yellow. Height: 30 cm (12 in.). Bloom: early season. Parentage: 'Knotty Pine' × 'Knotty Pine'.

Iris 'Southern Clipper' (S. Street 1970)
The soft blue flower has long falls that are decorated with pools of rich rose purple. The beards are white. Height: 30–36 cm (12–14½ in.). Bloom: early to midseason. Parentage: 'Southern Waters' × ('Green Spot' × 'Just So').

Iris 'Starbaby' (M. Smith 1993)
This violet plicata has short, open standards and ruffled falls. The style arms are stained with purple, while the short white beards are tipped with violet. Height: 35 cm (14 in.). Bloom: early season. Parentage: 'Peso' × 'Chubby Cheeks'. Cook-Douglas Medal Winner 2001.

Iris 'Serenity Prayer'

Iris 'Southern Clipper'

Iris 'Smart'

Iris 'Starbaby'

Iris 'Snow Troll'

Iris 'Sun Doll'

Iris 'Tarheel Elf'

Iris **'Sun Doll'** (B. Jones 1985)
This bright yellow self has small white beards that are heavily stained yellow. The hafts are marked with a pattern of white veins. Height: 36 cm (14½ in.). Bloom: midseason. Parentage: 'Tortuga' × 'Queen's Pawn'. Cook-Douglas Medal Winner 1992.

Iris **'Tarheel Elf'** (D. Niswonger 1982)
The rich mahogany flowers have distinctive large blue beards and silky standards that are also large. In contrast, the velvety falls are small and have ends that tip downwards. Height: 36 cm (14½ in.). Bloom:

midseason. Parentage: 'Little Black Belt' × 'Ruby Contrast'.

Iris **'Vavoom'** (A. Ensminger 1993)
The small flowers of this bicolour have vivid yellow falls and lacy, creamy white standards. The beards are white, and the hafts have a few white stripes. Height: 40 cm (16 in.). Bloom: late season. Parentage: ('People Pleaser' × ('Jillaroo' sibling × ('Limpid Pools' sibling))) × sibling. Cook-Douglas Medal Winner 2000.

Iris **'Webmaster'** (K. Keppel 1996)
The flower has round, velvety, yellow falls that are heavily veined and speckled, then edged with deep brown. The ruffled standards are almost entirely brown and splay open to reveal large style arms. The bushy beards are copper coloured. Height: 30 cm (12 in.). Bloom: midseason. Parentage: 'Firestorm' × 'Quote'.

Iris **'Westar'** (B. Jones 1984)
This white variety has round petals and soft blue beards that are long and slender. Height: 30 cm (12 in.). Bloom: midseason. Parentage: ('Kentucky Bluegrass' × 'Cotton Blossom') × (('Gingerbread Man' × 'Meadow Moss') × ('Meadow Moss' × 'Kentucky Bluegrass')).

Iris 'Vavoom'

Iris 'Webmaster'

Iris 'Westar'

Iris 'Westwell' (J. D. Taylor 1978)
This large, rosy violet plicata has
white beards tipped with violet at the
front and bronze at the back. The
falls are long, and the wide, almost violet standards overlap at the top.
Height: 28 cm (11 in.). Bloom: early
season. Parentage: 'Circlette' × 'Pli-
cutie'.

Iris 'Wimple' (W. & A. Godfrey 1999)
Soft lilac-blue in colour, the flowers
are gently ruffled and paler around
the edges. The beards are white.
Height: 30 cm (12 in.). Bloom: midseason. Parentage: 'Jeepers' × 'Violet
Lulu'.

Iris 'Yippy Skippy' (P. Black 1998)
This ruffled mauve-violet luminata
has large white beards sitting on
white pools, which gradually become
yellow as they reach the yellow hafts.
The standards open out to reveal
large, upright style arms. The flower
has a spicy scent. Height: 30 cm (12
in.). Bloom: midseason. Parentage:
includes 'Gentle Air', 'Chubby
Cheeks', 'Caesura', 'Betsey Boo', 'An-
tique Satin', 'Encanto', 'Gigglepot',
'Oriental Blush', and 'Gentle Air'.

Iris 'Westwell'

Iris 'Yippy Skippy'

Iris 'Wimple'

CHAPTER 6

Miniature Dwarf Bearded Irises

THIS GROUP CONSISTS of the smallest and earliest flowering of the pogon bearded irises. The plants produce dainty, rather fleeting flowers that open just above the short foliage to form a low mound of bright colour. Miniature Dwarf Bearded irises bloom at the same time as crocuses and the early flowering tulips. Because they are shallow rooted, needing sharp drainage, they are better grown in stony sites such as an alpine or scree garden. They could also be planted in stone troughs, among paving stones, or even along the top of a stone wall.

Each rhizome produces just one or two flowers, although three flowers are not unheard of. The blooms are carried singularly on short, sometimes barely visible, unbranched stems which grow between 5 and 20 cm (2–8 in.) tall. In rich soils, some varieties will grow taller than their registered height, to the height of the next category, the Standard Dwarf Bearded irises.

Miniature Dwarf Bearded irises begin to flower during midspring. In Britain this can be mid-April; in Canada it may be early May; and in Oregon it is the beginning of April.

Whatever the time, Miniature Dwarf Bearded irises generally bloom a week or so before the Standard Dwarf Bearded irises begin.

Development

Dwarf bearded irises were not known as Miniature Dwarf Bearded irises until the middle of the twentieth century when many new bearded irises were being introduced. Until then the smallest bearded irises in gardens were generally selections of *Iris lutescens* subsp. *chamaeiris*, then known as *I. chamaeiris*. The flowers of these hybrids are large compared with the height of the plant, and the falls are narrow, hanging downwards before curling under so that they cannot be seen from above.

Today most Miniature Dwarf Bearded hybrids originate from the European *Iris pumila*, a variable dwarf bearded species that produces a range of colours and holds its falls out horizontally so that the colour can be viewed from above. It is said that soldiers returning from the Crimean wars of the nineteenth century introduced this species into England. *Iris pumila* did not reach the United States until the 1930s when

Robert Schreiner imported seeds from three different European regions. He named three selections: *I.* 'Nana', with white flowers; *I.* 'Suina', a blue seedling; and *I.* 'Carpathia', yellow flowers with red beards. All three hybrids were later used extensively in breeding and became important ancestors of not only Miniature Dwarf Bearded irises but also Standard Dwarf Bearded and Intermediate Bearded irises.

As garden plants, the older varieties of Miniature Dwarf Bearded irises can be difficult to establish and keep from fading away. They need a site with extremely well drained soil, in full sun with just a little summer rainfall. Newer introductions, particularly those since the 1980s, have been raised from crosses using Standard Dwarf Bearded irises. This makes them more reliable and easier to establish. Although they need to be planted and divided carefully, these newer introductions are less likely to die off.

Over the years numerous Miniature Dwarf Bearded irises have been registered, but many are difficult to obtain especially in Britain. In the United States most growers tend to list just a handful of varieties, and therefore I must apologize for the shortness of my selection, which I feel reflects how difficult it is to get hold of even the best, award-winning hybrids.

Because Miniature Dwarf Bearded irises are shallow rooted, more so than all other bearded irises, they require very free draining soil. In the wild they grow in open, grassy areas, which means they should be planted in an open aspect where there is little competition from more robust neighbouring plants. To keep them perennial, lift, divide and replant them every two years, if not each year. Do this immediately after flowering or at the very latest in the early autumn. When dividing a clump, make sure that each division consists of at least three or four rhizomes. A plant with only one rhizome will generally take longer to establish and may well disappear before the spring. It does help to feed these irises immediately after planting or in early spring.

Caparne-Welch Medal

First given in 1950, this award commemorates the work done by British artist William J. Caparne, who introduced more than 100 Dwarf Bearded and Intermediate Bearded irises. Although mainly interested in orchids, Caparne worked extensively raising dwarf irises sometimes by putting them into a greenhouse and then crossing them with the pollen of another species. Later the name Welch was added to the award to honour another important hybridizer of dwarf irises. The Caparne-Welch Medal is given by the American Iris Society to Miniature Dwarf Bearded irises.

MINIATURE DWARF BEARDED IRIS SPECIES & THEIR COLLECTED FORMS

Iris alexeenkoi Gross 1950
Russia
The violet flowers have narrow falls that are slightly taller than the upright standards. The flowers are borne singularly and carry light violet or yellow beards. Height: 20 cm (8 in.).

Iris 'Atroviolacea' Toparo 1856
This purple-flowered iris was recorded in America as far back as 1856 and known as the 'cemetery iris' because it was carried across the country by pioneers who planted it on the graves of those who did not finish the journey. In Europe it has been sold for many years as a cultivar of *Iris pumila*. However, because of its form, it must be an old chameiris hybrid. The flowers are dull purple, the large beards white. The petals are crumpled and look like they need a good ironing. The style arms are large. Height: 15 cm (6 in.).

Iris attica Boissier & Heldreich 1859
Greece, Yugoslavia
This species has slender petals that can vary from yellow to purple in colour with contrasting spots on the falls of violet or plum. The beards can be white through to blue. Although the leaves are evergreen, the plant it is not particularly hardy in the damper climates of Britain or northeastern America. Therefore, it may be best to grow it in an alpine house or bulb frame along with other tender bulbs. Height: 10 cm (4 in.).

Iris furcata Bieberstein 1819
Caucasus, Moldavia, southwestern Ukraine
Widespread in the wild, this species is similar in character and colour to *Iris aphylla*. It produces purple flowers on short, branched stems. Height: 15 cm (6 in.).

Iris lutescens 'Nancy Lindsey' (S. Linnegar 1986)
This collected form of *Iris lutescens* was found growing in the wild by Nancy Lindsey, garden adviser to Queen Victoria. Sydney Linnegar gave it to me and told me that when he was a child, Nancy Lindsey lived in his village. Sydney was one of the few people allowed into Nancy's garden. This cultivar has large, soft yellow flowers. I am unsure where this form was collected but can confirm that it is an easy plant to grow. Height: 15 cm (6 in.).

Iris pseudopumila Tineo 1827
Italy, Yugoslavia, Malta
This species with slender petals has flowers of violet, purple, yellow, or a combination of these colours. Often the hafts are darker, and the beards are white, yellow, or bluish white. The foliage is evergreen and grows to above the height of the flowers. Although the plant is not difficult to grow, it has been noted that the rhizomes are liable to rot. Therefore, it may be better grown in a bulb frame. Height: 10 cm (4 in.).

Iris 'Atroviolacea'

Iris lutescens 'Nancy Lindsey'

Iris pumila. Photo by Sydney Linnegar.

Iris reichenbachii

Iris pumila Linnaeus 1753

Austria, Czechoslovakia, Hungary, Bulgaria through to the Urals

Research into the origins of this vastly diverse species suggests that it is a tetraploid from a natural hybrid of *Iris attica* and *I. pseudopumila*. Köhlein (1987) describes it as not being one species but a 'species complex'. The foliage dies back during winter, making it a very hardy plant. The flowers are borne singularly. They tend to vary in colour and shape, but are basically violet or yellow, the shades varying from blue-violet to bright red-purple and from soft to deep yellow. The falls exhibit large patches of colour that are darker tones of the petal colour, although on yellow flowers they are usually brown. Plicata patterning is not found in *I. pumila*. The beards also vary in colour. The standards, which are often wider than the falls, usually flare out to show the colour of the petals. The species is fragrant and has been extensively used in breeding modern dwarf irises. Height: to 20 cm (8 in.).

Iris reichenbachii Heuffel 1858

Serbia and Macedonia to northeast Greece

Each stem produces one or two flowers that can be dull yellow, purple, or violet with darker veins. The beards, which are thick, can be yellow or white, and they are often tipped with purple. The flowers have round petals and are lemon scented. Frequent division is required to keep this plant perennial. Height: 10–20 cm (4–8 in.).

Iris scariosa Willdenow ex Link 1820
Russia
Each stem produces two blooms that are either lilac or red-purple in colour and with brown-purple or yellow veins. The leaves are taller than the flowers. This species is not often found in cultivation as it is shy to flower and difficult to grow. Height: 10 cm (4 in.).

Iris suaveolens Boissier & Reuter (no date recorded)
Albania, Macedonia to Asia Minor
This species can be found in a variety of colours ranging from soft buff-violet, through mahogany, to purple and yellow. The falls curl under themselves, and the beards can be white or blue. The standards are broader than the falls. Height: 10 cm (4 in.).

Iris timofejewii Woronow 1924
Russia
Endemic to the eastern parts of the Caucasus, this species produces singular, violet flowers with white beards and long, club-shaped falls with yellow hafts. The upright standards are often notched around the edges. This iris is probably best grown in a bulb frame, as it likes excellent drainage and dry summers. Height: 15 cm (6 in.).

Iris suaveolens

MINIATURE DWARF BEARDED IRIS HYBRIDS

***Iris* 'Alpine Lake'** (A. & D. Willott 1980)
The small white flowers have oval falls that are washed in the centre with mid-blue. Height: 15 cm (6 in.). Bloom: mid to late season. Parentage: ('Carousel Princess' × 'Gunga Din') × seedling. Caparne-Welsh Medal Winner 1989.

***Iris* 'Brambleberry'** (M. Smith 1997)
This red-violet luminata has mauve-violet style arms and soft white beards. The petals are gently ruffled, and the flower is slightly scented. Height: 18 cm (7 in.). Bloom: mid to late season. Parentage: 'Rosie Lulu' × 'Privileged Character'.

***Iris* 'Bugsy'** (B. Hager 1992)
This truly miniature flower has soft yellow standards and short, round falls that are deepest maroon in colour. The falls are edged with a band of the same yellow and carry large orange beards. Height: 18 cm (7 in.). Bloom: midseason. Parentage: includes 'Abridged Version' sibling, 'Inca Toy', 'Atomic Blue', 'Curio', 'Prodigy', 'Red-Lilli', 'Pogo', 'Regards', 'Rickshaw', 'Lilli-Var', 'Bongo', 'Russet Dot', and 'Ditto'. Caparne-Welsh Medal Winner 2000.

***Iris* 'Coral Carpet'** (C. Chapman 1999)
This small-flowered soft orange variety has ruffled petals. The falls flare out horizontally exhibiting coral-coloured beards. Height: 23 cm (9 in.). Bloom: late season. Parentage: 'Pumpkin Center' × 'Chubby Cherub'.

***Iris* 'Dunlin'** (J. D. Taylor 1977)
The standards of this white-based plicata just touch at the top and are neatly stitched and washed with violet. A violet midrib runs down the

Iris 'Alpine Lake'

Iris 'Brambleberry'

Iris 'Bugsy'

Iris 'Coral Carpet'

Iris 'Dunlin'

centre of each standard. The falls, which are almost entirely white, have a little speckling around the hafts. Height: 15 cm (6 in.). Bloom: early season. Parentage: 'Mini-Plic' × 'Anne Elizabeth'.

Iris 'Grapelet' (T. Aitken 1989)
This variety looks like a miniature version of *Iris* 'Little Blackfoot'. The velvety, dark purple flowers have short dark violet beards and upright, shiny standards. In the Pacific Northwest of the United States, this plant will rebloom. Height: 13 cm (5 in.). Bloom: midseason and reblooming. Parentage: 'Clay's Caper' × 'Dixie Pixie'. Caparne-Welsh Medal Winner 1997.

Iris 'Hey There' (C. Lankow 1992)
This flower produces soft yellow standards and round, very pale blue-green falls. The beards are soft violet-blue. Height: 13 cm (5 in.). Bloom: early season. Parentage: 'Rain Dance' × 'Funny Face'. Caparne-Welsh Medal Winner 2001.

Iris 'Irish Doll' (A. Brown 1962)
This old but easily grown variety is basically white with large patches of bluish green on the falls. Height: 20

Iris 'Grapelet'

Iris 'Hey There'

Iris 'Irish Doll'

cm (8 in.). Bloom: early season. Parentage: white chamaeiris seedling (now known as *I. lutescens* subsp. *chamaeiris*) × 'Green Spot'. Caparne-Welsh Medal Winner 1969.

Iris 'Joanna Taylor' (J. D. Taylor 1971)
This variety produces white flowers with deep violet spots speckled across the falls and white beards. Height: 15 cm (6 in.). Bloom: early season. Parentage: seedling × 'Sea Fret' seedling.

Iris 'Lemon Puff' (Dunbar 1964)
In Britain this variety grows taller than its registered height and for this reason, for many years, I assumed it was a Standard Dwarf Bearded iris. It is easy to grow and establish. The neatly shaped, sparkling, palest yellow flowers are produced over many weeks. The beards are creamy white. Height: 18 cm (7 in.). Bloom: early to midseason. Parentage: 'Pigmy Gold' × 'Picture Yellow'. Caparne-Welsh Medal Winner

Iris 'Path of Gold' (Hodson 1941)
This important variety was one of the first 'improved' pumilas to be introduced. The flowers are strong yellow with golden yellow beards and paler-coloured standards. Height: 18 cm (7 in.). Bloom: midseason. Parentage: unknown.

Iris 'Scribe' (J. D. Taylor 1975)
This very small plicata has deep violet stitching that forms clear lines on the petals. Height: 15 cm (6 in.). Bloom: early season. Parentage: 'Mini-Plic' × 'Anne Elizabeth'.

Iris 'Self Evident' (B. Hager 1996)
The falls of this white flower are decorated with large purple spots. Height: 15 cm (6 in.). Bloom: early to late season. Parentage: (('Little You' × ('Inca Toy' × (BU68 pumila × 'Atomic Blue'))) × 'Ditto' sibling) × 'Jiffy' sibling.

Iris 'Joanna Taylor'

Iris 'Lemon Puff'

Iris 'Scribe'

Iris 'Path of Gold'

Iris 'Self Evident'

Iris 'Wise'

Iris 'Zipper'

Iris 'Wise' (T. Johnson 2001)
A profuse bloomer, this variety produces a broad clump of dark rosy violet flowers. The large beards are white. Height: 18 cm (7 in.). Bloom: midseason. Parentage: 'Beemused' × 'Tweety Bird'.

Iris 'Zipper' (D. Sindt 1978)
The distinctively shaped falls flare out into a point. The flowers are basically mustard-yellow with large bright blue beards. Height: 14 cm (5½ in.). Bloom: early to midseason. Parentage: 'Gingerbread Man' × 'Sun Sparkle'. Caparne-Welsh Medal Winner 1985.

CHAPTER 7

Aril Irises

ARIL IRISES ARE SO NAMED because of the white, fleshy collar, called an 'aril', that is located at the pointed end of the seed. The plants produce very beautiful flowers, usually in early to midsummer, often with exotic markings; however, because aril species originate from semi-arid areas of the Middle East, they are both difficult to grow and almost unobtainable in northern Europe and North America. For gardeners or collectors who live in areas with wet, cool summers, aril irises are best grown in a greenhouse or bulb frame. They can, however, be grown in the countries around the Mediterranean Sea and in California and the southwestern United States where the summers are drier and the winters warmer. Some arils are hardier than others, and those that originate from Turkey will generally survive temperatures as low as –20°C (–4°F).

Oncocyclus Irises
Section *Oncocylcus*

The oncos, as they are commonly called, grow in semi-arid areas of Israel, Jordan, Syria, Lebanon, Turkey, Iran, Iraq, and into the Caucasus Mountains of southern Russia. Here the summers are hot and dry with

rain falling only during the autumn and early summer. Some oncos are true desert plants; others can be found in mountains slopes and on high steppes where there is more rainfall and where the winters can be cold. The plants go dormant after they have flowered during the hottest summer months and grow during the cooler parts of the year, producing new red-skinned rhizomes in spring. Oncos do not require watering while they are dormant. The flowers are carried individually on the flower stems, and the leaves are sickle shaped. Finally, the oncos have shorter rhizomes than do the Regelia irises.

Botanists have subdivided the Oncocyclus irises further by flower form or by region. I have followed the division laid out by the Species Group of the British Iris Society in *A Guide to Species Irises* (1997), which places the 33 species currently known into geographical sections. Much is yet to be discovered and recorded about these plants, and I am sure that information about them will continue to be updated. Because most oncos are not available commercially, I have not described them in any detail. The few plants I do describe are simply in-

cluded to tempt the reader into exploring this beautiful group further.

ONCOCYCLUS IRISES BY REGION

Turkey, Iran, and Transcaucasia: Species with narrow leaves and short flower stems to 30 cm (12 in.) tall. Includes *Iris acutiloba*, *I. barnumae* Baker & M. Foster, *I. camillae* Grossheim, *I. iberica*, *I. meda* Stapf, *I. paradoxa*, *I. sari* Schott, *I. sprengeri* Siehe.

South Turkey, Syrian Desert, and further south: Dwarf and mid-sized species with stems to 30 cm (12 in.) tall. Includes *Iris assadiana* Chaudhary, Kirkwood & Weymouth, *I. bostrensis* Mouterde, *I. damascena* Mouterde, *I. heylandiana* Boissier & Reuter ex Baker, *I. mairiae* W. Barbey, *I. nectarifera* Guner, *I. nigricans* Dinsmore, *I. petrana* Dinsmore, *I. swensoniana* Chaudhary, Kirkwood & Weymouth, *I. yebrudii* Chaudhary.

South Turkey, Syria, Iraq, Lebanon, and Israel: Large species with flower stems to 45 cm (18 in.) tall. Includes *Iris antilibonatica* Dinsmore, *I. aurantiaca* Dinsmore, *I. basaltica* Dinsmore, *I. bismarkiana* Regal ex E. Damman & C. Spenger, *I. cedretii* Dinsmore ex Chaudhary,

I. gatesii, *I. haynei* Baker, *I. hermona* Dinsmore, *I. kirkwoodii* Chaudhary, *I. lortetii* W. Barbey, *I. sofarana* Foster, *I. susiana*, *I. westii* Dinsmore.

Mediterranean coastal plains of Israel: *Iris atropurpurea* Baker.

Negev, Sinai, and Jordan Deserts: *Iris atrofusca* Baker.

CULTIVATION

All arils require a warm, sunny, dry spot away from summer rain and with sharp drainage. A sloping site is ideal, or under the eaves of a house. Alternatively, arils can be grown in a greenhouse, bulb frame, or raised bed. In Britain, they can also be treated like dahlias: lift them after flowering as they go dormant (in June), clean them up, dry them out, then place them in a box with sand or vermiculite, and store them in a warm, dry place until they are ready to plant out during the early autumn (September to October).

When grown outdoors, arils should be planted just as they break dormancy. This is generally as summer is turning to autumn, around late September in the United Kingdom and in October in warmer areas of Europe and the United States. In New Mexico, California, and similar areas, the best time to plant arils is when the heat of summer is beginning to relinquish. In Mediterranean climates with dry summers, arils can be left outside all year but should be protected from any irrigation. Protect any growth made during the autumn from winter weather.

To grow them in a greenhouse, place arils in deep pots or terracotta drainpipes that are large enough to accommodate the long, fleshy roots that emerge from the rhizome. Use a medium that is two parts coarse sea sand or crushed limestone, one part loam or chalk soil, and one part sterilized leaf mould or peat-based compost. In the wild the plants grow in soil that ranges from loose sand to sticky clay, the latter becoming rock hard in summer. Half of the pot should be plunged into a bed of sand. Plants grown in pots should be repotted in fresh soil at least every three years.

Arils can be grown in a raised bed in the greenhouse or outside. If they are grown outside, make sure that the bed is covered by glass to keep out most of the rain. Water must not be allowed to seep in from below ground due to capillary action. To prevent this, line the bottom and the sides of the bed with heavy-duty plastic, cover it with a layer of course gravel just as you would fill patio containers, then top up the bed with the soil mix as outlined previously.

The instructions for watering aril irises, especially those grown undercover, are somewhat exacting. In Britain arils should not be watered until the late autumn when new roots have begun to grow but not new leaves. Water well for a few times, then water sparingly to keep the soil arid for much of the winter while the roots are growing. Too much watering will cause the roots to rot. Resume more frequent watering in late winter, around February, and feed plants with a fertilizer that is high in potash, such as one used for feeding tomatoes, or with a granular slow-release type. Water just enough to keep the soil moist until after the plants have bloomed and formed new rhizomes, which usually happens around the end of June.

ONCOCYCLUS IRIS SPECIES

Iris acutiloba C. A. Meyer 1832
Turkey, Iran, Transcaucasia
The flowers range from cream to soft violet and have brown or grey veins.

Both the falls and standards are pointed, and the standards are much larger than the falls. The falls are marked with two spots and have brown beards. Height: 7 cm (3 in.). Bloom: May.

Iris gatesii M. Foster 1890
South Turkey, Syria, Iraq, Lebanon, Israel
This large-flowered species has subtly coloured petals that can be white, pink, or cream. The petals are covered with tiny spots and veins of mahogany or black. The markings are denser on the falls. The broad standards are pushed into a globular shape by the strong midrib and are paler in colour than the falls. The falls are shorter and curl gently under. On these sit dark signals and sparse, dark coloured beards. The style arms are the same colour as the standards. Height: 50 cm (20 in.). Bloom: April to June.

Iris iberica G. F. Hoffman 1808
Turkey, Iran, Transcaucasia
The large flowers have globular-shaped standards that overlap at the top and falls that curl under. The white or soft violet petals are heavily veined or stippled with purple or maroon. The long style arms can cover

Iris acutiloba

REGELIA IRIS HYBRIDS

***Iris* 'Byzantine Art'** (L. Baumunk 2001)
The flower is domed and has soft caramel falls and white standards with heavy veins of lavender. The mahogany-red signal is strongly washed into the falls. The big bronze beards are suffused with lavender. Height: 55 cm (22 in.). Bloom: early season. Parentage: *I. korolkowii* 'Concolor' × *I. iberica*.

***Iris* 'Dardanus'** (Van Tubergen 1962)
This beautiful variety is known as a Regeliocyclus, a cross of Regelia iris and Oncocyclus iris. It has round, vertical falls that are basically white and heavily overlaid with purple veins, then smeared with a wash of purple. The purple standards are tongue shaped with paler edges and white insides. The style arms are fluted, and the signals black. Readily available, this iris is one of a series that was produced by van Tubergen in Holland for use as a cut flower. Even today it is possible to buy aril irises during spring from a good florist. Sadly they are usually unnamed. They do make excellent cut flowers as they travel well while still in bud. Height: 90 cm (36 in.). Bloom: May. Parentage: unknown.

Iris 'Byzantine Art'

Iris 'Dardanus'

CHAPTER 8

Arilbred Irises

THE EXOTIC AND BEAUTIFUL, subtly coloured arilbred irises are worth growing in the garden, even if the only spot is in a greenhouse. Their close relatives, the aril irises, although breathtakingly beautiful, can be extremely difficult to grow in wetter, cooler areas of the world such as northern Europe. Because the arilbreds are hybrids between the garden hybrids of bearded irises and either Oncocyclus or Regelia irises, which also possess beards, they contain the genes that help them to survive in damper conditions. Most arilbreds today tend to have a parentage that contains both types of aril irises; however, they are still not as tough as their bearded hybrid ancestors, which makes them prone to fungal diseases such as leaf spot and rhizome rot.

Some arilbreds can be used in borders as one would use the bulbous Dutch irises. They are better planted in a spot where leaf growth is of less importance than the flowers. The taller arilbreds flower at much the same time as Tall Bearded irises; the shorter ones, often referred to as arilmeds, flower together with the Intermediate Bearded irises and require similar cultural methods.

History of the Development of Arilbred Irises

Arilbreds have been around for over a hundred years. In fact, the history of arilbred development can be traced through only four important parents.

Arilbreds were first launched into the horticultural world during the late 1890s. Lovers of aril irises were keen to grow the beautiful plants, but as the arils originated from areas with extremely low rainfall, they were difficult to establish and keep going in much of northern Europe and also North America. Therefore, hybridizers began to cross the hardier and more easily cultivated bearded irises with aril irises, which also have beards, resulting in arilbreds.

The first arilbred to be named was *Iris* 'Alkmene' in 1896, a cross between *I. paradoxa* and *I. sweertii* (syn. *I. plicata*). These earlier arilbreds were diploids and not very fertile, which meant it was difficult to produce aril-looking hybrids. It was not until 1910 when the Dutch firm of van Tubergen introduced the first fully fertile tetraploid arilbred with the imaginative name of *I.* 'Ib-Mac' that things began to move forward. A cross between *I. iberica* and the tetraploid Tall Bearded *I. germanica* var. *macrantha* (now known as *I. germanica* 'Amas'), *I.* 'Ib-Mac' was used as a parent of *I.* 'Esther the Queen', which was registered some 56 years later.

It took a further fifteen years before the next great leap occurred. In 1925 two Californians—William Mohr and his friend Professor Mitchell—crossed *Iris* 'Parisiana', a Tall Bearded plicata from the French breeder Vilmorin, with the immensely handsome Oncocyclus *I. gatesii*. This resulted in *I.* 'William Mohr', parent of a series of arilbreds with the name 'Mohr'. Phillip Loomis, a heart specialist from Colorado, used *I.* 'William Mohr' for many of his crosses. In 1942 he introduced *I.* 'Elmohr', the first and only arilbred to be awarded a Dykes Medal. In form, however, *I.* 'Elmohr' looks more like a Tall Bearded iris.

The next advance occurred in 1940 with the arrival of *Iris* 'Capitola'. A cross between *I.* 'Ib-Mac' and *I.* 'William Mohr', *I.* 'Capitola' was for many years the only Oncocyclus-looking arilbred. As a result it was regularly used as a parent. One of its progeny is Keith Keppel's brightly coloured arilbred *I.* 'Nineveh'. Clarence White who, like Loomis, made thousands of crosses between Tall Bearded and aril irises, introduced *I.* 'Capitola' but registered only 30 hybrids in his three decades of work.

Defining an Arilbred

Arilbreds have been redefined several times since the 1970s. Currently they are divided by the amount of aril ancestry and by what kind of aril species each hybrid contains. This information can be found in a code attached to a hybrid at the time of registration. It not only assists the hybridizer, but will also inform the gardener which hybrids are the easiest to grow. The codes are as follows:

OB: Hybrids of Oncocyclus arils.
RB: Hybrids of Regelia ancestry.
OGB (Oncogelia bred): Hybrids of Regelia and Oncocyclus irises. These have half aril and half pogon ancestry and are the easiest to establish in cooler, wetter climates.

Occasionally a hybrid will have a + or – attached to the letters of its code. These symbols indicate the amount of aril ancestry in a given hybrid. For instance, a hybrid coded OGB– will have only one-quarter or one-third aril ancestry, whereas one coded OGB+ will have more than half aril ancestry.

For a hybrid to be called an arilbred the flowers must have certain characteristics. A Regelia hybrid must have at least two of the following characteristics: flowers with long standards

and falls, thin beards on all the petals, and a spot on the falls. An Onco hybrid has wide, rounded petals with standards that form a dome and falls that are decorated with a distinctive signal, although they sometimes have narrow falls.

Cultivation

Some arilbreds can be difficult to grow; therefore, it is important to select the right varieties for the growing conditions. Almost any variety can easily be established in areas where Tall Bearded irises need to be watered for much of the growing season. In cooler areas it might be better to choose award-winning varieties that have been tried and tested over a long period. Arilbreds with the code OGB are also easier in cooler areas, as they require the same growing conditions as the typical bearded iris.

The only thing to remember is that arilbreds must be planted in a rich, warm soil with sharp drainage during the summer months and in full sun. I have grown them in both sandy soil and a clay loam and have had no difficulty in either location. If you do not have these conditions, plant arilbreds in a raised bed, on top of soil that is ridged up, or in a warm, dry border near the house. Like all bearded irises, arilbreds do not like an acid soil. Add lime to the soil to achieve a non-acid pH.

Arilbreds also like frequent division, ideally every two years. This should be done two or three months after blooming. In cooler areas, the hybrids that contain more aril than bearded hybrids are better grown in a greenhouse. Arilbreds growing outdoors in areas that get a reasonable amount of frost must be provided some protection during winter.

Clarence G. White Award

This medal is one of two given to arilbreds by the American Iris Society. The Clarence G. White Award was first awarded in 1993 to the best arilbred iris with half or more aril ancestry in the parentage. During the 1950s White created the family of fertile arilbreds that still dominates the breeding of these beautiful plants.

William Mohr Medal

Since 1993 the William Mohr Medal has been given by the American Iris Society to the best arilbred with less than half aril parentage in its lineage.

ARILBRED IRIS HYBRIDS

Iris **'Afrosiab'** (Volfovich-Moler 2002) RB. This cross between a Regelia and a Tall Bearded iris has light purple standards that are broadly edged with brown. The bright rose-purple falls are covered with dark veins and edged with a broad band of brown. The long soft blue beards are tipped with orange. Height: 100 cm (40 in.). Bloom: early season. Parentage: *I. stolonifera* × 'Mary Frances'.

Iris **'Big Black Bumblebee'** (Danielson 1965) OGB+. The smooth, dusky purple-pink falls are evenly veined, and the lilac standards have deeper-coloured veining. The signals are black-mauve, and the beards are bronze. Height: 60 cm (24 in.). Bloom: early to midseason. Parentage: 'Theseus' × WO1 seedling. Clarence G. White Award Winner 1970.

Iris **'Chocolate Mint'** (R. Tasco 1997) OGB. The falls are cream, and the very pale blue standards are deeper in colour around the dark brown beards. Height: 89 cm (35½ in.).

Iris 'Afrosiab'

Iris 'Concerto Grosso'

Iris 'Big Black Bumblebee'

Iris 'Desert Attire'

Iris 'Chocolate Mint'

Iris 'Desert Moonlight'

Bloom: mid to late season. Parentage: 'Apricot Brandy' × 'Bold Sentry'. Clarence G. White Medal 2004.

Iris 'Concerto Grosso' (H. Mathes 1998)
OGB. The flower is described as oxblood red, the standards are greyer, the signals mauve-black, and the beards dark blue. Height: 50 cm (20 in.). Bloom: early season. Parentage: (('Gelee Royale' × sibling) × 'Anacrusis' sibling) × 'Invention'.

Iris 'Desert Attire' (H. Shockey by Irene Shockey 1997)
OGB. The buff-peach falls are veined and stippled with maroon. The signals are a shiny maroon,and the soft lilac standards have fine, violet veins. The white whiskers are tipped with yellow and form three rows on the falls. Height: 60 cm (24 in.). Bloom: midseason. Parentage: includes 'Seraph's Jewel', 'Queen Sheba', 'Stars Over Chicago', 'Welcome Reward', 'Syrian Moon', 'Heart Stealer', 'Onlooker', 'Desert Princess', 'Heart Stealer', and 'Kalifa Gulnare'.

Iris 'Desert Moonlight' (L. Rich by James Whitely 1990)
OGB. On closer observation the cream standards are in reality white with heavy veins of yellow. The bright yellow falls curl underneath and are decorated with chestnut-brown signals. Both the style arms and beards are yellow. Height: 64 cm (25½ in.). Bloom: mid to late season. Parentage: (onco hybrid × 'Garden Gold') × (((onco × Tall Bearded) × 'Welcome Reward') × ('Welcome Reward' × (onco × AB))).

Iris **'Desert Plum'** (B. Hager 1991) OGB. The standards are dark violet, the falls brown-plum, and the signals rich maroon. The bronze style arms are visible between the standards, and the beards are bronze-black. The flowers are scented. Height: 86 cm (34½ in.). Bloom: mid to late season. Parentage: includes 'Syrian Moon', 'Bagdad Beauty', 'Pink Formal', 'Welcome Reward', 'Orchid and Flame', 'Kalifa Hirfa', 'Bethlehem Song', and 'Moon Star'.

Iris **'Domingo'** (G. F. Wilson 1996) OGB. This neatly domed flower has white standards with yellow midribs. On the soft yellow falls sit large smudges of red-brown. The beards are yellow. Geoff Wilson, from Nottingham, England, is one of the few British hybridizers who have attempted to work with arilbreds. Because of his work,we now have a range of reliably hardy arilbreds. Height: 81 cm (32½ in.). Bloom: early season. Parentage: 'Syrian Moon' × 'Onlooker'.

Iris **'Down Payment'** (H. Danielson 1987) The lavender-white flowers have falls that are smeared with red-brown and soft purple. The beards are brown. This is an aptly named plant as we find that the stems tend to topple over because of the size of the flowers. Height: 76 cm (30½ in.). Bloom: early to midseason. Parentage: 'Ghost Story' × 'Dee Mouse'.

Iris **'Elmohr'** (P. Loomis 1942) OB–. The small, smoothly shaped flowers are rose purple in colour with yellow beards and no visible signals. Height: 91 cm (36½ in.). Bloom: midseason. Parentage: 'William Mohr' × seedling. Dykes Medal Winner USA 1945.

Iris 'Desert Plum'

Iris 'Elmohr'

Iris 'Domingo'

Iris 'Esther The Queen'

Iris 'Down Payment'

Iris 'First Chapter'

Iris 'Esther The Queen' (E. Hunt 1967) OGB. Variable in its colour, this flower has lilac standards suffused with deeper streaks and rose-brown falls marked with red-brown streaks. The beards are brown-black, and the style arms match the falls. Height: 90 cm (36 in.). Bloom: early to midseason. Parentage: ('Ardrun' × 'Ib-Mac') × 'Kalifa Gulnare'. C. G. White Award Winner 1971.

Iris 'First Chapter' (G. F. Wilson 1994) OGB. The falls are rose plume in colour, and the long, narrow standards are violet. The signal is maroon-black, and the V-shaped beards are bronze. The flower smells like nutmeg. Height: 84 cm (33½ in.). Bloom: early to midseason. Parentage: 'Onlooker' × 'Tornado Warning'.

Iris 'Harem Girl' (W. Wilkes, introduced by W. Hawkinson 1976) OGB. The large soft pink standards are handsomely patterned with mauve veins. The soft copper falls curl under and are heavily veined and stippled with dark purple. The signals are maroon-black, and the beards are bronze. This iris was first introduced in 1962. Height: 102 cm (41 in.). Bloom: midseason. Parentage: 'Mam Ahmid' × 'Kalifa Gulnare'.

Iris 'Kalifa Gulnare' (C. White 1954) OGB. The parent of many arilbreds, this iris has white standards suffused with soft lavender. The corn yellow falls are heavily stained and flecked with red-brown, and the very large beards are bronze. I last grew this cultivar in the early 1980s, when the photograph was taken. Height: unknown. Bloom: unknown. Parentage: unknown.

Iris 'Kalifa's Horn' (R. Annand 1995) OGB–. In my opinion this is a rather ugly flower. The petals are large and gently ruffled and laced around the edges. In colour they are soft lilac with splashes of soft purple. The falls are suffused with ochre from the hafts, and the bronze beards extend into long, pointed horns. Height: 97 cm (38¾ in.). Bloom: mid to late season. Parentage: 'Sky Hooks' × ('William Mohr' × 'Kalifa Gulnare'). William Mohr Medal Winner 2001.

Iris 'Kalifa's Robe' (B. Hager 1989) OGB. This smoothly shaped flower has strongly domed rose-purple standards and soft terracotta falls. The large signals are brown-black, and

Iris 'Harem Girl'

Iris 'Kalifa's Horn'

Iris 'Kalifa Gulnare'

Iris 'Kalifa's Robe'

the beards are black. Height: 81 cm (32½ in.). Bloom: early to midseason. Parentage: includes 'Rare Form', 'Heart Stealer', 'Syrian Moon', 'Bagdad Beauty', 'Pink Formal', 'Welcome Reward', 'Orchid and Flame', 'Kalifa Hirfa', 'Bethlehem Song', and 'Moonstar'.

Iris 'Kiosk' (B. Hager 1985)

OGB. This pure yellow flower has standards with paler edges and signals that are large, round, and brown-black. Height: 90 cm (36 in.). Bloom: midseason. Parentage: includes 'Bethlehem Song', 'Welcome Reward', 'Moonstar', 'Syrian Moon', 'Bagdad Beauty', 'Pink Formal', 'Orchid and Flame', and 'Kalifa Hirfa'.

Iris 'Lady Mohr' (Salbach 1944)

OGB–. This incredibly reliable aril-bred thrives in fields in the middle of England. It has large, round soft violet-white standards and long, sparkling ochre falls. The whisker-like beards are soft brown, and the blooms are carried on long, branched stems. According to Judith Berrisford (1961), this is 'one of the most exciting irises ever raised' as it combines 'the strange beauty of the Oncocyclus with the height and dignity of the Tall Bearded irises'. Height: 101 cm (40½ in.). Bloom: early season. Parentage: 'William Mohr' × unknown.

Iris 'Lancer' (H. Shockey 1994)

OGB. This smoothly shaped lilac-coloured flower has deeper-coloured midribs on the standards and large maroon-purple spots on the falls. It also has a light sweet scent. Height: 71 cm (28½ in.). Bloom: midseason. Parentage: 'Seraph's Jewel' × 'Queen Sheba'. Clarence G. White Award Winner 2002.

Iris 'Mohr Pretender' (L. Rich 1977)

OGB. The very soft blue flowers are decorated with purple signals that wash into eyelash-like stripes down the falls. The beards are brown. Height: 86 cm (34½ in.). Bloom: midseason. Parentage: (('William Mohr' × seedling) × ('Welcome Reward' × seedling)) × (Kerr seedling × ((('Fair Enough' × 'July Beauty') × 'Whole Cloth') × sibling)). Iris 'Mohr Pretender' (L. Rich 1977).

Iris 'Nineveh' (K. Keppel 1965)

OGB. This beautiful variety grows well in England. The falls are purple-terracotta and the standards vibrant rose purple. The beards are dark brown, and there are no signals. Height: 76 cm (30½ in.). Bloom: early season. Parentage: 'Bang' × 'Capitola'. William Mohr Award Winner 1969.

Iris 'Onlooker' (B. Hager 1984)

OGB. The pale lilac standards are marked with fine veins of deep lilac, while the large ochre falls exhibit maroon-black signals. The style arms are also ochre, and the beards are bronze. Height: 66 cm (26½ in.). Bloom: midseason. Parentage: (('Bethlehem Star' × 'Welcome Reward') × 'Moon Star') × unknown.

Iris 'Oyez' (C. G. White 1938)

OGB. This delightfully patterned flower has a cream-coloured background and broad veins of black-maroon decorating the entire flower. The style arms are rust-brown. The short brown beards sit behind the small maroon-black signals. Raised by Clarence White, this is one of many thousands of crosses, most of which were unsuccessful. Height: short. Bloom: midseason. Parentage: unknown.

Iris 'Kiosk'

Iris 'Lady Mohr'

Iris 'Lancer'

Iris 'Mohr Pretender'

Iris 'Oyez'

Iris 'Nineveh'

Iris 'Pink Betterment'

Iris 'Saffron Charm'

Iris 'Onlooker'

Iris 'Pink Betterment' (L. Peterson 1984)
OGB. The flowers have rich terracotta-pink falls and black whiskery beards that spread along the back of the petals. In front of these are triangular dark brown signals. The standards are rose-lavender, and the style arms are orange-buff. Height: 66 cm (26½ in.). Bloom: midseason. Parentage: 'Esther's Son' × 'Heart Stealer'.

Iris 'Saffron Charm' (Benbow 1953)
OGB–. This gently ruffled, laced hybrid has soft ochre falls and lilac-white standards. The long beards are bronze coloured. There are no signals. Height: 71 cm (28½ in.). Bloom: early season. Parentage: Regeliocyclus ancestry.

Iris 'Sheba's Jewel'

Iris 'Vera-Anne'

Iris 'Sheik'

Iris 'Walker Ross'

Iris 'Sunset Trail'

Iris 'Sheba's Jewel' (H. Shockey 1994) OGB. The pure white flower has large maroon signals and white beards that are tipped with yellow. Height: 71 cm (28½ in.). Bloom: midseason. Parentage: 'Seraph's Jewel' × 'Queen Sheba'. Clarence G. White Award Winner 2000.

Iris 'Sheik' (B. Hager 1976) OGB. This large glowing flower has violet standards and chestnut falls and style arms. The beards are yellow, and the shiny petals have lightly laced edges. Height: 86 cm (34½ in.).

Bloom: early season. Parentage: 'Turkish Tracery' × 'Welcome Reward'. C. G. White Award Winner 1980.

Iris 'Sunset Trail' (G. R. Wilson 1991) OGB. The smooth falls are soft copper in colour with a large wash of chestnut-brown radiating down the petals from the chestnut-brown beards. The standards are rose violet with deeper veining. Height: 65 cm (26 in.). Bloom: early season. Parentage: 'Turkish Tangent' × 'Warrior's Mantle'.

Iris 'Vera-Anne' (L. Ransom 1995) RB. The falls of this golden yellow flower soften to grey-white in the centre. Red-brown veins emerge from the hafts, working their way down the petals. The whiskery, grey-white beards are tipped with yellow. Height: 45 cm (18 in.). Bloom: early to midseason. Parentage: 'Vera' × 'Third Charm' or 'Triplicate'.

Iris 'Walker Ross' (W. Ross by Chuck Chapman 1996) OGB–. The petals of this lilac-blue, gently ruffled flower have a white background etched with violet-blue veins. The beards are dark blue. Height: 76 cm (30½ in.). Bloom: early to midseason. Parentage: 'Spinning Wheel' × seedling.

ARILMED IRIS HYBRIDS

Arilmed irises are crosses between aril species and median bearded hybrids that are shorter than Tall Bearded irises. Culturally, arilmeds are treated as median bearded irises.

Iris 'Omar's Gold' (C. Boswell 1995) OGB–. The standards are soft violet, and the falls are gold- and toffee-coloured, washed with dark purple-brown flecks. The beards are coffee coloured, and the flower has a light flowery scent. Height: 45 cm (18 in.). Bloom: midseason. Parentage: ('Puppet Baby' × 'Moon Spot') × 'Onlooker'. William Mohr Medal Winner 2002.

Iris 'Omar's Stitchery' (C. Boswell 2000)

OGB. The ruffled white flower has falls that are perfectly lined with violet and stitched with the same colour around the edges. The standards have flecks of soft lilac. Height: 60 cm (24 in.). Bloom: midseason. Parentage: 'Dunlin' × L. rich seedling: ((*I. atropurpurea* × (*I. mariae* × Judean Cream)) × (*I. stolonifera* × ((*I. lortetii* × *I. susiana*) × *I. nazarena*))).

Iris 'Omar's Touch' (C. Boswell 1985)

OGB–. The flower has bright purple standards and maroon-brown falls that are deeper in the centre. The beards are bright yellow. Height: 46 cm (18½ in.). Bloom: midseason. Parentage: ('Gingerbread Man' × *I. balkana*) × 'Welcome Reward'. William Mohr Medal Winner 1992 and 1997.

Iris 'Omar's Gold'

Iris 'Omar's Stitchery'

Iris 'Omar's Touch'

PART TWO BEARDLESS IRISES

BEARDLESS IRISES ARE A DIVERSE GROUP of plants. There are many more species of beardless irises than bearded ones. These can be found growing throughout the Northern Hemisphere in forests, on the sides of mountains, along coast lines, in swamps and wet meadows, and in dry, scrubby regions. Therefore, they are the most versatile group with plants for the most difficult garden locations.

Some beardless irises are suitable for growing in ponds as well as along the edges of ponds. Others are ideal for growing in borders along with a mixture of other garden plants, including the most vigorous perennials. Some are small enough to grow in rockeries or alpine gardens, while others are tall enough to use as a backdrop at the back of a border. There are plants for acid and alkaline soils, for shady areas, and for dry, sunny borders.

By and large, beardless irises do not produce the large glamorous blooms associated with bearded irises, and fewer cultivars are available among the different species. The most colourful blooms can be found among the Louisiana, Japanese, and Pacific Coast irises, all of which can be difficult to grow, depending on your climate, as they require either a warm climate, or a wet or acid soil. However, the Siberian irises are the most tolerant of all the iris groups, as they will thrive in a range of conditions. On the whole, beardless irises are less prone to the diseases that afflict bearded irises. Most groups produce flowers during midsummer.

Classification of Beardless Irises

The list begins with the larger groups and ends with groups of only one or two species.

Siberian Irises: These are suitable for borders, wild gardens, and along the edges of ponds, but not for growing in water.

Laevigata Irises: A water-loving group of irises, these tend to be vigorous and are suitable for growing in the shallow parts of ponds and in gardens with moisture-retentive soil.

Japanese Irises: This large-flowered race of irises can be grown in any soil that remains moist, including along the edges of ponds.

Louisiana Irises: Generally these are best for warmer gardens where they require a moist or boggy soil such as that found around ponds.

Pacific Coast Irises: These are ideal for lightly shaded wooded areas and rockeries, or in borders with acid soils.

Spuria Irises: These contain the tallest irises. The foliage is upright and ideal for planting at the back of a border. Other members of the group are small enough for rockeries. Spurias produce their flowers later than most other irises.

Crested Irises: Generally evergreen, these are suitable for shady areas, but most will only grow in warmer areas of the world.

Iris sanguinea

Iris foetidissima: This species is ideal for shady parts of the garden. The seeds are attractive enough to pick for winter displays.

Iris lactea: A tolerant species, this iris can be grown in most types of soils including along coasts.

Rocky Mountain Irises and *Iris setosa*: These are suitable for wet soils.

Winter Flowering Iris: *Iris unguicularis* is perfect for drier, warmer soils.

Iris verna: This small plant is ideal for rockeries.

Cultivation

Specific growing details are given with each group of beardless irises, but here are a few general growing guidelines. Beardless irises make their root growth during the autumn. In Britain they can be successfully transplanted in autumn and spring; however, in hotter climates, they are best planted in autumn. In general, beardless irises can be left undivided for many years, but if the flowers begin to dwindle in number the plants should be lifted, divided, and replanted. In most cases, species with small rhizomes should be replanted in large clumps, while species with large rhizomes can be replaced in single clumps or fans. Most beardless irises must be watered after planting. Almost all of them should be planted at least 25 mm (1 in.) deep, or deep enough to seriously cover the growing tips. Be aware that most beardless irises take time to establish and will not produce great quantities of flower until the second growing season.

CHAPTER 9

Siberian Irises
Series *Sibiricae*

Siberian irises are graceful plants and perhaps the most elegant of all irises. The flowers can be delicate. Some are produced on long, slender stems, while others are flat and carried on more solid stems. All Siberian irises produce upright clumps of slim, grassy foliage. In Britain they usually flower at the same time as the midseason Tall Bearded irises, but in some areas, such as Oregon, they open earlier. Flower colours once limited to tones of blue, purple, and white now include yellow and pink. Siberians are very tolerant of many conditions and can be grown in a wider range of locations than bearded irises. They prefer a site in partial shade, in soil that does not dry out during the summer as long as it is not too acid.

Sibs, as they are generally called, can be divided into two groups. The first group, consisting of the most common and easiest-to-grow species, includes the traditional blue-flowered types that are derived from *Iris sanguinea* and *I. sibirica*. In the wild *I. sanguinea* grows in damp areas and along rivers that stretch from Russia (including Siberia) to northern China, into Korea, and Japan. *Iris sibirica*,

the plant from which this group inherits its name, does not actually grow in Siberia. Its natural range starts in northern Italy and spreads to Turkey, then up into southeastern Russia. Many Siberian irises presently in cultivation are diploids, but due to the pioneering work of Currier McEwen an increasing number of tetraploids are being introduced. Diploid sibs have delicate stems and narrow foliage, whereas tetraploid sibs have more hefty stems and larger flowers with greater substance.

The second group of Siberian irises comes from China and the Himalayas where the plants grow in marshy areas and wet meadows. All members of this group—*Iris chrysographes* is an example—have 40 chromosomes, unlike irises derived from *I. sanguinea* and *I. sibirica*, which have only 28 chromosomes.

After much discussion during the late 1960s and 1970s, the Society for Siberian Irises in North America decided in 1977 to divide the series *Sibiricae* into two groups based on the number of chromosomes. The groups were given the inelegant names of 28-Chromosome Siberians and 40-Chromosome Siberians. The

40-chromosome irises have since come to be known as Sino-Siberians, a name that relates to their wild origins. Because of the different chromosome count, the two groups do not cross easily, and if they do, the offspring are usually infertile.

A Brief History of the Development of Siberian Irises

Siberian irises have been grown in Europe for centuries. Carl Linnaeus and Carl Thunberg recorded *Iris sibirica* and *I. sanguinea* during the eighteenth century. These species were not just ornamental plants but also used in herbal recipes for the cure of ulcers, to alleviate problems particular to woman, and even to remove freckles. By the end of the nineteenth century English nurserymen such as Peter Barr, Robert Wallace, and Amos Perry were selecting new hybrids. During the 1920s and 1930s, Bertrand Farr, Cleveland Morgan, Isabella Preston, and Frances Cleveland were doing the same in the United States and Canada. As no great advances in substance or colour of the flower were made for many decades, many of these plants are still being sold today.

Not until *Iris* 'White Swirl' was introduced in 1957 did the flowers of Siberian irises gain flaring petals. Nearly all hybrids introduced since that time have this parent in their ancestry. Then during the 1960s Currier McEwen treated the seedlings of his Sibirica crosses with a solution of colchicine, a drug used to alleviate gout. It resulted in diploid seedlings becoming tetraploid. Up until then all Sibirica irises were diploids with pendent-shaped falls and erect standards. By turning the plants into tetraploids, the flowers became larger, the falls more horizontal, and the stems thicker. The next important step was the introduction of a new colour with *I.* 'Dreaming Yellow' and *I.* 'Floating Island'. Both produce yellow flowers with creamy yellow falls that become white with age.

Most of the Siberian irises introduced in the twentieth century have been hybrids between *Iris sanguinea* and *I. sibirica*; however, a group of hybridizers has worked with Sino-Sibs, which readily cross with each other and with members of the series *Californicae*. One of the most notable introductions was *I.* 'Margot Holmes'. Introduced in 1927 by Amos Perry, it won the British Dykes Medal that year. Tom Tamberg in Germany has been working with these crosses since the mid 1970s. Despite being extremely beautiful, most Sino-Sibs are difficult to establish and maintain. Therefore, sadly these are very rarely available commercially.

Siberian species (28 chromosomes): *Iris sanguinea, I. sibirica, I. typhifolia.*

Sino-Siberian species (40 chromosomes): *Iris bulleyana, I. chrysographes, I. clarkei, I. delavayi, I. dykesii, I. forrestii, I. phragmitetorum, I. wilsonii.*

Cultivation of Species with 28 Chromosomes

Iris sibirica and *I. sanguinea* and their hybrids prefer a spot in full sun in a soil that is neither too acid nor too alkaline, too wet nor too dry. These plants can cope with their feet being in water for short spells, and for that reason they are often seen growing along the edges of streams and pools where flooding is likely at some time in the year. Nevertheless, it is important to plant them in ground above the water level. These irises can grow in partial shade, especially in hotter areas where the soil will remain moist. Once established they do not mind a soil that dries out, provided the dry spell is not prolonged.

PLANTING

It does not seem to matter whether Siberian irises are planted in spring or autumn. In areas where the ground gets deep frosts, spring planting may be more suitable. It is important to replant large clumps and to not allow the roots to dry out before and after planting. When it comes to planting, simply make sure that the hole is deep enough to cover the roots and the bottom 2.5 cm (1 in.) of the leaves, then water the plants well. In dry springs it may be necessary to keep plants watered for several weeks until they have established.

Siberian irises will take some time to establish after planting; therefore, do not expect a great number of blooms for at least one season. Space sibs at least 45 cm (18 in.) apart. They do not need dividing as often as bearded irises but will appreciate being occasionally fed with any general fertilizer. These extremely hardy plants tolerate low temperatures. Therefore, no winter protection is needed even in areas with long winters. However, plants grown in regions of deep frosts need some protection; a mulch of oat straw is advisable.

MAINTENANCE

In Britain, Siberian irises get few diseases and need very little attention once established. They can be left undisturbed throughout the year, but it is probably better to tidy them up by removing old flower stems. I tend to leave the foliage on until very early spring. This provides a hiding place for small insects such as ladybirds during the winter. As soon as the months become lighter and the small, pointed green shoots appear, I then remove all the dead leaves; however, it does not harm, and may keep fungal spores at bay, to remove the foliage earlier.

Cultivation of Species with 40 Chromosomes

This group is not as easy to grow or as hardy as the first group of Siberian irises. A lot of water is required, especially during the growing season, and this group prefers a soil that is more acid than alkaline. This explains why I found them nearly impossible to grow in a sandy, well-drained soil. Because the Sino-Sibs come from areas with cool summers, they are best grown in gardens that are neither too cold nor too hot. They do not thrive in the southern United States but will succeed in the cooler northeastern states and in northern Europe. Currier McEwen wrote in his book *Siberian Iris* (1996) that he lost plants when the temperature went as low as −26°C (−15°F). Therefore, if you wish to grow these beautiful plants in colder areas, be sure to mulch them well over the winter months.

Morgan-Wood Medal

The Morgan-Wood award is given by the American Iris Society and was first called the Morgan Award. It dates back to 1951. It was given to honour the work of F. Cleveland Morgan. Later its name was changed. The medal is given to Siberian irises.

SIBERIAN IRIS SPECIES & THEIR COLLECTED FORMS

Iris bulleyana Dykes 1910
Southwest China

This iris was thought to be a natural hybrid between *Iris chrysographes*, *I. forrestii*, and *I. wilsonii*, but the true species has now been found in China, where it grows in moist areas on hillsides and in meadows. The flowers range from pale to mid violet or blue-purple; however, most specimens of *I. bulleyana* grown in gardens are pale yellow, suffused with violet, and these should be sold as 'Bulleyana'. The standards are upright, while the falls droop downwards and are marked with creamy white stippling. This species usually produces two flowers per stem, and the leaves are grey-green underneath. Height: to 60 cm (24 in.). Bloom: June and July.

Iris chrysographes Dykes 1911
Southwest China, northern Myanmar

This plant of marshy areas produces velvety, dark black-purple or bluish-purple flowers on unbranched stems. The blooms are marked with golden signals that are broken into short lines, giving the species its name *chrysographes*, meaning 'gold markings'. Height: 45 cm (18 in.). Bloom: June and July (in Britain.).

Iris chrysographes var. *rubella*

The flowers are a velvety, rich crimson.

Iris bulleyana

Iris chrysographes

Iris chrysographes var. *rubella*

Iris chrysographes 'Black Form'

This smoothly shaped, velvety purple-black flower has very fine lines down its hafts and in the signal area.

Iris chrysographes 'Black Knight'

The black-purple flower is velvety with yellow speckling that forms lines on the falls. The style arms are large.

Iris clarkei Baker ex Hooker f. 1892

Himalayas, northern Myanmar

The flowers have pendant-like falls of deepest sky-blue with white markings covering the hafts and extending halfway down the falls. The slim standards are violet-blue. The slender, twisted leaves are grey-green beneath. This is the only species in its section that has solid stems. Sometimes the flowers can be red-purple. The plant thrives in bogs and along the margins of streams or ponds. Height: to 60 cm (24 in.). Bloom: June and July.

Iris delavayi Micheli 1895

Bhutan and southwest China

In the wild this plant can be found growing in wet or marsh meadow areas high in the mountains. Therefore, in cultivation it also requires a permanently damp soil. The branched stems carry deep violet flowers that are decorated with white lines in the centre of the falls. The standards tend to splay out. This species is the tallest one in this section. Height: 150 cm (60 in.). Bloom: May to July.

Iris dykesii Stapf 1932

Not known in the wild, this iris is probably a hybrid of *Iris chrysographes* and *I. delavayi*. Found in the garden of W. R. Dykes, it was named for him after his death by Otto Stapf of the Royal Botanic Gardens Kew. Most of the plants sold today look more like *I.*

chrysographes. The flowers are similar in colour—deep purple-violet—and the falls display the familiar broken pattern of gold. Height: 80 cm (32 in.). Bloom: June.

Iris forrestii Dykes 1910

Southwest China and northern Myanmar

This species produces scented flowers that are yellow with broken lines of brown-purple on its oval falls. The standards are upright. The foliage is glossy green with a grey-green back. Height: 40 cm (16 in.). Bloom: May and June.

Iris sanguinea Hornemann ex Donn 1811

Siberia, Korea, Japan, northern China

This species was once known as *Iris orientalis*. The flowers are blue-purple with darker veins on the yellow hafts. The standards are short and upright, the falls are broad and round. The blooms are borne on stems that are usually unbranched with leaves that are as tall as the flowers. The reddish spathes, unlike the spathes of other species, do not become papery after flowering. They droop over to show off the flowers. In the wild this species is found in damp meadows and along the edges of rivers and lakes. Height: 70 cm (28 in.). Bloom: May and June.

Iris sibirica Linnaeus 1753

Northern Italy through to Central and Eastern Europe, from northeastern Turkey into Russia

The flowers are borne on straight, slender stems with one or two branches. They range from white to blue in colour and are smaller than the flowers of *Iris sanguinea*. They have narrow, upright standards and long falls that are usually marked with blue veins over a paler background and white signal. Height: to 120 cm (48 in.). Bloom: May to July.

Iris chrysographes var. *rubella*

Iris chrysographes 'Black Knight'

Iris clarkei

Iris sibirica 'Alba', the white form of
I. sibirica

Iris typhifolia

Iris typhifolia Kitagawa 1988
Northeastern China to Manchuria
One of the most important of the recently described species, *Iris typhifolia* was known only as an herbarium
plant until it was introduced to
Britain in 1989. Professor Zhao Yu-
tang in China sent seeds to the Royal
Botanic Gardens Kew, some of which
went to Bob Wise in England. Bob became the first individual in the West
to grow the plant to flowering stage. I
have described the plant that is growing at Kew in the rock gardens. It has

large rich blue flowers that have a
rosy hue around the hafts and slender, upright, violet-blue standards. At
first its hardiness was questionable;
however, for most part it does seem
to be reliably hardy, but in some in-
stances it may not survive wet winters in cooler parts of the world. In
size the plants may vary, but all have
one thing in common: they flower a
good two weeks before all known Siberian cultivars. Height: 60–90 cm
(24–36 in.). Bloom: May to June.

Iris wilsonii C. H. Wright 1907
Western China
In the wild this species grows along
streams and at the edges of forests.
It produces scented, yellow flowers
with brown-black markings on the
falls. The standards flare out extravagantly, and the leaves grow to the
same height as the flowers but droop
over at the top. Height: 70 cm (28
in.). Bloom: May and June.

SIBERIAN IRIS HYBRIDS

Iris 'Active Duty' (H. Stahly 1999)
The flower is deep wine red with a
white signal edged by a faint blue
halo. It has round falls and narrower
standards that flare open to reveal
light wine red style arms. Height: 94
cm (37 in.). Bloom: midseason.
Parentage: 'Temper Tantrum' × unknown.

Iris 'Ann Dasch' (S. Varner 1977)
This deep blue-purple flower is
deeper in colour around the edges.
The falls are round, and the splaying
standards are crinkled on the outside. The hafts are long, yellow, and
distinctively marked with veins.
Height: 97 cm (38¾ in.). Bloom: mid
to late season. Parentage: ('Gatineau'
× 'Dreaming Spires') × seedling.
Morgan Medal Winner 1983.

Iris 'Active Duty'

Iris 'Ann Dasch'

Iris 'Caesar's Brother' (F. Cleveland Morgan 1932)
Still popular with our customers today, this iris produces rich blue-purple flowers with short yellow-and-white signals on each fall. The standards flare outwards above the broad, twisting falls. Height: 99 cm (39½ in.). Bloom: midseason. Parentage: thought to be 'Nigrescens' × 'Blue King'. Morgan Medal Winner 1953.

Iris 'Cambridge' (M. Brummit 1964)
The flowers open from soft blue buds into large ruffled blooms with round, light blue-violet petals that have veins of a deeper colour. The hafts are gold, and the signal has a cream base. The back of the bud is edged with blue. Height: 91 cm (36½ in.). Bloom: midseason. Parentage: 'White Swirl' × 'Gatineau'. Dykes Medal Winner UK 1971.

Iris 'Carmen Jeanne' (C. Helsley 1993)
The short round, velvety petals are deep blue-violet in colour and heavily ruffled. The signals are cream and gold, while the style arms are a wash of violet. Height: 71 cm (28½ in.). Bloom: early to midseason. Parentage: 'Mabel Coday' × ('Marlya' × 'Steve').

Iris 'Cleedownton' (J. Hewitt 1998)
The flowers have large, flaring, wavy violet-blue falls edged with white lines and flushed with violet. The signals are gold and white, the standards pale blue, and the style arms even paler blue. The spathes are red. The plant is a tetraploid. Height: 86 cm (34½ in.). Bloom: midseason. Parentage: 'Harpswell Happiness' × 'Dance Ballerina Dance'.

Iris 'Cool Spring' (Kellogg 1939)
The clear blue flowers are carried on long branched stems. The violet veins on the falls extend halfway

Iris 'Caesar's Brother'

Iris 'Cleedownton'

Iris 'Cambridge'

Iris 'Cool Spring'

Iris 'Carmen Jeanne'

Iris 'Coronation Anthem'

down the falls, which flare out horizontally and are paler in colour towards the bottom. Height: 84 cm (33½ in.). Bloom: midseason. Parentage: unknown. Morgan Medal Winner 1966.

Iris 'Coronation Anthem' (R. Hollingworth 1990)

The flowers are large, ruffled, and violet-blue, more violet along the edges. The standards are semi-flaring and between them sit arching pale blue and violet style arms that have small teeth along their middles. The signals are cream and brown. The

plant is a tetraploid. Height: 81 cm (32½ in.). Bloom: midseason. Parentage: 'Jewelled Crown' × ('Super Ego' × 'Anniversary'). Morgan-Wood Medal Winner 1997.

Iris 'Crème Chantilly' (C. McEwen 1981)

The very ruffled creamy white flowers have open standards and large style arms. On the falls sit yellow signals that are veined with green. The plant is diploid and has pale green foliage. Height: 91 cm (36½ in.). Bloom: midseason. Parentage: 'Anniversary' × ('Big Blue' × unknown).

Iris 'Dance Suzy' (M. Schafer & J. Sacks 1999)

This plant produces a rather flat, creamy yellow flower with falls that are deeper in colour compared with the standards. Height: 74 cm (29½ in.). Bloom: early to midseason. Parentage: 'Careless Sally' × (('Percheron' × 'Butter and Sugar') × sibling).

Iris 'Dawn Waltz' (M. Schafer & J. Sacks 1998)

This variety has round, ruffled, pink-lavender falls with golden signals and short very pale lavender standards. The style arms are white. Height: 69 cm (27½ in.). Bloom: early to midseason. Parentage: ('Reprise' × 'Mad Magenta') × ('Isabelle' × 'Silver Illusion').

Iris 'Dream on Dream' (R. Barker 1999)

The flowers are white and lightly speckled with purple. The standards, which lie flat matching the height of the white style arms, have soft blue midribs and violet at the base. The falls dip down, have long corn yellow hafts, and are ruffled long the edges. The flowers open below the level of its leaves. Height: 61 cm (24½ in.). Bloom: midseason. Parentage: unknown.

Iris 'Crème Chantilly'

Iris 'Dance Suzy'

Iris 'Dawn Waltz'

Iris 'Dream on Dream'

Iris 'Dreaming Spires' (M. Brummitt 1964)

The large, flaring, violet-blue flowers have paler, crinkled edges to the petals and almost black hafts that are veined with white. The standards are more violet than blue and splay out slightly. The style arms are a softer blue. The colour of the flower blends nicely with the grey-green foliage. Height: 91 cm (36½ in.). Bloom: midseason. Parentage: 'White Swirl' × 'Tycoon'.

Iris 'Dreaming Yellow' (C. McEwen 1969)

This important introduction is one of the first white-and-yellow sibiricas. The flowers have short white standards and fairly narrow, creamy yellow falls. Height: 79 cm (31½ in.). Bloom: mid to late season. Parentage: 'Dreaming Spires' × unknown.

Iris 'Emma Ripeka' (F. Love 1990)

This large-flowered variety has violet-blue falls that flare out horizontally. The falls curl upwards, forming a point at the end. Their colour, which is unevenly spread across the petals, becomes deep violet around the cream signal. The sky-blue standards sit straight up, and the style arms are a very pale blue. The plant is tetraploid, and the foliage is grey-green. Height: 91 cm (36½ in.). Bloom: midseason. Parentage: a self-crossing seedling. Dykes Medal Winner New Zealand 1994.

Iris 'Dreaming Yellow'

Iris 'Dreaming Spires'

Iris 'Emma Ripeka'

Iris 'Exuberant Encore' (C. McEwen 1985)

In our fields, after a wet summer, this variety produced flowers continually over a period of six weeks. The large blooms are rich violet-blue with flaring standards and soft green hafts that are pattered with brown veins. Height: 61 cm (24½ in.). Bloom: very early to very late season and reblooming. Parentage: ('My Love' × 'Violet Repeat') × 'Blue Encore'.

Iris 'Flight Of Butterflies' (J. Witt 1972)

This delicate flower has violet-blue standards and white falls that are covered with a butterfly wing pattern of violet-blue. The small blooms are carried on long, slender stems. Height: 91 cm (36½ in.). Bloom: midseason. Parentage: unknown.

Iris 'Fourfold Lavender' (C. McEwen 1982)

The flowers could be described as white and heavily stained with pale lavender. The edges of the round, horizontal falls are white, the signals gold. The style arms are white. Height: 71 cm (28½ in.). Bloom: midseason. Parentage: (('Orville Fay sib' × 'Blue Brilliant' seedling) × ('Snowy Egret' seedling × 'Dreaming Yellow')) × unknown.

Iris 'Grand Junction' (F. McCord 1968)

The large deep mid-blue flowers are veined with violet and have white spots rather than signals. The undersides of the petals are white and blue in equal proportions. The style arms are also white. Height: 71 cm (28½ in.). Bloom: midseason. Parentage: 'Tunkhannock' × 'Tycoon'. Morgan Medal Winner 1974.

Iris 'Hoar Edge' (J. Hewitt 1990)

The flaring falls are deep blue, heavily tinged with violet, edged with a broad white band, and splattered all over with white. The standards splay out and are deep violet-blue. The large style arms are pure violet in colour, and on the hafts are yellow veins. The foliage of this tetraploid variety is blue-green. Height: 75 cm (30 in.). Bloom: early to midseason. Parentage: 'Laurenbuhl' × seedling.

Iris 'Exuberant Encore'

Iris 'Fourfold Lavender'

Iris 'Flight Of Butterflies'

Iris 'Grand Junction'

Iris 'Hoar Edge'

Iris 'Indy' (R. Hollingworth 1984)
The rose-violet flower has large falls with a flush of blue radiating down the petals and dark gold hafts. It has shorter, open standards. Height: 81 cm (32½ in.). Bloom: very early season. Parentage: (('Dreaming Spires' × 'Tealwood') × unknown) × ('Dreaming Spires' × unknown).

Iris 'Jewelled Crown' (R. Hollingworth 1985)
This ruffled variety has round petals that are rich red-purple in colour with wide white patches sitting in front of golden signals. Purple veins decorate the signals. The style arms are softer in colour, and the midribs up the inside of the standards are yellow. This hybrid is a colchicine-induced tetraploid. Height: 61 cm (24½ in.). Bloom: midseason. Parentage: 'Ruffled Velvet' × 'Showdown'. Morgan-Wood Medal Winner 1993.

Iris 'Kathleen Mary' (C. Bartlett 1999)
This lightly ruffled, white variety has flaring petals and yellow signals. It is a tetraploid. Height: 75 cm (30 in.). Bloom: mid to late season. Parentage: 'Harpswell Happiness' × McEwen seedling.

Iris 'Kingfisher' (W. R. Dykes 1923)
This very early introduction has bright, deep blue flowers that open from deeper blue buds. The pale blue style arms are tinted with violet, and the hafts are marked with deep gold then white. The spathes are tinted with red. Height: 83 cm (33 in.). Bloom: early to midseason. Parentage: unknown.

Iris 'Lady Walpole' (M. Schafer & J. Sacks 1996)
The flaring, pale blue standards are washed from the base with violet, and the rose-violet falls are round and ruffled. These are bleached

Iris 'Indy'

Iris 'Kingfisher'

Iris 'Jewelled Crown'. Photo by Jennifer Hewitt.

Iris 'Kathleen Mary'

Iris 'Lavender Bounty'

Iris 'Lady Walpole'

Iris 'Langthorns Pink'

Iris 'Lavender Light'

Iris 'Mad Magenta'

around the edges and have white signals. Height: 81 cm (32½ in.). Bloom: early to midseason. Parentage: ('Lady Vanessa' × 'Springs Brook') × ('Springs Brook' × (('Atoll' × 'Ruffled Velvet') × 'Ruffled Velvet')).

***Iris* 'Langthorns Pink'** (Cannon)
Small, lilac-white flowers open from lilac buds. The falls are flushed a deeper colour and sitting on them are corn yellow signals. Height: 78 cm (31 in.). Bloom: early to midseason. Parentage: unknown.

***Iris* 'Lavender Bounty'** (C. McEwen 1981)
This very ruffled variety has soft lavender-pink standards and falls. The hafts are gold-brown, and the signals are white. Height: 91 cm (36½ in.). Bloom: very early season. Parentage: 'Augury' × 'Lavender Light'.

***Iris* 'Lavender Light'** (C. McEwen 1973)
This variety has violet-tinted buds that open into gently ruffled, soft lilac flowers with cream signals and dark gold hafts. The style arms are streaked with violet, and the flowers are carried on well-branched stems. Height: 97 cm (38¾ in.). Bloom: early season. Parentage: 'Morning Magic' × 'Fairy Dawn'.

***Iris* 'Mad Magenta'** (B. Warburton 1986)
The colour of this variety is quite distinctive. It is registered as magenta, although I would describe it as magenta-violet. The flowers have ruffled, round, flaring falls and short open standards. The small signals are gold and white. Height: 66 cm (26½ in.). Bloom: mid to late season. Parentage: 'Percheron' × 'Silver Rose'.

Iris 'Madeleine Hamilton' (J. Hewitt 2002)

The flowers of this tetraploid variety are large, ruffled, and blue-violet with open standards and pale blue style arms. Large cream signals sit on the wavy edged falls. Height: 86 cm (34½ in.). Bloom: midseason. Parentage: uncertain, possibly 'Hoar Edge' × 'Reddy Maid'.

Iris 'Mrs Rowe' (A. Perry 1916)

This charming but old variety produces small, delicate flowers with pale pink-violet falls, almost white standards, and hafts marked with gold. The blooms are borne on slender stems. Height: 100 cm (40 in.). Bloom: midseason. Parentage: unknown.

Iris 'My Love' (E. Scheffy 1948)

This variety produces fairly large deep sky-blue flowers with upright, flaring standards and semi-flaring falls that are washed and veined with violet. The hafts are gold and heavily veined with deep purple. Height: 100 cm (40 in.). Bloom: early season and reblooming. Parentage: unknown.

Iris 'Mrs Rowe'

Iris 'My Love'

Iris 'Madeleine Hamilton'

Iris 'Night Breeze'

Iris 'Oban'

Iris 'Night Breeze' (C. Wyatt 1978)
The blue-violet flowers have pointed cream signals. The petals are gently ruffled. Height: 117 cm (46 in.). Bloom: late season. Parentage: 'Placid Waters' × 'Swank'.

Iris 'Oban' (H. Foster 1989)
The large violet-blue flowers have short standards and purple-tinged falls that are finely edged with white. The signals are white and yellow, and the style arms are pale blue. This is a tetraploid variety. Height: 97 cm (38¾ in.). Bloom: midseason. Parentage: 'Silver Edge' × 'Reddy Maid'.

Iris 'Off She Goes' (M. Schafer & J. Sacks 1998)
This very ruffled variety has round, flaring soft lavender falls and short pale violet standards. The white style arms are the same length as the standards, and the falls have gold signals and green hafts. Height: 71 cm (28½ in.). Bloom: early to midseason. Parentage: ('Reprise' × 'Mad Magenta') × ('Isabelle' × 'Silver Illusion').

Iris 'Orville Fay' (C. McEwen 1969)
This second-generation tetraploid has rich blue flowers with gold signals that are covered with dark blue veins. Height: 91 cm (36½ in.). Bloom: mid to late season. Parentage: ('Violet Flare' × unknown) × ('Pirouette' × unknown). Morgan Award 1976.

Iris 'Over In Gloryland' (R. Hollingworth 1992)
As velvety as a dinner jacket, the falls are also round and dark royal purple. The signals are cream coloured. This is a tetraploid variety. Height: 86 cm (34½ in.). Bloom: midseason. Parentage: 'Jewelled Crown' sibling × (('Dreaming Spires' × unknown) × ('Cambridge' × unknown)). Morgan-Wood Medal Winner 2000.

Iris 'Perry's Blue' (A. Perry 1912)
This famous iris has sapphire-blue flowers with deeper blue veins. The falls are edged with white, the hafts are dark gold, and the signals cream. The standards twist slightly and are richer in colour. The large style arms are a soft blue. Height: 101 cm (40½ in.). Bloom: early to midseason. Parentage: unknown.

Iris 'Off She Goes'

Iris 'Over In Gloryland'

Iris 'Orville Fay'

Iris 'Perry's Blue'

Iris **'Phosphorflamme'** (S. Steffen 1935)
This small flower with evenly sized petals has deep blue falls with cream-and-yellow signals. It is an unregistered seedling, which, according to the Siberian Iris Checklist 2003, may have first been exhibited in 1935 by Mr Steffen of Germany. Height: 102 cm (41 in.). Bloom: mid to late season. Parentage: unknown.

Iris **'Pink Haze'** (W. McGarvey 1969)
The falls are lavender-pink, flaring, and arching, with wavy edges. The short standards are paler than the falls and even paler around the borders. The style arms are almost white, and the signals ochre. This iris was not introduced until 1980. Height: 97 cm (38¾ in.). Bloom: midseason. Parentage: ('Royal Ensign' × 'Royal Ensign') × ('White Swirl' × 'Royal Ensign' seedling). Morgan-Wood Medal Winner 1984 and 1988.

Iris 'Phosphorflamme'

Iris 'Pink Haze'

Iris 'Plisseé'

Iris 'Prussian Blue'

Iris 'Purple Mere'

Iris 'Reddy Maid'

Iris 'Reprise'

Iris **'Plisseé'** (T. Tamberg 1995)
This tetraploid variety has bright deep blue flowers with round, very ruffled, flaring falls that are finely edged with a stitching of white. The petals are small, and the blue style arms are similar in size to the standards. The foliage is blue-green. Height: 90 cm (36 in.). Bloom: mid-season. Parentage: ('Lake Niklas' × ('Cambridge' × seedling)) × 'Silberkante'.

Iris **'Prussian Blue'** (T. Tamberg 1993)
The flowers of this aptly named tetraploid hybrid are deep blue with large, round, flaring falls and semi-flaring standards. On the falls sit signals of gold and white. The style arms also flare out and are violet-blue in colour. Height: 85 cm (34 in.). Bloom: mid-season. Parentage: 'Germantet One' × 'Blue Burgee'.

Iris **'Purple Mere'** (P. Hutchinson 1959)
The flowers are deep violet-blue with clear veins of cream forming the signals. The petals are lightly ruffled around the edges, and the standards open out to reveal soft blue style arms. Height: 89 cm (35½ in.). Bloom: mid to late season. Parentage: 'Caezar' × 'Gatineau'.

Iris **'Reddy Maid'** (C. McEwen 1978)
The rich wine red flowers of this tetraploid variety have cream signals and soft green hafts. Height: 76 cm (30½ in.). Bloom: early to midseason. Parentage: ('Ewen' × ('Polly Dodge' × ('White Swirl' × 'Eric the Red'))).

Iris **'Reprise'** (B. Warburton 1986)
This truly violet flower has short semi-flaring standards. The falls lack signals and instead have dark blue patches. The style arms are soft blue and rosy violet. The plant is said to be reblooming. Heiht: 81 cm (32½ in.). Bloom: mid to late season. Parentage: 'Silver Rose' × 'George Henry'.

(30 in.). Bloom: early to midseason. Parentage: 'Reprise' × 'Springs Brook'.

Iris 'Snow Queen' (Barr 1900)
This form of *Iris sanguinea* was collected by Peter Barr in Japan and listed in 1900. The small pure white flowers have greenish-yellow markings on the hafts. These markings are almost hidden by the white style arms. The foliage is soft green. It is doubtful whether the plants sold as *I.* 'Snow Queen' are correctly labelled. As it is quite tall, the form currently available could be a white form or cultivar of *I. sibirica*. Height: 84 cm (33 in.). Bloom: mid to late season.

Iris 'Snowcrest' (M. Grace 1932)
The large white flowers have yellow hafts. This hybrid resembles a bigger flowering form of *Iris* 'Snow Queen'. Height: 70 cm (28 in.). Bloom: early to midseason. Parentage: unknown.

Iris 'Soft Blue' (C. McEwen 1979)
The soft sky-blue flowers have large, flaring, and arching, ruffled falls that pale towards the edges. Gold markings surround the hafts, and the standards splay out into a V shape. The plant is said to be reblooming. Height: 76 cm (30½ in.). Bloom: very early season. Parentage: 'On and On' sibling × 'My Love'.

Iris 'Sparkling Rose' (B. Hager 1967)
The standards of this slender-petalled, rose-mauve flower flare. The hafts are gold-brown, and the cream signals are flushed with blue. Height: 97 cm (38¾ in.). Bloom: midseason. Parentage: 'Towanda Redflare' × 'Eric the Red'.

Iris 'Steve' (S. Varner 1974)
The flowers have rich blue-purple falls and softer coloured standards that lie flat over the falls. Inside these lie blue-tinted, violet style arms. Height: 86 cm (34½ in.). Bloom: mid

Iris 'Snow Queen'

Iris 'Sparkling Rose'

Iris 'Snowcrest'

Iris 'Soft Blue'

Iris 'Steve'

Iris 'Summer Sky'

Iris 'Steve Varner'

Iris 'Teal Velvet'

to late season. Parentage: 'Tealwood' × 'Blue Moon'.

***Iris* 'Steve Varner'** (H. Briscoe 1976) This variety produces large, ruffled soft blue flowers with softer coloured standards that open outwards. The falls, which are flushed and veined with violet, are paler around the edges, while the pale blue-violet style arms have a midrib of soft blue. Height: 74 cm (29½ in.). Bloom: midseason. Parentage: 'White Swirl' × 'Barbara's Choice'. Morgan Medal Winner 1982 and 1988.

***Iris* 'Summer Sky'** (F. Cleveland Morgan 1935) The delicate flowers have softest sky-blue petals. The standards are deeper in colour than the falls, and the hafts are yellow. The flowers are borne on slender, upright stems. Height: 71 cm (28½ in.). Bloom: midseason. Parentage: unknown.

***Iris* 'Teal Velvet'** (C. McEwen 1981) The velvety flowers of this tetraploid are very dark red-purple with style arms of a similar colour. Yellow signals extend from yellow-green hafts. Height: 85 cm (34 in.). Bloom: very early to midseason. Parentage: 'Ruffled Velvet' × 'Tealwood'.

Iris 'Thelma Perry' (A. Perry 1923)
Amos Perry introduced many Siberian irises, including this one with soft blue flowers. The long falls are decorated with cream-and-gold signals which extend halfway down the petals. The standards are violet at the base, and the style arms are soft blue flushed with violet. Height: 91 cm (36½ in.). Bloom: midseason. Parentage: unknown.

Iris 'Troika' (N. Scopes 1993)
The ruffled flowers have velvety, rich purple falls with finely lined edges that curl upwards. Height: 97 cm (38¾ in.). Bloom: mid to late season. Parentage: 'Floating Island' × 'Silver Edge'.

Iris 'Tropic Night' (F. Cleveland Morgan 1937)
The violet-mauve flowers have slender, upright standards and round falls with a large white signal in front of the brown hafts. Height: 91 cm (36½ in.). Bloom: midseason. Parentage: 'Caezer' × unknown. Morgan Medal Winner 1954.

Iris 'Tycoon' (F. Cleveland Morgan 1938)
This rich violet-blue flower has hafts that are heavily veined with black-purple, just allowing the soft yellow signals to come through. Height: 90 cm (36 in.). Bloom: midseason. Parentage: unknown. Morgan Medal Winner 1951.

Iris 'Violet Mere' (P. Hutchinson 1963)
The violet flower has round falls that are heavily veined with deeper purple and finely edged with blue. On the falls sit distinctive signals that go from gold by the hafts to cream at the base. The standards sit open, showing off the light blue style arms. Height: 107 cm (43 in.). Bloom: late season. Parentage: 'Purple Mere' × 'Blue Mere'.

Iris 'Thelma Perry'

Iris 'Tycoon'. Photo by Jennifer Hewitt.

Iris 'Troika'

Iris 'Tropic Night'

Iris 'Violet Mere'

Iris 'Violet Repeat'

Iris 'Violet Repeat' (M. Brummitt 1967)
The falls of this bright reddish-violet flower are heavily veined with violet. Height: 91 cm (36½ in.). Bloom: midseason and reblooming. Parentage: 'White Swirl' × 'Eric the Red'.

Iris 'Weisse Etagen' (T. Tamberg 1984)
The creamy white flowers have upright standards and oval, flaring falls with yellow hafts. Height: 91 cm (36½ in.). Bloom: early to midseason. Parentage: a combination of McEwen tetraploid seedlings.

Iris 'Welfenprinz' (M. Ahlburg 1990)
The bright yellow falls pale to cream after the first day. Nearer the hafts the falls are darker in colour, and they flare outwards. The standards and style arms are cream. Height: 70 cm (28 in.). Bloom: midseason. Parentage: (seedling × 'Butter and Sugar') × (('Dreaming Yellow' × 'Cambridge') × seedling).

Iris 'White Amber' (M. Schafer & J. Sacks 2001)
This flower is very different in colour. The flaring, round falls are pink-buff with yellow signals lined with soft brown veins. The buff-white standards are very short and the same

Iris 'Weisse Etagen'

Iris 'Welfenprinz'

Iris 'White Amber'

length as the lemon-coloured style arms. Height: 65 cm (26 in.). Bloom: early season. Parentage: (('Reprise' × 'Mad Magenta') × ('Isabelle' × 'Silver Illusion')) × (('Isabelle' × 'Silver Illusion') × 'Snow Prince').

Iris **'White Swirl'** (F. Cassebeer 1957) Initially registered as *Iris* 'Frank Stubbs' in 1954, this is the first Siberian iris with falls that flared outwards and one of the most important to be introduced. The gently ruffled flowers are pure white with yellow hafts but no signals on the falls. Height: 102 cm (41 in.). Bloom: late season. Parentage: unknown. Morgan Medal Winner 1962.

Iris 'White Swirl'

CHAPTER 10

Laevigata Irises
Series *Laevigatae*

A VERY USEFUL GROUP of irises, in the wild all the laevigatas grow in wet conditions, including shallow, standing water. The group includes *Iris ensata*, the Japanese iris whose glamorous hybrids can be found in a separate chapter; the thug *I. pseudacorus*, also known as the yellow flag; and *I. versicolor* and *I. virginica*, the American blue flag irises. Members of the series *Laevigatae*, as defined by Dykes, cross-pollinate with each other. As a group they produce broad leaves, which when held up to the light reveal small, blackish spots along the veins—telltale signs that these plants will grow in moist soils.

LAEVIGATA IRIS SPECIES & THEIR COLLECTED FORMS

Iris ensata Thunberg 1794
Japan, northern China, Korea, eastern Russia
For many years this plant has been known as *Iris kaempferi*. It is the original 'Japanese iris'. The flowers range from red-purple to deep purple with long golden yellow signals on the oval falls and short, erect standards. This rhizomatous plant produces upright, dark green leaves that, unlike those of *I. laevigata*, have very promi-

nent midribs. The blooms are carried on straight, but sometimes poorly branched, stems. In the wild the plant grows in acid soils in damp, grassy areas along rivers and lakes rather than in water. Interestingly, the seed capsules do not split open, as most iris seedpods do, but tend to rot away. Height: 90 cm (36 in.). Bloom: June and July.

Iris ensata 'Variegata'
A plant with white-striped leaves that remains handsome until late in the year. The flowers are rich purple. Height: 90 cm (36 in.). Bloom: June and July.

Iris ensata

Iris ensata 'Variegata'

Iris laevigata F. Fischer 1837

Central Russia, China, Korea, Japan

In the wild this iris can be found growing around the edges of lakes and rivers. It was introduced into Europe from Japan. The blue-purple flowers have silky, triangular petals and a yellow signal on the falls. The standards are short and upright, and the flowers sit just above the foliage on erect stems with upright branches. The slender, smooth, grey-green leaves grow into a thick clump. This very hardy plant can be grown in shallow water. When grown in a pond the plant should be placed in basket with the top no more than 15 cm (6 in.) below water level. It will, however, also thrive in a border provided the soil is rich, fertile, on the acid side, and remains moist during the growing season. Flowers appear as those of the Tall Bearded irises fade. Other noteworthy hybrids include 'Colchesterensis' and 'Weymouth Midnight'. Height: 80 cm (32 in.). Bloom: late June and into July.

Iris laevigata 'Snowdrift'

This pure white flower has delicate, drooping falls and flaring white standards that are taller than its short standards. The yellowish signals turn into long lashes. It is probably a white form of *Iris ensata*, but as information about this is limited I shall list it under the name by which I purchased it. Height: 74 cm (29½ in.). Bloom: mid to late season.

Iris pseudacorus Linnaeus 1837

Europe, North Africa into southwest Asia, China

This well-known plant, also known as the yellow flag, grows throughout Europe on land that stays wet for much of the year. It produces thick rhizomes and mid-green leaves that form dense clumps. It has bright yellow flowers carried on tall, well-

Iris laevigata 'Colchesterensis'

Iris laevigata 'Snowdrift'

Iris laevigata 'Weymouth Midnight'

Iris pseudacorus

Iris pseudacorus 'Alba'

Iris pseudacorus 'Alba'

Iris pseudacorus 'Flore Pleno'

branched stems. The falls usually, but not always, have dark brown markings, and the standards are spoon shaped. In Britain the plant will grow anywhere, even in a well-drained sandy soil, and it is a useful plant for growing in bogs or large pools. In Australia it has been outlawed as a thug, because it grows so vigorously, suffocating the surrounding natural wild plants. It is nonetheless an excellent pod parent and has been crossed with other members of the series *Laevigatae* with interesting results. Height: 120 cm (48 in.), if not more. Bloom: May to July.

Iris pseudacorus 'Alba'

Not really white at all, the small flowers are very pale cream and have a dark cream flush in the centre of the falls. The flush is ringed by a charcoal-grey halo. The foliage is soft green. Height: 96 cm (38½ in.). Bloom: May to July.

Iris pseudacorus var. *bastardii*

(Spach) Dykes
Llanfairfechan in North Wales
This variety has bright yellow flowers that fade to cream with age. Height: 96 cm (38½ in.). Bloom: May to July.

Iris pseudacorus 'Flore Pleno'

Not the most elegant of flowers, it is nonetheless interesting. The bright yellow flowers are of the 'hose-in-hose' type, which means a second set of petals sprouts out of the first. Height: 96 cm (38½ in.). Bloom: May to July.

Iris pseudacorus var. *bastardii*

Iris pseudacorus 'Gubijin' (H. Shimizu 1999)

Grown from seed supplied by the British Iris Society seed exchange, this iris is included here because it is responsible for a new group of irises, the beautiful 'Eye Lash' irises that have recently been raised by Hiroshi Shimizu of Japan. Shimizu's aim, when choosing this plant, was to find a clone of *Iris pseudacorus* that would readily cross with *I. ensata*. The plant is named after a Chinese princess who tragically died in B.C. 202. The Chinese tale tells about how a yellow flower bloomed on her grave. Height: 110 cm (44 in.). Bloom: May to July.

Iris pseudacorus 'Variegata'

Yellow striped in the spring, the leaves of this handsome plant become uniformly green over summer. Height: 96 cm (38½ in.). Bloom: May to July.

Iris versicolor Linnaeus 1753

Eastern North America, eastern Canada southwards to Texas

An American equivalent to the European *Iris pseudacorus*, *I. versicolor* is also known as the blue flag. This species grows in wet areas of northeastern America, but, like the European yellow water iris, it will thrive in any type of soil, whether wet or dry. Up to nine elegant flowers, ranging in colour from lavender to soft blue-purple, are produced on long, arching, slender, well-branched stems. The flowers have slim petals, and the standards are shorter than the falls. The falls are veined with soft yellow. The broad, grey-green foliage is stained at the base with purple and grows into broad, gracefully arching clumps. Medicinally, it is still used as a drug for purging the liver and intestines. Height: 80 cm (32 in.). Bloom: July.

Iris pseudacorus 'Gubijin'

Iris versicolor. Photo by Sydney Linnegar.

Iris pseudacorus 'Variegata'

Iris virginica var. shrevei

Iris virginica Linnaeus 1753

Eastern coastal United States south to Virginia, Florida, Georgia, North and South Carolina, and southeastern Louisiana

The second of the American 'blue flag' irises is not as hardy as the first, and it requires a more acidic soil that is wetter. The two species are often confused, but *Iris virginica* can be recognized by the hairs that sit on the yellow signals on the falls and by the laced standards that are the same size as the falls. The flowers are large with long, slender petals and range from white to lavender and violet-blue with purple-blue veins on the falls. These are borne on long, slender, arching, unbranched stems. Dark green leaves arch over at the top. Height: 100 cm (40 in.). Bloom: May to July.

Iris virginica var. shrevei E. S. Anderson 1936

Great Lakes area of Minnesota, Wisconsin, and Michigan (United States) up into Ontario (Canada)

The flowers are broader and more rounded than *Iris virginica*. The variety will grow in soil that is not so acid and is more suitable for the average garden. Height: 80 cm (32 in.). Bloom: May to July.

CHAPTER 11

Japanese Irises
Series *Laevigatae*

Japanese irises, still sometimes referred to as Kaempferi irises, are usually thought of as water dwellers, which they are not. The wild species of Japanese irises can be found growing in damp meadows where the soil is slightly acid. In fact, these extremely decorative, late-flowering irises will grow in a wide range of locations. They can cope with full sun or partial shade and also a dry soil, as long as they are watered well during the growing season.

Today's hybrids hardly resemble their wild ancestor *Iris laevigata*. Over the centuries they have been hybridized so much that it can be difficult to describe a flower. The colour is limited to shades of white, violet, purple, blue, and mauve, which is often speckled, stippled, or splashed across the surface in a very complicated manner. Most modern hybrids have round flowers with overlapping, ruffled petals and remind me of crumpled handkerchiefs. The texture varies from silky to thick and quilted, and the falls are almost always decorated with a yellow flash that looks as though it was applied by a Japanese paintbrush. The flowers have short standards and style arms that resemble the stems of the Chinese vegetable pok (bok) choy.

Japanese irises are versatile garden plants and produce thick clumps of heavily ribbed leaves that, when planted in drifts, look wonderful around the edge of a pond. The flowers are also excellent for cutting.

History

Iris ensata has been cultivated in Japan for over 500 years. The simply shaped flowers were considered a symbol of good omen and used extensively for decoration and in festivals and ceremonies.

The early cultivars of Japanese irises have a long and elaborate history. New cultivars were frequently jealously guarded, and their availability was often limited to the areas in which they originated. Tokyo became an important region for irises. Here they were often planted in large drifts, frequently in paddy fields where they created a magnificent spectacle during the flowering season. The plants were raised from seed collected from the wild, sown directly into the ground, and as they came into flower, the fields were flooded so that the full beauty of the flowers was reflected in the water. This practice explains why a mistaken belief exists that Japanese irises should be grown in water. For many years only noblemen were allowed to visit the iris gardens and fields. Then, during the late 1860s, after the restoration of the Japanese emperor, the public was also allowed to enjoy the splendour of the paddy fields for a small fee. By the 1930s these irises became known as Edo irises, after the old name for Tokyo.

About the same time another strain of Japanese irises was being developed. These were shorter in size and ideal for growing in pots. They were known as Ise irises, after the Japanese district in which they were raised. The single flowers were softly coloured with pendant-like falls and flaring standards.

The third group of Japanese irises to gain fame was the Higo irises. These had more elaborate flowers than the earlier cultivars. The style arms were broader and more erect, and the falls had large crests. These irises were largely grown for indoor decoration, and the growing requirements were quite exact. They were initially grown outside, and as the buds began to open, the pots were taken into the house, placed on a black wooden plate, and set against a red cloth in front of a gold screen. Because of this custom, the number of the flower colours was limited to only those that would harmonize with red, black, and gold. Higo irises were jealously guarded. Prior to 1914 a ban existed, preventing them from being sold outside of the Japanese province in which they had been developed. When this ban was lifted, they were exported to Europe and then America. Since then, and as a result of crossing Edo, Ise, and Higo irises, hundreds of hybrids have been introduced.

Sadly, even today there is still a very limited number available in Europe. In North America they are more popular, due mainly to the work of W. A. Payne of Indiana and Walter and Louise Marx of Oregon. Their work began during the 1930s and continued for over 40 years. During the latter years of the twentieth century, Currier McEwen in the United States and Suichi Hirao in Japan began to introduce tetraploid varieties.

Cultivation

Japanese irises will grow in climates from just about subtropical to cool temperate areas like northern Europe. They are found in soils ranging from acid to neutral, and because they are heavy feeders, they prefer soils rich in humus. If the leaves turn yellow, the soil is probably not acid enough. Japanese irises like the soil to be moist; therefore, in hotter areas they perform better in dappled shade. For a good succession of flowers, moisture is particularly important just before and during the flowering period.

Japanese irises need to be divided every three years. Plant them in a good-sized clump, then cover the rhizomes completely and water well. Do not feed them for the first season.

Unlike most irises, Japanese irises can be grown in a pot. The soil should be rich, and the pot as large as possible. Just make sure that the plants are kept moist. It is a good idea to place the pot in standing water. Japanese irises in Britain do not suffer from any notable diseases; however, in North America they may suffer from thrips or iris borer.

Japanese irises are divided into three groups depending on the number of petals per flower. Terms used for these groups in the descriptions are as follows:

3F: Single flowers
6F: Double flowers
9–12F: Very double and variable in the number

Payne Award and Medal

The top award for Japanese irises given by the American Iris Society, this medal is named after U.S. hybridizer W. Arlie Payne (1881–1971), who introduced many exceptional cultivars. From 1966 to 1992 the highest award a Japanese iris could receive was the Payne Award, but in 1993 the award was elevated to medal status.

Clumps of Japanese irises in the garden

Iris 'Ack-countable'

Iris 'Ack-scent Pink'

JAPANESE IRIS HYBRIDS

Iris 'Ack-countable' (W. Ackerman 1988) 6F. The white petals are peppered with irregular streaks of violet-mauve and have yellow signals down the midribs. Violet-mauve is brushed around the style arms, and the edges of the petals are laced. Height: 107 cm (43 in.). Bloom: midseason. Parentage: involves two seedlings.

Iris 'Ack-scent Pink' (W. Ackerman 1988) 6F. The ruffled white flower is heavily tinged with lavender-pink. The signals are greenish towards the centre, and the white style arms are washed around the edges with lavender-pink. Height: 86 cm (34½ in.). Bloom: midseason. Parentage: involves two seedlings.

Iris 'Anytus' (S. Innerst 1981) 6F. The only other colour of this white-flowered variety comes from the large golden yellow signals and seeps down the veins on the petals. Height: 97 cm (38¾ in.). Bloom: midseason. Parentage: unknown × 'Reign of Glory'.

Iris 'Ashton Velvet' (W. Ackerman 1997) 3F. This short variety produces many flowers. The standards are purple, the falls white with purple veins. The purple is deeper around the very golden signal. Inside the standards is a cluster of oddly sized, upright style arms that are also purple. Height: 71 cm (28½ in.). Bloom: midseason. Parentage: (irradiated seed × self) × 'Taffeta and Velvet'.

Iris 'Ashton Velvet'

Iris 'Anytus'

Iris 'Asian Warrior' (T. Aitken 1993)
3F. This flower has thick, very dark rose-purple petals. On the falls, lighter coloured lashes radiate down from the yellow signal. These are surrounded by white. The large white style arms are edged with rose purple. Height: 91 cm (36½ in.). Bloom: mid to late season. Parentage: 'Stranger in Paradise' × 'King's Court'.

Iris 'Bellender Blue' (B. Bauer & J. Coble 1993)
3F. The velvety, rich purple-blue flowers have a silky sheen and a yellow signal that is almost covered by its style arms. Height: 127 cm (51 in.). Bloom: early season. Parentage: 'Prairie Chief' × unknown. Payne Medal Winner 2000.

Iris 'Caprician Butterfly' (W. Marx by D. Rogers 1984)
6F. The flowers are white with purple veins etched into the petals. These veins taper off before they get to the edge of the petals. The flares are long and yellow, and the style arms are deep purple. Height: 91 cm (36½ in.). Bloom: midseason. Parentage: unknown. Payne Medal Winner 1990 and 1994.

Iris 'Caprician Chimes' (W. Marx by D. Rogers 1984)
6F. Described as pansy purple, the ruffled petals have large triangular signals and large white style arms. Height: 91–122 cm (36–49 in.). Bloom: mid to late season. Parentage: unknown.

Iris 'Continuing Pleasure' (C. McEwen 1982)
6F. A beautiful plant, this variety has ruffled, soft blue flowers with white style arms. The blue is gently washed over the petals, and the short signals are yellow. Height: 97 cm (38¾ in.). Bloom: mid to very late season and

Iris 'Asian Warrior'

Iris 'Caprician Chimes'

Iris 'Bellender Blue'

Iris 'Crystal Halo'

Iris 'Caprician Butterfly'

Iris 'Continuing Pleasure'

Iris 'Dame Fortune'

reblooming. Parentage: (seedling ×
('World's Delight' × 'Pink Frost')) ×
(('Star at Midnight' × 'Garden
Caprice') × unknown).

Iris 'Crystal Halo' (W. Marx 1958)
6F. This variety has distinctive deep
red-purple flowers. The petals are
painted with broad, bright yellow signals, and the edges of both the petals
and the purple style arms are
bleached to white. Height: 122 cm
(49 in.). Bloom: mid to late season.
Parentage: unknown.

Iris 'Dame Fortune' (W. Payne 1958)
6F. This variety has violet flowers.
The colour on the petals is unevenly
washed across the surface, and the
petals are rimmed with a fine white
line. The triangular golden signals
are surrounded by a violet halo, and
the style arms are also violet. Height:
107 cm (43 in.). Bloom: midseason.
Parentage: unknown.

Iris 'Diomedes' (S. Innerst 1991)
6F. This variety produces a smoothly
coloured, blue-violet flower with
golden signals. In front of the signals
is a light sanding of pale blue, and in
the centre of the flower sits a cluster
of light blue style arms that are edged
with violet. Height: 102 cm (41 in.).
Bloom: mid to late season. Parentage:
unknown.

Iris 'Double First' (C. McEwen 1986)
6F. This white-flowered variety has
green signals that leach their colour
into veins that cross the petals. It has
short style arms. Height: 91 cm (36½
in.). Bloom: early to late season.
Parentage: involves Hirao seed
among others.

Iris 'Ebb and Flow' (S. Hirao by B.
  Hager 1988)
6F. This tall variety has lavender
flowers that are tinged with blue. The
yellow signal is lighter at the edges,
and the white style arms have soft violet crests. Height: 102 cm (41 in.).
Bloom: mid to late season. Parentage:
unknown.

Iris 'Electric Rays' (T. Aitken 1990)
6F. The rich violet-blue, ruffled flowers have electric-blue veining and a
wide band of bright blue around the
edges. The edges of the petals are
ruffled, and the tall style arms are
white tipped with blue. Height: 102
cm (41 in.). Bloom: midseason.
Parentage: 'Knight in Armor' × 'Reign
of Glory'. Payne Medal Award 1997.

Iris 'Diomedes'

Iris 'Ebb and Flow'

Iris 'Double First'

Iris 'Electric Rays'

our stains the deep veins. The violet style arms are deeper around the edges. Height: 86 cm (34½ in.). Bloom: midseason. Parentage: ("Marihiri" × 'Valiant Prince') × 'Frostbound'.

Iris 'Japanese Sandman' (G. Bush 1979)
6F. This vigorous, free-flowering variety has double white flowers that are heavily veined with violet. The green-yellow signals change to yellow, and then white. The violet style arms are tipped with white. Height: 91 cm (36½ in.). Bloom: mid to late season. Parentage: unknown.

Iris 'Koshui-no-Asa' (H. Shimizu by Carol Warner 1998)
9–12F. This basically white flower is heavily washed with sky-blue and has golden signals. The petals are so ruffled that they seem to be jumbled up. They also vary in number. Height: 81 cm (32½ in.). Bloom: midseason.

Iris 'Magic Ruby' (Payne 1962)
6F. The ruffled flowers are solid plum purple with bright yellow flashes, and the short style arms are washed with purple. Height: 122 cm (49 in.). Bloom: early to midseason. Parentage: ('Sishono' × 'Mahogany') × ('Otomere' × 'Iso-no-nami').

Iris 'Mist Falls' (Marx Gardens 1967)
6F. Basically white, the petals are evenly sanded with lavender-blue. The speckling stops just short of the edge, leaving a white rim. The style arms are self coloured. Height: 122 cm (49 in.). Bloom: midseason. Parentage: 'Halls of Marble' × seedling.

Iris 'Oba' (H. Shimizu by Carol Warner 1999)
6F. This very pink variety has white edges and white style arms with pink edges. The yellow signals are broad

Iris 'Japanese Sandman'

Iris 'Mist Falls'

Iris 'Koshui-no-Asa'

Iris 'Oba'

Iris 'Magic Ruby'

Iris 'Oriental Elegance'

and edged with white. The petals are ruffled unevenly. Height: 86 cm (34½ in.). Bloom: mid to late season. Parentage: 'Yuki Arashi' × "Sakura-no-Sei".

***Iris* 'Oriental Elegance'** (Payne 1965)
6F. This ruffled, lilac flower has standards that sit neatly above the falls. All the petals are veined with deeper lilac. As they open, the flowers are blue, and with time they pale around the edges. The style arms are violet, and the long yellow flares are rimmed with a dark rose-plum halo. Height: 124 cm (50 in.). Bloom: mid-

season. Parentage: 'Dame Fortune' × 'Debonair Prince'.

***Iris* 'Oriental Eyes'** (A. Vogt 1984)
6F. The petals of this ruffled, soft violet flower are deeper in colour below the broad, golden flares. The flares are surrounded by purple halos, and the violet style arms are paler at the edges. Height: 102 cm (41 in.). Bloom: midseason. Parentage: 'Oriental tracery' × 'Tomino'. Payne Medal Winner 1988 and 1993.

***Iris* 'Pink Frost'** (Marx 1955)
6F. The large ruffled flowers are soft pink with long yellow signals that are broadly edged with white. The style arms also are white. Height: average. Bloom: midseason.

***Iris* 'Pooh Bah'** (B. Hager 1999)
6F. The very large ruffled flower has mauve petals with distinctive white veins. The style arms are white with mauve tips, and the short signals yellow. Height: 97–102 cm (38–41 in.). Bloom: midseason. Parentage: 'Mai Ogen' × 'Hozan'.

***Iris* 'Prairie Glory'** (A. Hazzard 1972)
3F. This very gently ruffled variety has round, white falls that are veined heavily with red-violet. The yellow signals are edged with a wash of red-violet. Above the signals sit upright, deep red-purple standards that are edged with white. In between the standards and falls lie large style arms that are red-purple tipped with white. Height: 76 cm (30½ in.). Bloom: early season. Parentage: 'La Favorite' × unknown.

Iris 'Oriental Eyes'

Iris 'Pooh Bah'

Iris 'Pink Frost'

Iris 'Prairie Glory'

***Iris* 'Prairie Twilight'** (A. Hazzard 1977)
3F. The falls of this gently ruffled
flower are densely peppered with
blue-lavender and edged with a thin
white rim. The upright standards are
more violet, and the large, deep violet
style arms fade to white in the centre.
Height: 91 cm (36½ in.). Bloom:
early season. Parentage: 'Gekka-No-
Nami' × unknown.

***Iris* 'Purple Parasol'** (C. McEwen 1977)
6F. This very glossy, ruffled purple
flower has broad, golden yellow signals that end in pointed rays. Height:
122 cm (49 in.). Bloom: midseason.
Parentage: seedling × 'Great Blue
Butterfly'. Payne Medal Winner 1980.

***Iris* 'Raspberry Candy'** (B. Bauer & J.
  Coble 1999)
6F. The white petals are veined and
washed with red-violet. Around the
broad yellow signals is a red-violet
halo with more colour washed into
the surrounding petals. The upright
style arms are deep red-violet.
Height: 86 cm (34½ in.). Bloom:
early to midseason. Parentage:
'Geisha Gown' × 'Iapetus'.

***Iris* 'Raspberry Gem'** (A. Miller 1988)
6F. This variety has round, rosy
mauve flowers and long sword-like
flares that are surrounded by electric-
blue. The petals are edged with a
wire-like rim of white, and they have
flat, violet style arms. Height: 102 cm
(41 in.). Bloom: mid to late season.
Parentage: 'Kimiko' × 'Storm and Sea'.

***Iris* 'Raspberry Glow'** (T. Aitken 1992)
6F. The thick petals are bright raspberry purple above, much paler
below, with rivers of soft blue and
long, slender yellow signals. The
style arms are yellow-white and
edged with deep raspberry purple.
Height: 117 cm (46 in.). Bloom: mid
to late season. Parentage: 'Hue and
Cry' × 'Electric Rays' sibling.

Iris 'Prairie Twilight'

Iris 'Purple Parasol'

Iris 'Raspberry Gem'

Iris 'Raspberry Glow'

Iris 'Raspberry Candy'

Iris 'Rolling Seas' (T. Aitken 1994)
6F. The flowers are bright blue, although they might look violet in the photograph. The veins are softer coloured, the style arms pink-violet, and the long, pointed signals are golden yellow. Height: 122 cm (48 in.). Bloom: mid to late season. Parentage: unknown.

Iris 'Rose Frappe' (A. Miller 1988)
3F. The large white falls are lightly veined all over with red-violet, and the flaring red-violet standards are bleached around the edges. The flaring violet style arms are also edged with white. The long signals are yellow. Height: 107 cm (43 in.). Bloom: midseason. Parentage: 'Kimiko' × 'Storm at Sea'.

Iris 'Rose Prelude' (W. Marx 1959)
6F. The deep pink-lavender colour of the flowers is uneven. The petals are crumpled, and the short yellow flares are surrounded by white halos which extend into long white veins. The style arms are also white with soft lavender crests. Height: 91 cm (36½ in.). Bloom: early season. Parentage: unknown.

Iris 'Rolling Seas'

Iris 'Rose Frappe'

Iris 'Rose Prelude'

Iris 'Rose Queen' (ca. 1915)
3F. Introduced under the name of *Iris laevigata* 'Rose Queen', this flower has smooth, soft pink petals. The colour is more concentrated nearer the hafts, and the petals are veined with deeper pink. The long signals are yellow, and the pink style arms are almost as long as the standards. Height: 97 cm (38¾ in.). Bloom: midseason.

Iris 'Rosewater' (B. Bauer & J. Coble 1995)
6F. The deep rose-violet flower has long signals surrounded by blue-violet halos. The style crests are dark violet, the style arms a lighter colour. The thick petals have a bumpy texture similar to calico. Height: 96 cm (38½ in.). Bloom: late season. Parentage: 'Gayety' × 'Jocasta'.

Iris 'Shining Prince' (S. Hirao 1991)
6F. The dark violet flower has sharp, bright yellow signals and long white veins radiating down the petals. The style arms are white and edged with dark violet. Height: 94 cm (37 in.). Bloom: midseason. Parentage: unknown.

Iris 'Sing the Blues' (L. Reid 1997)
6F. The ruffled, soft blue flowers pale dramatically to white at the edges. The greenish-yellow signals form long rays and are edged by soft yellow halos. The style arms are yellow-white with blue washed crests. Height: 91–107 cm (36–43 in.). Bloom: mid to late season. Parentage: 'Warai-Hotei' × ((striped seedling × 'Royal Crown') × 'Midnight Whisper').

Iris 'Southern Son' (C. McEwen 1989)
6F. The bright violet-blue flower has very long yellow flares that extend into a paler wash down the falls. The style arms are violet-pink, the crest

Iris 'Rose Queen'

Iris 'Sing the Blues'

Iris 'Rosewater'

Iris 'Southern Son'

Iris 'Shining Prince'

Iris 'Time and Tide'

Iris 'Tropical Storm'

violet-blue. Height: 91 cm (36½ in.). Bloom: mid to late season. Parentage: includes 'Garden Caprice', 'Frostbound', and 'Continuing Pleasure'.

Iris 'Time and Tide' (F. Maddocks 1968) 3F. The rich violet flowers have short green-yellow signals, which are almost hidden by the large white halo that runs into white veins on the falls. The standards are white, and style arms are edged with rich violet. Height: 102 cm (41 in.). Bloom: mid to late season. Parentage: involves seedlings.

Iris 'Tropical Storm' (B. Bauer & J. Coble 1996) 6F. The ruffled petals are thickly sanded with rose violet, the sanding almost disappearing entirely towards the edges, leaving them almost white. The very long sword-like flares are bright yellow. Height: 107 cm (43 in.). Bloom: midseason. Parentage: ('Lace Ruff' × 'Peloponnesus') × 'Hagoromo'.

Iris 'Winged Sprite' (Payne 1965) 6F. The petals of this very blue variety are washed with white veins and have a broad band of blue-violet around the edges. The long signals are green-yellow and surrounded by white halos. Height: 107 cm (43 in.). Bloom: early to midseason. Parentage: involves seedlings.

Iris 'Yaemomiji' (H. Shimizu 1994) 6F. This variety produces very round, neatly ruffled flowers with red-violet petals that are evenly stippled with streaks of white. The yellow flares are very large and green at the base. The white style arms are edged with red-violet. Height: 89 cm (35½ in.). Bloom: early to midseason. Parentage: "Sakura-no-Sei" × 'Sekiyo'.

Iris 'Winged Sprite'

Iris 'Yaemomiji'

CHAPTER 12

Louisiana Irises
Series *Hexagonae*

THE UNITED STATES IS BLESSED with many native irises, all of which are beardless. None are more striking than those found in the southern United States. The five species of Louisiana irises grow in a region that stretches from the Mississippi River Delta westwards to the Texas-Louisiana state line, north to Missouri and Ohio, and as far east as South Carolina. In this area they grow in swamps and pools and along riverbanks which, being obviously wet, are also rich in nutrients. They also grow in damp meadows and hillsides. The water provides a perfect medium for distributing the seeds, washing them along, and allowing them to settle then grow into great colonies. This also means that over time different species have naturally cross-pollinated, often to become one, and produce a vast array of colours and flower forms.

Although three species were described by the early nineteenth century, it was not until much later that the Louisianas were grown in gardens. During the 1930s and 40s many forms were collected, especially the best clones, often by those who joined guided collecting trips or were members of garden clubs. Of the hundreds of plants collected and planted in gardens, few were registered. Since then much of the natural habitat in which these irises grew has disappeared. Also, because Louisianas naturally produced so many different colours, few had been hybridized prior to 1940. Dykes introduced *Iris* ×*fulvala*, a cross between *I. fulva* and I. *brevicaulis*, in the early twentieth century, but it was not until the late 1940s that hybridization became more important than collecting.

When Dykes wrote *The Genus* Iris (1913), he included only three species of Louisiana irises, but subsequently Percy Viosca Jr., a professional biologist, added *Iris fulva*, *I. giganticaerulea*, and other hybrids. Lowell F. Randolph later excluded the hybrids, but there is still some doubt surrounding the classification of Louisianas as they stand today.

Hybrids of the Louisiana irises can be found in many colours. They produce six to eight blooms per stem and are around 15 cm (6 in.) wide. Each flower will last for up to three days, opening one or two at a time over a period that can last up to eight weeks. The stems vary from straight to zigzag. Like other water-loving irises, Louisiana irises have standards that droop downwards. The petals can be pendent, recurved, open, overlapping, double or semi-double. They are found in tones of blue, lavender, yellow, white, pink, and orange-red; the latter colour is not found among any other group of irises. The foliage varies from light green to dark blue-green, although the tetraploid hybrids tend to be dark green.

Many hybrids have been raised in North America; however others have been introduced from Australia, notably by Heather Pryor and John Taylor, where they are raised in regions with a similar climate to that of Louisiana. Generally speaking, most Louisiana irises will not survive in areas where the temperature drops below −5°C (−20°F) in winter. In recent years tetraploid varieties have come on the market, allowing Louisiana irises to be grown further north, in Europe and the more northern regions of North America. Much of the work to convert diploid plants to tetraploid was done by Joseph Mertzweiller, using the chemical colchicine. The seeds of diploid plants were soaked in the chemical to convert them to tetraploid. The resulting plants, which were first introduced in 1973, were bigger and had flowers with increased substance to the petals and a greater range of colours and shapes.

Cultivation

Louisiana irises need a humus-rich, slightly alkaline to slightly acid soil that remains moist. In cooler climates such as that of northern Europe they should be grown in drier soils with as much sun as possible, while in hotter climates they can be grown under the light shade of trees. Louisiana irises are greedy feeders, so if they are grown near trees make sure there is no competition from the roots. In hot regions Louisiana irises can grow in bog gardens, along the shallow parts of a pool, or even planted in baskets set in a pool of shallow water. If you intend growing these in a pond, make sure an ample amount of foliage sits above the water line.

Louisiana irises are best planted in the autumn, but in colder areas spring planting might be preferable. Clumps should be divided at least

every three years. At other times it is important not to disturb or cut back the leaves especially during hot weather. In warmer areas it is also important to fertilize plants six to eight weeks before flowering. The only disease Louisiana irises are likely to suffer from is rust. The symptoms are red powdery deposits on the leaves and are most likely caused by excess nitrogen in the soil.

A clump of *Iris* ×*fulvala*

Roots of Louisiana irises

LOUISIANA IRIS SPECIES

Iris brevicaulis Rafinesque 1817
South Louisiana

For many years this species was known as *Iris foliosa*. The flowers, which have a white or yellow triangular spot on the falls, range from pale to violet-blue, and very occasionally white forms appear. The flowers sit below the height of the leaves on short, stout, zigzagging stems. Height: to 30 cm (12 in.). Bloom: June.

Iris fulva Ker-Gawler 1812
South Louisiana, Arkansas, Missouri, Ohio

The flowers can vary from brick to coppery red and can sometimes be yellow. They are borne on jointed stems. The species is limited to the lowlands along the Mississippi River from the southeastern counties of Missouri and the southwestern counties of Illinois to the Mississippi Delta of Louisiana. Height: 80 cm (32 in.). Bloom: June.

Iris brevicaulis

Iris giganticaerulea J. K. Small 1929
South Louisiana
The flowers range from bright blue to lavender-blue through to pure white. As its name suggests, this species is the largest of the group, producing flowers on straight stems above the foliage. Height: 100 cm (40 in.). Bloom: March and April.

Iris hexagona Walter 1788
Florida, Georgia, Carolinas along the Atlantic coast
In colour the flowers vary from mid-blue to violet-purple and lavender. All have a red-lilac or yellow ridge and are carried on upright stems. Although the species is said to grow in Florida, after travelling regularly to that state for a period of five years and never seeing it, I suspect it is most commonly found in the northern part of the state. This short species produces stems about the same height as the leaves. Height: 90 cm (36 in.). Bloom: June and July.

Iris nelsonii Randolph 1966
Louisiana
In the wild this species is restricted to the area of Abbeville, New Orleans, and was once known as one of the the 'Abbeville Reds'. It is thought to be a natural hybrid of *Iris fulva* and *I. giganticaerulea*. The flowers range from purple to a red that is brighter than that of *I. fulva*, and sometimes yellow. It is known to hybridize with *I. pseudacorus*, *I. spuria*, *I. versicolor*, and *I. virginica*. The blooms are held above the leaves. Height: to 100 cm (40 in.). Bloom: a week or two later than *I. fulva* and *I. giganticaerulea* during June

LOUISIANA IRIS HYBRIDS

Iris 'Ann Hordern' (H. Pryor 1997)
Essentially a soft lemon, the flowers are tinted around the edges with pink, and the greenish-yellow signals wash the colour further into the petals. The edge of the petals is scalloped and ruffled. As the flower ages it becomes entirely pink. Height: 102 cm (41 in.). Bloom: mid to late season. Parentage: 'Desert Jewel' × 'Noble Planet'.

Iris 'Ann Hordern'

Iris 'Big Easy' (M. Dunn 1995)
The wine-purple flowers have large golden yellow signals on the falls and deep orange-tinted style arms. The edge of the petals is wavy. Height: 91 cm (36½ in.). Bloom: mid to late season. Parentage: 'Plantation Beau' × 'Wine Country'.

Iris 'Black Gamecock' (F. Chowning 1978)
This glossy black flower has a maroon sheen and stick-like, yellow signals. The blooms are borne on unbranched stems that grow to the

Iris 'Big Easy'

Iris 'Black Gamecock'

same height as the light green, evergreen foliage. This variety is reliable in Britain, consistently producing flowers each year. Height: 61 cm (24½ in.). Bloom: late season. Parentage: unknown.

Iris 'Boy Crazy' (M. Dunn 1994)
The deep blue-purple flowers have fine yellow signals and petals that are heavily veined with deep blue-purple. Height: 86 cm (34½ in.). Bloom: midseason. Parentage: 'C'est Chic' × 'Easter Tide'.

Iris 'Captain Gates' (H. Pryor 1998)
This tightly ruffled, round flower is deep purple in colour with deeper purple veins and triangular signals. The yellow style arms are tipped with rose violet, and the ruffled petals are very finely edged with white. Height: 100 cm (40 in.). Bloom: mid to late season. Parentage: 'Koorawatha' × 'Sea Lord'.

Iris 'Charlotte's Tutu' (H. Pryor 1994)
The soft rosy maroon flower has large triangular, lime-yellow signals and very ruffled edges. The style

arms are deep pink, and dark veins emanate from the signals. Height: 97 cm (38¾ in.). Bloom: early to midseason. Parentage: 'Desert Jewel' × 'Noble Planet'.

Iris 'Cherry Cup' (R. Morgan 1988)
This rust-red flower has smooth, slender petals that are finely bleached around the edges. The small signals are mustard coloured. Height: 66–71 cm (26–28½ in.). Bloom: midseason. Parentage: 'F. A. C. McCulla' × 'Little Miss Sims'.

Iris 'Boy Crazy'

Iris 'Charlotte's Tutu'

Iris 'Captain Gates'

Iris 'Cherry Cup'

Iris 'Clown About' (R. Morgan 1991)
This very gently ruffled flower has
slim petals that are corn yellow. A
heavy wash of rust-maroon leaches
from the green-yellow signals down
to the lower part of the falls. The
standards are delicately washed with
soft rose-brown, and the style arms
are green. Height: 71 cm (28½ in.).
Bloom: midseason. Parentage:
'Gypsy Moon' × 'Bayou Comus'.

Iris 'Crushed Ice' (H. Pryor 1995)
This large pure white flower has long
yellow signals and very fine ruffles
along the edges of its broad petals.
Height: 100 cm (40 in.). Bloom: early
to midseason. Parentage: 'Dural
White Butterfly' × 'Alluvial Gold'.

Iris 'Delta Twilight' (M. Dunn 1995)
The signal of the soft lavender flower
is reduced to a green hue that covers
the hafts of the petals and the style
arms. The oval petals are covered
with fine veins. Height: 91 cm (36½
in.). Bloom: midseason. Parentage:
'Fat Tuesday' × 'Cammeray'.

Iris 'Dural White Butterfly' (J. C. Taylor
1989)
The pure white flower has petals patterned with fine green-lemon veins
and edged with small ruffles. Known
to thrive in southern Britain, this variety is one of the few non-bearded
irises to be awarded a Dykes Medal.
Height: 120 cm (48 in.). Bloom: mid
to late season. Parentage: 'Screen
Gem' × 'Helen Naish'. Dykes Medal
Winner Australia 1993.

Iris 'Empress Josephine' (D. Haymon
1989)
The flowers have velvety, dark red-
purple petals and broad, solid yellow
signals. The edges are ruffled, reveal-
ing the softly coloured undersides to
the petals, and the dark style arms
are rimmed with cream. Height: 81

Iris 'Clown About'

Iris 'Dural White Butterfly'

Iris 'Crushed Ice'

Iris 'Empress Josephine'

Iris 'Delta Twilight'

Iris 'Even Handed'

Iris ×fulvala

cm (32½ in.). Bloom: mid to late season. Parentage: 'Full Eclipse' × 'Ann Chowning'.

Iris 'Even Handed' (M. Dunn 1994) This big ruffled flower is lavender-blue in colour with small, sharply pointed signals and lightly ruffled edges to the petals. Height: 94 cm (37 in.). Bloom: midseason. Parentage: 'Plantation Beau' × 'Easter Tide'.

Iris ×fulvala (W. R. Dykes) This hybrid produces wine-purple flowers with large green hearts. Very hardy and vigorous, it grows almost anywhere in my nursery in England, producing the best flowers when grown in a soil that does not dry out. Height: to 91 cm (36½ in.). Bloom: July. Parentage: *I. fulva* × *I. brevicaulis*.

Iris 'Gate Crasher' (J. C. Taylor 1991) This variety has deep dusky pink falls, paler pink standards, and soft yellow style arms. The petals are finely edged with buff, and the triangular signals are golden. Height: 110 cm (44 in.). Bloom: midseason. Parentage: 'Dazzling Star' × 'Helen Naish'.

Iris 'Geisha Eyes' (C. Amy 1987) The flower has round, smooth blue-purple petals, narrow purple-tinted style arms, and large green-yellow signals. From above, the colours form a distinctive star-shaped pattern. Height: 76 cm (30½ in.). Bloom: mid to late season. Parentage: 'Acadian Miss' × 'Valera'.

Iris 'Hot and Spicy' (H. Pryor 1995) The soft terracotta red flowers are bleached to a paler colour around the edges. The style arms are lime green, and the triangular signals are golden yellow. Height: 89 cm (35½ in.). Bloom: midseason. Parentage: 'Gladiator's Gift' × 'Desert Jewel'.

Iris 'Jacaranda Lad' (H. Pryor 1996) This rich lavender-blue flower has pointed yellow signals that are edged with deep purple, a colour that runs down the centre of the falls. The petals are ruffled, and the style arms are tinted with green, rose violet, and violet. Height: 102 cm (41 in.). Bloom: midseason. Parentage: 'Sea Wisp' × 'Spanish Ballet'.

Iris 'Gate Crasher'

Iris 'Hot and Spicy'

Iris 'Geisha Eyes'

Iris 'Jacaranda Lad'

Iris 'Jazz Ballet' (J. C. Taylor 1986)
The very rich violet flowers have tri-angular golden yellow signals veined with purple and forming an Art Nouveau–like pattern. The petals are ruffled and edged with white. Height: 80 cm (32 in.). Bloom: mid to late season. Parentage: 'Secret Spell' × 'Helen Naish'.

Iris 'Jazz Hot' (H. Pryor 1994)
The large, round soft brick red flowers have ruffled petals edged with white. These are suffused with green from the hafts and form a large central star around the green style arms. The signals are yellow. Height: 89 cm (35½ in.). Bloom: mid to late season. Parentage: 'Gladiator's Gift' × 'Desert Jewel'.

Iris 'Joie de Vivre' (H. Pryor 1995)
This very frilly flower has maroon petals that are flushed with copper and decorated with flaring yellow signals that are raised up. The petals are paler underneath. Height: 89 cm (35½ in.). Bloom: mid to late season. Parentage: 'Gladiator's Gift' × 'Desert Jewel'.

Iris 'Koorawatha' (J. Taylor 1986)
The gently ruffled, lemon flower has lemon style arms, long yellow signals, and petals covered with fine veins. Height: 71 cm (28½ in.). Bloom: midseason. Parentage: 'Dural Charm' × 'Clara Goula'.

Iris 'La Stupenda' (H. Pryor 1994)
The very large flowers have ruffled, yellow petals that are edged with dark rose-pink and covered with deep veins which break into many branches. The yellow style arms are washed with rose on either side of the midribs. Height: 96 cm (38½ in.). Bloom: late season. Parentage: 'Desert Jewel' × 'Noble Planet'.

Iris 'Jazz Ballet'

Iris 'Koorawatha'

Iris 'Jazz Hot'

Iris 'La Stupenda'

Iris 'Joie de Vivre'

Iris 'Lemon Petticoats'

Iris 'Love Me Do'

Iris 'Lemon Petticoats' (H. Pryor 1996)
This bicolour has lemon falls and cream standards. The texture of the petals is similar to crepe paper. The long yellow signals extend down the length of the petals. The style arms are soft yellow, and the buds dark lemon. Height: 97 cm (38¾ in.). Bloom: early season. Parentage: 'Alluvial Gold' × 'Gladiator's Gift'.

Iris 'Love Me Do' (B. Pryor 1996)
The purple-pink flowers have triangular, lime green signals and deeper veins etched into the petals. The edges are rimmed with white and

curl up to reveal the white undersides to the petals. Height: 81 cm (32½ in.). Bloom: mid to late season. Parentage: 'Volcanic Wildfire' × 'Spanish Ballet'.

Iris 'Malibu Magic' (J. Taylor 1990)
The heavily textured flower is soft violet-blue, a colour that is unevenly veined and washed over a white background. The signals are a faint lime green, and the edges of the petals are very ruffled. Height: 110 cm (44 in.). Bloom: midseason. Parentage: 'Flight of Fantasy' × 'Helen Naish'.

Iris 'Mischief Maker' (B. Pryor 1997)
Dusky blue-pink in colour, the broad, ruffled petals are rimmed with white and in the centre washed with soft lemon. Long brown veins extend from the hafts and over the long lime green signals. The style arms are soft lemon. Height: 81 cm (32½ in.). Bloom: early to midseason. Parentage: 'Volcanic Wildfire' × 'Spanish Ballet'.

Iris 'Professor Barbara' (J. Mertweiller 1990)
This very smooth lemon flower has falls that are edged with little ripples and small standards that almost sit upright. The grass green signals are edged with bright yellow and send green veins radiating down the falls. This tetraploid was an important advancement among yellow Louisianas. Height: 81–86 cm (32–34½ in.). Bloom: midseason. Parentage: ('Professor Ike' × 'Wheelhorse' colchicine-treated chimera) × (a seedling with a colchicine-treated chimera × 'Professor Ike').

Iris 'Sinfonietta' (R. Raabe 1986)
The flowers are rich gentian-blue in colour, with green-yellow steeple-shaped signals and blue style arms that are washed with lime green at

Iris 'Professor Barbara'

Iris 'Malibu Magic'

Iris 'Sinfonietta'

Iris 'Mischief Maker'

LOUISIANA IRISES ● **255**

Iris 'Soft Hearted'

the base. The falls are round, and the long slender standards have gently ruffled edges. Height: 85 cm (34 in.). Bloom: early to midseason. Parentage: 'Bethany Douglas' × ('Clara Goula' × 'Gatewood Princess').

Iris 'Soft Hearted' (M. Dunn by J. Ghio 1999)

This violet-blue variety has round petals that do not quite touch, unlike those of most modern cultivars. The petals are distinctively edged with blue-white, and the short yellow signals are shaped like daggers. Height: 91 cm (36½ in.). Bloom: mid to late season. Parentage: ('Plantation Beau' × 'Easter Tide') × 'Sea Consul'.

Iris 'Star Power' (M. Dunn 1993)

The royal purple flower has velvety, ruffled petals that are so large they almost hide the thin yellow signals. The style arms are also velvety and purple. Height: 91 cm (36½ in.). Bloom: midseason. Parentage: ('Bajazzo' × 'Full Eclipse') × 'Clara Goula'.

Iris 'Venus Vortex' (H. Pryor 1998)

This rosy maroon flower has yellow signals that are edged by white. The yellow extends into the petals, and the white breaks into veins. The ruffled edges are bleached and curl upwards to reveal the soft peach undersides to the petals. The style arms are buff. Height: 114 cm (46 in.). Bloom: midseason. Parentage: 'Saturn Swirl' × self.

Iris 'Wizard of Aussie' (H. Pryor 1997)

The russet-brown flower has golden brown standards and rich yellow style arms. The broad, golden yellow signals break into veins at the bottom. The blooms are held above the foliage, and the colours are unstable. Height: 114 cm (46 in.). Bloom: early to midseason. Parentage: 'Volcanic Wildfire' × ('Frank Chowning' × 'Desert Jewel').

Iris 'Star Power'

Iris 'Wizard of Aussie'

Iris 'Venus Vortex'

CHAPTER 13

Pacific Coast Irises
Series *Californicae*

PACIFIC COAST IRISES are not the easiest irises to grow in most parts of the world, and I for one have had little success with them. These natives of the western coast of North America produce flowers in a combination of colours that are not available among most other irises. Known as Pacificas, Californians, Pacific Coast irises (PCI), or Pacific Coast natives (PCN), these irises grow into low, leafy clumps with slender, often tangled rhizomes and long, leathery, deep green leaves. The blooms are borne on slender stems. The Californian species produce delicate flowers, while many of the hybrids, especially the modern ones, have short standards and round falls that are often ruffled and overlapping. In the wild they grow in forested areas or along the low parts of mountainous regions usually in light shade, with the exception of *Iris douglasiana*, which seems to break most of the Californian iris rules. The blooming period is from April to May, and in cooler areas flowering may continue to June. All the species of this group will hybridize readily with members of the series *Sibericae*, producing what is known as Cal-sibs.

One of the earliest hybridizers to work with Pacific Coast irises was Lee Lenz of the Rancho Santa Ana Botanic Gardens in California. During the mid-twentieth century he collected plants from the wild and introduced many crosses. Marjorie Brummitt in England also introduced 32 varieties between 1955 and 1982, usually with the prefix 'Banbury'. Today, Joe Ghio of California has done much to keep the hybrid Californian iris in the eye of the public. By 1995, Ghio had introduced 185 Pacific Coast irises, in addition to many other types of irises. Sadly, however, despite hundreds of named varieties being introduced, Pacific Coast hybrids are not readily available. Commercial growers are few and far between, and the hybrids they list rarely coincide with one another. Thankfully these beautiful little plants are easy to grow from seed.

Cultivation

There is one basic rule for growing Pacific Coast irises: plant them in acid soil. (The single exception is *Iris douglasiana*, which prefers alkaline or neutral soil.) The soil should be well drained and humus-rich. In cooler climates, such as northern Europe, these irises can be grown in full sun. In warmer, drier climates they prefer partial shade. Gardeners who find it difficult to grow Pacific Coast irises outdoors may find it easier to establish plants in containers. A large clay one is ideal.

Pacific Coast irises should be replanted when they produce new white roots, generally during the autumn, but they can also be planted in spring. If an old clump needs dividing, pot it up for overwintering

Iris douglasiana roots

before planting it out in the spring. In cooler climates, such as that of Britain, Pacific Coast irises might be better left in a greenhouse throughout the winter. The foliage of plants grown outside should be cut back to ground level in autumn to minimize any fungal diseases that might appear the following year. Applying mulch during the winter can help plants survive the winter. Pacific Coast irises do not usually like fertilizer, but if you feel it is needed, use one for acid-loving plants that is very low in nitrogen.

Sydney B. Mitchell Medal

The Sydney B. Mitchell Medal is the top award of the American Iris Society for Pacific Coast irises. Mitchell was the first president of the California Horticultural Society, an author of gardening books, and one of the earliest gardeners to use the Pacific Coast iris in a garden setting.

PACIFIC COAST IRIS SPECIES & THEIR COLLECTED FORMS

Iris bracteata S. Watson 1885
Northern California and Southern Oregon
This large-flowered species produces blooms in various tones of yellow with maroon or brown veins. The flowers sit below the level of the leaves, which are broader than most, grey-green at the top end, and yellow-green towards the base. The species grows naturally in shady, dry areas and is sometimes known as the Siskiyou iris. Height: to 60 cm (24 in.).

Iris douglasiana Herbert 1841
Coastal areas from California to southern Oregon
This species produces a dense evergreen clump of broad, sword-like, deep green leaves that flops over at the top. Long, slender, branched stems carry flowers that range from deep red-purple to lavender and white. The falls have yellow, purple, or blue veins. A vigorous plant in the wild, *Iris douglasiana* can be found growing in grassy pastures, on cliff tops, and near the beach. It thrives in my garden in England and is also known as the Douglas iris. Height: 28 cm (11 in.).

Iris hartwegii Baker 1876
California
This sparsely leaved plant produces open, spreading clumps of slender foliage. The soft yellow or lavender flowers are also slender. Various forms are known: subsp. *australis* has purple, blue-violet, or bright blue flowers; subsp. *columbiana* produces yellow flowers with deeper veining; and subsp. *pinetorum* has soft yellow flowers. All the forms originate from woody areas on hillsides or mountains, where it is sunny or partially shaded. Height: to 30 cm (12 in.).

Iris innominata L. F. Henderson 1930
Northwest California to southwest Oregon
A parent, together with *Iris douglasiana*, of many of today's hybrids, *I. innominata* produces wide clumps of slender, rich green leaves and slender stems of gently coloured blooms. Flower colour ranges from yellow through soft buff-orange. Most flowers are heavily veined with maroon, brown, or purple.

Iris munzii R. C. Foster 1938
Central California
This species produces the largest flowers in the series. In colour the blooms range from pale lavender to red-violet, but in cultivation they can be turquoise to deep sky-blue. The evergreen foliage is grey-green. This species is only found growing in one small region of California, around the foothills of the southern Sierra Nevada, and is sometimes known as Munz's iris. Height: to 70 cm (28 in.).

Iris purdyi Eastwood 1897
North California
This species grows naturally in open places of coniferous forests. Today it is under threat of extinction because of man's development. The flowers are usually soft yellow with brown-purple veins, although sometimes they are white. The flowers are carried on distinctive stems, which are covered with overlapping, inflated, red-tinted bracts. The narrow, dark grey-green leaves form a low, spreading clump. Height: 20–40 cm (8–16 in.).

Iris tenax Douglas ex Lindley 1829
Southwest Washington to west Oregon
The foliage is light green and lax, and the long, slender, unbranched stems carry flowers with long, slim petals. In colour the blooms range from deep purple-blue to pink, white, and

Iris douglasiana

Iris douglasiana, white form

yellow. This species grows in open grassy areas, including roadside verges, in a small region of northwestern America. It is also known as the Oregon iris. Height: 70 cm (28 in.). Bloom: April and May.

Iris tenuissima Dykes 1912
North California

Naturally growing in dry, sunny wooded areas, this species produces a flower with six narrow petals that flare out sideways to form a star pattern. The blooms are pale in colour, either white or cream, with veins of lavender, mahogany, or brown. The evergreen leaves are grey-green. Height: to 40 cm (16 in.).

PACIFIC COAST IRIS HYBRIDS

Iris 'Agnes James' (C. Starker 1939)
This white-flowered variety has narrow petals with long yellow signals that extend into yellow veins. Height: to 30 cm (12 in.). Bloom: midseason.

Iris 'Amiguita' (E. Nies 1947)
The light blue flower has slender petals with large purple spots that wash into the surrounding petals. The signals are pale gold, and the midribs blue. Height: 30 cm (12 in.). Bloom: midseason. Mitchell Award 1974.

Iris innominata

Iris tenax 'Alba'

Iris tenax

Iris 'Agnes James'

Iris 'Amiguita'

Iris 'Baby Blanket' (J. Ghio 1998)
The round flower is pink-buff in colour with vibrant blue signals slipping down the falls. The edges of the petals are tightly ruffled, and the style arms are serrated around the edges. Height: 41 cm (16½ in.). Bloom: midseason. Parentage: includes many unnamed seedlings and 'Greeting Card'.

Iris 'Blue Moment' (D. Meek 1992)
This soft lavender flower has vibrant purple halos around the long gold signals that melt into the ruffled petals. Height: 38 cm (15 in.). Bloom: mid to late season. Parentage: includes *I. tenax*, *I. innominata*, and 'Native Warrior'.

Iris 'Broadleigh Ann' (Bootle & Wilbraham 1973)
The soft chestnut flowers have round falls that are heavily patterned with gold veins and rimmed with gold. The slim standards are softer in colour and yellow at the edge. This cultivar is one of many Pacific Coast irises with the prefix of 'Broadleigh'. Height: 30 cm (12 in.). Parentage: unknown.

Iris 'Broadleigh Medusa'
The wine red flower has large pale gold signals that emerge from the hafts. The signals are covered with wine red veins. The falls tuck under themselves at the end, and the large standards flare open. Height: 20 cm (8 in.). Bloom: early season.

Iris 'Cinnamon Blush' (D. Meek 1995)
This very ruffled flower has short, round petals that open cinnamon and fade to tan with age. The falls have large creamy gold signals. Height: 30 cm (12 in.). Bloom: midseason. Parentage: ((*I. tenax* × *I. innominata*) × 'Encircle') × 'Tunitas'.

Iris 'Fallen Plums' (J. Marchant 1990)
This variety has very ruffled, rich red plum petals with edges that are bleached to white and veined with deep purple. The style arms are pink-buff. Height: 28 cm (11 in.). Bloom: midseason. Parentage: seedlings.

Iris 'Floating World' (N. Scopes 1993)
The round, white falls are heavily edged, streaked, and lined with rose purple, a colour that is deeper around the yellow signals. The rose-pink standards are laced. This variety grows into a very upright plant. Height: 38 cm (15 in.). Bloom: midseason. Parentage: unknown.

Iris 'Greenan Gold' (D. Meek 1972)
The falls of this yellow flower are marked with very small, light brown dots and curl down around the edges. The ruffled standards are paler in colour, and the style arms are bright yellow. Height: 38 cm (15 in.). Bloom: early to midseason. Parentage: ((*I. tenax* × *I. innominata*) × 'Encircle') × 'Tunitas'.

Iris 'Joey' (J. Gatty 1978)
This buff flower has slender standards and round falls with long hafts. The blooms are decorated with round chrome yellow signals and surrounded by a broad wash of red-brown. The style arms are also buff. Height: 25 cm (10 in.). Bloom: midseason. Parentage: unknown.

Iris 'Baby Blanket'

Iris 'Blue Moment'

Iris 'Broadleigh Ann'

Iris 'Broadleigh Medusa'

Iris 'Cinnamon Blush'

Iris 'Fallen Plums'

Iris 'Greenan Gold'

Iris 'Floating World'

Iris 'Joey'

Iris 'Moresco' (B. Blyth 1983)
This variety produces very ruffled, lavender-blue flowers with falls that are veined with purple and decorated with large bright gold signals. Height: 46–51 cm (18–20½ in.). Bloom: midseason. Parentage: unknown.

Iris 'Pacific Rim' (B. Jones 1990)
The ruffled edges of this crisp, white triangular flower are heavily speckled with deep blue and veined from the hafts with yellow. Height: 38 cm (15 in.). Bloom: midseason. Parentage: unknown. Mitchell Medal Winner 1998.

Iris 'Peacock Pavane' (N. Scopes 1993)
The violet flowers have frilly, round falls and standards that flop between the falls. On the falls sit soft yellow signals that are surrounded by a halo that is first violet, then white. The falls are covered with violet lines. Height: 38 cm (15 in.). Bloom: midseason. Parentage: 'Spring Daze' × unknown.

Iris 'San Lorenzo Valley' (J. Ghio 1992)
Very short, round petals form a flat, white flower. The falls have yellow signals that are surrounded by a blue-purple halo and covered with neat purple veins. The standards and style arms are white. Height: 36 cm (14½ in.). Bloom: mid to late season. Parentage: 'Idyllwild' × 'Fault Zone'.

Iris 'Short Order' (J. Ghio 1982)
This soft orange-yellow flower is nearer to peach than orange and has soft brown veins covering its yellow signals. The plant forms a bushy clump. Height: 15 cm (6 in.). Bloom: early to midseason. Parentage: 'Banbury Tapestry' × 'San Vicente'.

Iris 'Star of Wonder' (J. Ghio 2003)
This frilly, vibrant copper-yellow flower has petals coated with maroon. Height: to 30 cm (12 in.). Bloom: midseason. Parentage: unknown.

Iris 'Umunhum' (J. Ghio 1998)
The burnt orange flowers have violet signals and ruffled edges. Height: 41 cm (16½ in.). Bloom: very early season. Parentage: 'Ultimate Suntan' × seedling.

Iris 'Warragne' (B. Blyth 1987)
This pink-maroon flower has gently ruffled petals that are softer in colour around the edges. On the white signals sits a covering of maroon veins that travel down the petals. Height: 30 cm (12 in.). Bloom: midseason. Parentage: unknown.

Iris 'Moresco'

Iris 'Peacock Pavane'

Iris 'Pacific Rim'

Iris 'San Lorenzo Valley'

Iris 'Star of Wonder'

Iris 'Umunhum'

Iris 'Short Order'

Iris 'Warragne'

CHAPTER 14

Spuria Irises
Series *Spuriae*

ONCE CALLED THE 'butterfly irises', spurias have flowers that bear some resemblance to the blooms of bulbous Dutch irises, which are mainly used for cutting. The similarity does not stop there, and I can vouch for their success as cut flowers; however, these are not bulbous irises but rhizomatous, and the wild species are distributed from Europe to the Far East.

As a group, Spuria irises are generally divided into two sections: the tall ones and the dwarf ones. The blooms have long, slender petals with long, arching style arms, but the colour range is limited to blues, lavender, yellows, brown, and white. The flowers tend to open in ones or twos at an awkward angle up stiffly erect stems that emerge from a thick clump of upright, often twisted foliage. Sadly these very hardy plants are still not as popular as they deserve to be. They produce flowers at the same time as peonies but continue for much longer, lasting for up to four weeks. Bees love them, burying their way under the style arms to get to the nectar. Spurias are ideal for planting at the back of an herbaceous border. The handsome, upright foliage will provide a perfect background for early, more brightly coloured flowers.

One of the first hybrids goes back to the late nineteenth century. The English iris lover Sir Michael Foster introduced *Iris* 'Monspur', a name derived by combining its two parents, *Iris monnieri* and *I. spuria*. The hybridizing of spurias has not been as active as that of bearded or Siberian irises, and the number of named varieties is limited. Today most tall hybrids sold are still crosses of *I. crocea*, *I. orientalis*, and *I. monnieri*. Through the efforts of people like Walker Ferguson, Eleanor McCown, Ben Hager, and Dave Niswonger, these plants have been kept alive in the eyes of the iris-buying public.

Cultivation

All the books will tell you that Spuria irises need a sunny spot with good drainage and a deep, moist soil. Having grown the hybrid spurias for over 20 years, I have found they are not that fussy about the soil requirements. Indeed, in the West Midlands of England, these plants have grown to between 120 and 150 cm (48–60 in.) tall, a lot taller than the prescribed height. They do not seem to mind clayish or sandy soils, drying out in summer or being very wet in winter, or soils that are slightly acid, alkaline, or neutral. They do like a deep soil so that the rhizomes can work their way down into the earth, and they will multiply better in a soil that remains moist for much of the year. As to light, spurias grow in full sun or partial shade. The species other than *Iris crocea*, *I. orientalis*, and *I. monnieri* are probably a little fussier and should be grown in a way that reflects their natural home.

When planting Spuria irises make sure the rhizome is set deeply, around 5 cm (2 in.) below the surface of the soil. Newly planted spurias will take a little while to settle down and establish. They should not be allowed to dry out during or after planting. Transplanting is probably best done in autumn, but plants do not seem to resent spring planting. They can be left undivided for many years, but if they like your soil a clump will slowly multiply to a point where division might be necessary. If plants require fertilizing, do this after they have flowered or in the spring, using a well-balanced, slow-release fertilizer or very well rotted compost.

SPURIA IRIS SPECIES

Iris crocea Jacquemont ex Baker 1877
Kashmir

Once known as *Iris aurea*, this tall species can be found growing near cemeteries high up in Kashmir. It produces up to six large golden yellow flowers with petals that are crimped around the edges. Height: to 150 cm (60 in.). Bloom: June and July.

Iris graminea Linnaeus 1753
Northeastern Spain, southeastern Europe, Caucasus, Crimea

Nicknamed the 'plum tart' iris because of its scent, this low-growing iris makes me wonder how many gardeners would get on their knees to stick a nose in it. The flowers are charming and have long, slender petals. The soft blue falls are veined white, the standards are soft purple, and the style arms are large and arching. The plant blooms profusely at the base of a thick clump of slender rich green foliage. Height: to 60 cm (24). Bloom: May and June.

Iris kerneriana Ascherson & Sintenis 1884
Northern Turkey, Armenia

Go and see this species growing on rock gardens at the Royal Botanic Gardens Kew and I defy anyone to not think it a very handsome plant. This iris produces creeping clumps of slender, bright green leaves and soft yellow flowers that sit in or just above the foliage. The smooth blooms have slightly twisted standards and falls that arch and then tip down. They are decorated with large yellow flashes, and the petals are of a good substance. Difficult to establish, this species needs a good moist soil especially during the growing season and prefers one that is either neutral or slightly acid. It does not like being disturbed. Height: to 45 cm (18 in.). Bloom: May and June.

Iris lilacina Borbás
Origin unknown

I have not seen this plant growing, but it is described, as one might guess, as having lavender flowers. Where it originates from is a mystery. It could come from Kashmir, central Asia, or even Romania; however, it can be found in cultivation in Britain, New Zealand, Australia, and the United States. Height: 100 cm (40 in.). Bloom: June to July.

Iris longipedicellata Czeczott 1932
Turkey

This native of marshy areas in the mountains of Turkey produces yellow flowers. Height: 40 cm (16 in.). Bloom: July.

Iris graminea

Iris kerneriana

Iris monnieri De Candolle 1808

Origin unknown

Like *Iris crocea*, *I. monnieri* produces bright yellow flowers. The species was discovered by Augustin de Candolle growing in a garden near Versailles, France, and named after the owner of the garden, a Mr Lemonnier. This iris probably comes from the southern Greek islands of Rhodes and Crete. It could also be a hybrid as seeds germinating from this plant are recorded to resemble *I. orientalis*. Height: 100 cm (40 in.). Bloom: June and July.

Iris orientalis P. Miller 1768

Turkey, the Aegean Islands of Lesbos and Sámos, northeastern Greece

For many years this tough species was listed under the name of *Iris ochroleuca*. It is a long-established garden plant and, more recently, it has been extensively used in the hybridization of new cultivars. The flowers are white and have a large yellow spot on the falls. It is sometimes known as the swamp iris. Height: to 125 cm (49 in.). Bloom: June and July.

Iris pontica Zapalowicz 1906

Southeast Romania, Ukraine, Russia

The flowers are deep blue-purple with winged hafts mottled with brown over a yellow background. The leaves grow taller than the flowers, which reach 14 cm (5½ in.) tall. This dwarf variety could be a good rockery plant and is suitable for growing in a pot. It requires a rich clay loam with crushed limestone. Height: 4 cm (1½ in.). Bloom: end of May.

Iris sintenesii Janka 1876

South Italy, Balkans, Southwest Russia, Turkey

The flowers have white falls veined with purple and purple-blue standards. Like all short spurias, this species produces leaves that grow above the height of the flowers. It forms spreading clumps and in the wild can be found in scrubland as well as in grassy areas. In the garden this iris does not like a site where the ground is baked hard during the summer. Height: 30 cm (12 in.). Bloom: June to July.

Iris spuria Linnaeus 1753

Europe, Middle East, central Asia

Iris spuria has many subspecies: *carthaliniae*, *demetrii*, *halophila*, *maritima*, *musulmanica*, *notha*, *sogidiana*, and *spuria*. In general terms, it is a widely distributed species that can be found growing throughout Europe into Scandinavia and down to Spain, from France to Russia, and through Iran to Turkey and then across to China. The flowers range from soft blue, purple-blue, blue-violet, and purple to grey-lilac and white with varying colours of veining. In the wild the different forms are to be found growing in areas that vary from wet to dry, near the sea to up on well-drained hillsides. Height: 75–100 cm (29–40 in.); var. *sogidiana*, 35 cm (14 in.). Bloom: June to July.

Iris orientalis

SPURIA IRIS HYBRIDS

Iris 'Archie Owen' (B. Hager 1970)

This bright yellow variety has soft lemon style arms. Height: 97 cm (38¾ in.). Bloom: midseason. Parentage: 'Windfall' × ('Golden Lady' × 'Morningtide').

Iris 'Cambridge Blue' (M. Foster 1882)

This plant can also be found listed under the name *Iris* 'Monspur Cambridge Blue'. The flowers are bright blue with large golden spots on the falls that are covered with veins of blue. The very upright standards are ruffled around the edges. Height: 150 cm (60 in.). Bloom: early season. Parentage: *I. monnieri* × *I. spuria*.

Iris 'Cinnamon Roll' (D. Niswonger 1979)

This chocolate-brown iris produces flowers with frilly edges and yellow signals that extend from the hafts. It has soft yellow style arms that are ribbed with brown. Height: 107 cm (43 in.). Bloom: midseason. Parentage: 'Intensity' × 'Elixir'.

Iris 'Dress Circle' (B. Hager 1984)

This gently ruffled flower has violet-blue falls marked with a large yellow spot that pales to lemon, then is edged by violet-blue. The standards are bright blue with violet veins. The style arms also are violet. Height: 91 cm (36½ in.). Bloom: mid to late season. Parentage: ('Marilyn Holloway' × 'Allegory') × ('Farolito' × 'Port of Call').

Iris 'Headway' (B. Hager 1985)

This silky, golden yellow variety is almost pure in colour except for a few brown veins. The style arms are softer yellow. Height: 114 cm (46 in.). Bloom: midseason. Parentage: 'Eagle' × 'Forty Carats'.

Iris 'Archie Owen'

Iris 'Dress Circle'

Iris 'Ila Crawford'

Iris 'Cambridge Blue'

Iris 'Headway'

***Iris* 'Highline Halo'** (E. McCown 1975)
The flowers are yellow and edged with white. The white style arms are flushed with yellow down the midrib, and the petals are edged with little ruffles. Height: 102 cm (41 in.). Bloom: midseason. Parentage: ('Imperial Song' × 'Thrush Song') × 'Highline Lavender'.

***Iris* 'Ila Crawford'** (B. Hager 1976)
The white flower has round falls with a large yellow spot that is washed into the surrounding petals. The style arms are white tinted with yellow down the midrib, and the petals are edged with little ruffles. Height: 91 cm (36½ in.). Bloom: midseason. Parentage: 'Marilyn Holloway' × 'Allegory'.

Iris 'Cinnamon Roll'

Iris 'Highline Halo'

Iris 'Imperial Bronze' (E. McCown 1970)
The flowers, which open down the stem, are rich yellow and heavily overlaid with nutmeg-brown veins. The style arms are yellow and tinged with nutmeg. Height: 102 cm (41 in.). Bloom: midseason. Parentage: 'Driftwood' × 'Imperial Night'.

Iris 'La Senda' (W. Ferguson 1972)
The flowers are soft grey-lilac with large yellow spots on the falls and white style arms that have a soft lilac midrib. Height: 122 cm (49 in.). Bloom: very late season. Parentage: 'Pink Candles' × seedling.

Iris 'Lady Butterfly' (B. Charles Jenkins 1994)
More ruffled than many spurias, this flower has little ripples around the edges of its soft yellow petals. The style arms are also lemon yellow. Each fall has a small deep yellow signal. Height: 107–124 cm (42–49 in.). Bloom: early season. Parentage: 'Lively One' × 'Candle Lace'.

Iris 'Lighted Signal' (B. Charles Jenkins 1990)
This richly coloured flower has bright blue-purple petals. The large golden signals on the falls wash into the falls to form a blend of purple and yellow. The style arms are heavily washed with soft purple. Height: 102–122 cm (41–49 in.). Bloom: midseason. Parentage: 'Ping and Pang' white × 'Terra Nova'.

Iris 'Marilyn Holloway' (B. Hager 1970)
The standards are pale grey-blue, and the falls are yellow edged with grey-blue. The ruffled petals are veined deeply, and the style arms are white tinged with yellow and violet. Height: 97 cm (38¾ in.). Bloom: mid to late season. Parentage: 'Windfall' × 'Port of Call'.

Iris 'Imperial Bronze'

Iris 'Lighted Signal'

Iris 'La Senda'

Iris 'Marilyn Holloway'

Iris 'Lady Butterfly'

Iris 'Media Luz'

Iris 'Purple Smoke'

Iris 'Media Luz' (B. Hager 1967) This variety produces soft lavender flowers with yellow signals and long soft lavender style arms. The falls have a cream undertone. Height: 101 cm (40½ in.). Bloom: late season. Parentage: 'Dutch Defiance' × 'Wadi Zem Zem'.

Iris 'Purple Smoke' (B. Charles Jenkins 1995) The standards are purple, and the falls are yellow and heavily stained and veined with yellow. The edges of the petals are ruffled, and the style arms a smoky purple. Height: 107–

130 cm (43–51 in.). Bloom: midseason. Parentage: 'Live One' × 'Now This'.

Iris 'Red Oak' (W. Ferguson 1965) The smoothly shaped maroon-brown flower has yellow hafts and softer self-coloured style arms. In my experience, this hybrid grows taller than its registered height. Height: 91 cm (36½ in.). Bloom: midseason. Parentage: 'Shift to Red' × seedling.

Iris 'Rodeo Blue' (B. Charles Jenkins 1994) This mid-blue variety has small petals with very slight ruffles around the edges. The large yellow signals are covered with blue veins. Height: 97–114 cm (38–46 in.). Bloom: early season. Parentage: 'Bali Bali' × 'Lenkoran'.

Iris 'Vintage Year' (D. Niswonger 1979) The very dark blue-purple flower has petals with ruffled edges and a yellow spot is sprayed onto the centre of each fall. The style arms are purple with edges that are almost white. Height: 102 cm (41 in.). Bloom: midseason. Parentage: 'Proverb' × (Purple Knight × Anacapa).

Iris 'Walker Ferguson' (W. Ferguson by J. Collins 1975) This dark red-brown variety has round falls that are rich in colour and yellow signals that are eaten into by brown veins. The standards are a silky red-brown, and the brown style arms are broadly edged with lemon. Height: 94 cm (37 in.). Bloom: midseason. Parentage: seedling × 'Crow Wing'.

Iris 'Red Oak'

Iris 'Vintage Year'

Iris 'Rodeo Blue'

Iris 'Walker Ferguson'

CHAPTER 15

Other Beardless Species

The irises in this chapter are among the most effective plants for using in difficult situations around the garden. Some of the iris groups will grow in dry shade, while others will thrive in hot, dry borders. Most of them produce handsome clumps of evergreen foliage.

Crested Irises
Section *Lophiris*

The majority of crested irises originate from China and Japan, but a few species grow wild in the United States. As a group these irises bear little resemblance to other members of the iris family. Instead of upright, sword- or linear-shaped leaves, which the majority of irises possess, crested irises produce broad leaves that form arching or floppy fans. The flower stems are generally divided into segments with each segment producing a flower stem and a further set of leaves. The flowers are usually flat and, when looked at from above, star shaped. In colour they range from white to dark lavender with style arms that have fringed crests. Some species also have fringed edges to the petals. The falls are decorated with raised humps, known as the crest—

hence the name crested iris—and dots of purple, white, and splashes of white. The rhizomes are thin and grow horizontally, but in some species these grow upwards, bearing some resemblance to bamboo.

Crested irises are sometimes called Evansia Irises. This name commemorates Thomas Evans, who first described them in 1794. Since that time there has been much discussion about where crested irises should be placed in relation to other irises. In 1913 William Dykes considered them to be a section of the genus *Iris*. George H. M. Lawrence in 1953 thought of them as a subsection. Since then, the Russian botanist G. Rodionenko has placed them in their own subgenus of *Crossiris* and divided them into three separate sections: *Crossiris*, *Lophiris*, and *Monospatha*. In this book, however, I am following the system favoured by the British Iris Society Species Group as laid out in 1997. There is also some discussion about which are and which are not species. *Iris confusa*, *I. japonica*, *I. formosana*, and *I. wattii* have been grown in Chinese and Japanese gardens for so long that botanists widely suspect these species to

be hybrids. In appearance they are very similar, and it is not unheard for the different species to become muddled.

All these species can be found growing in moist, warm climates of the world, which means that most are not hardy in northern climates. Where they are hardy, they should be grown in a shady, moist spot in soil that is slightly acid.

Iris confusa Sealy 1937
Western China

The flowers of this species range from white to soft lavender with yellow-orange crests and purple dots on the falls. The leaves, which are broad, shiny, and evergreen, are carried on bamboo-like stems. This vigorous plant grows along the fringes of forests and on grassy slopes. In Britain it is inclined to be tender and should therefore be grown in a pot and placed, during winter, in a cool greenhouse. The form 'Martyn Rix' is hardier and I have grown it outside two years, although it is yet to flower. In Melbourne, Australia I have seen *Iris confusa* covering the ground beneath shrubs. Height: 30 cm (12. in.). Bloom: April and May.

Iris cristata Solander 1789

Southeastern and central United States

Generally the flowers are pale lilac with ruffled edges, crimped orange crests, and white central patches that are edged by purple; however, there are blue, violet, pink, and white forms. The wide light green leaves, which emerge from nodes on the bamboo-like stems, form a spreading carpet. In the wild this species can be found growing on rocky hillsides and in moist woods on neutral or slightly acid soils. In cultivation it should be grown in a cool, semi-shady situation with well-drained soil. To maintain vigour, the plant should be divided frequently. It is commonly known as the crested iris. Height: 10 cm (4 in.). Bloom: April to May.

Iris formosana Ohwi 1934

Taiwan

Probably the only truly tropical iris, this native of Taiwan is not hardy in northern climates. It is similar in many respects to *Iris japonica*, but has shorter leaf stems and larger white flowers. The latter are speckled with yellow-orange and dotted with purple. Height: 100 cm (40 in.). Bloom: April to May.

Iris gracilipes A. Gray 1858

Japan, China

This woodland species requires a rich, acid soil, which does not dry out. It has very branched stems with starry, small lilac or pink-mauve flowers that are veined with lilac and covered with large white patches. The crests are orange. The arching foliage is grassy, light green and turns yellow in autumn. The species is reasonably hardy in more temperate climates. Height: to around 20 cm (8 in.). Bloom: May.

Iris japonica Thunberg 1794

Central China, Japan

This species produces white flowers that are washed with soft blue and patterned with violet and orange dots. The edges of the petals are fringed, and the crest is divided into three raised ridges, the middle one being yellow. The blooms, which are produced for up to four weeks, are carried on well-branched stems. The creeping aerial rhizomes produce roots at intervals and carry evergreen, shiny, broad, and deep green leaves. This species is sometimes known as the Japanese iris and is the most commonly cultivated crested iris in Britain. I grow this plant in an open, lightly shaded and reasonably moist border; however, in some years it fails to flower.

As a rule, beardless irises do not cross with bearded irises. However, during the mid-twentieth century, a hybrid named *Iris* 'Paltec' was successfully raised from a cross between a bearded iris (probably *I. pallida*) and *I. japonica*.

Other forms of *Iris japonica* are available; the most popular of these is 'Ledger's Variety', which is said to be hardier than the species. Height: to 60 cm (2 ft.). Bloom: April to late May.

Iris confusa

Iris formosana

Iris japonica

Iris japonica 'Bourne Graceful'
(J. Ellis 1975)

The large flowers are palest mauve with deep violet spots around the yellow crests. The falls droop down. Height: to 102 cm (41 in.). Bloom: May. Parentage: *I. japonica* 'Capri Form' × *I. japonica* 'Ledger's Variety'.

Iris japonica 'Fairyland'

This short, spreading plant bears white flowers on upright stems. Height: 30 cm (12 in.). Parentage: *I.* 'Uwodu' (an American form) × *I. confusa*.

Iris japonica 'Purple Heart' (M. Ogisu)

This form was collected by Japanese botanist Mikinori Ogisu. The leaves have dark purple bases, and the flower stems also are dark purple. The flowers are white with deep purple spots on each fall. Height: to 75 cm (30 in.).

Iris milesii M. Foster 1893
Himalayas

This hardy species was named after Frank Miles who first raised it from seed collected by his cousin at Simla in India. The rhizomes are fatter than those of most other Evansia irises. The flower stems carry small leaves that envelope each branched flower stem. The soft violet flowers are speckled with purple and have fringed white crests. Although they do not last long, the blooms are produced in profusion over a period of weeks, and the foliage sprouting at the base of the plant is wide and light green. Height: to 90 cm (36 in.). Bloom: June.

Iris tectorum Maximowicz 1871
Japan, central and southwestern China

The flowers are deep blue-lilac with ruffled, broad petals, white crests, and brownish-purple flecks. The rhizomes are fat, while the broad leaves

Iris japonica 'Bourne Graceful'   Iris milesii

Iris japonica 'Fairyland'

Iris japonica 'Purple Heart'   Iris tectorum

Iris tectorum 'Burma Form'

Iris tenuis

Iris wattii 'Sylvia'

Iris tenuis S. Watson 1881

Oregon (United States)

Once listed in the series *Californiacea*, this species was transferred in 1959 by Lee W. Lenz into the section *Lophiris*. The white flowers have barely noticeable crests, and the pale green leaves are very narrow. This iris is not widely grown as a garden plant, but I was lucky enough to see it blooming one April in Oregon. It grows only in one small region of northern Oregon, where it is endemic along the Clackamas River in Clackamas County, not far from Mount Hood. It can be found growing in cool shady spots, among dense undergrowth where it forms large colonies. In the garden it requires a slightly acid, humus-rich, well-drained soil, in a shady position. Height: 30 cm (12 in.). Bloom: late April and May.

Iris wattii Baker 1886

Assam, southwestern China

This large plant produces upright bamboo-like stems, which are branched all the way up. It has lavender-blue flowers with ruffled falls and white centres that are dotted with orange and lavender spots. The evergreen leaves are heavily ribbed. This species was named after George Watt, who found the plant growing on the summit of a hill in eastern India. However, the form most sold today is one collected by the Englishman Major Lawrence Johnson in Yunnan, China. The species is not hardy in northern climates and therefore should be grown in a greenhouse. Height: 2 m (6 ft.). Bloom: April.

Iris wattii 'Sylvia'

Taller than *Iris wattii*, this cultivar produces an abundance of pale blue-violet flowers. It is thought to be a clone of *I. wattii*, probably collected

are ribbed and soft green. This species was introduced into Europe from Japan during the early nineteenth century, where it could be seen growing on the thatched roofs of houses. For that reason, it is often called the Japanese roof iris. In China it is cultivated extensively and simply known as 'the iris', and in the wild it can be seen growing along roadsides and on steep hillsides. A white form is also available.

Iris tectorum can be grown in full sun or partial shade in a well-drained soil. As it is vigorous, it needs to be divided every three or four years. It is also suitable for growing in a large pot, but it will need to be repotted frequently. Height: 40 cm (16 in.). Bloom: May.

Iris tectorum 'Burma Form'

I saw this iris growing under trees in southwestern Australia. It produces broad swathes of mid-green, upright leaves with dark violet flowers that are flecked and veined with purple and have white crests. Height: 40 cm (16 in.). Bloom: May.

by Major Lawrence Johnson. It cross-pollinates with other Evansia irises, and hybrids have been raised from crosses with *I. tectorum* and *I. milesii*.

Series *Foetidissimae*

The only member of the series, *Iris foetidissima* is known commonly as gladwyn or gladdon iris, a name that most probably comes from the Latin *gladius*, meaning 'sword' and referring to the leaf shape. A tough plant, this species will grow in alkaline to slightly acid soil, in deep shade to full sun. The soil can be moist or dry, heavy or light in structure. *Iris foetidissima* is particularly useful for growing in shady, dry sites where little else will thrive, although in these conditions the flowers and therefore the seeds may not be produced in abundance. When transplanting these plants, like most beardless irises, it is better not to let the rhizomes dry out. It is unnecessary to cut back the leaves for replanting.

Iris foetidissima Linnaeus 1753
Europe, North Africa
This species is admired more for the upright clumps of long, glossy, deep green leaves than for the flowers. When crushed the leaves smell like cooked meat. The flowers appear, almost without being noticed, during the summer. They are rather insignificant, about 8 cm (3 in.) across, and usually grey-fawn in colour with different-coloured veins. Grey-blue and white flowers are also known. Once the flowers have finished, the seeds start to form. Later in the year the pods open to reveal two rows of pea-sized seeds that remain adhered to the pod for many months, eventually scattering during spring. The seeds are usually brilliant red, but yellow and more rarely white forms are available. Height: 60 cm (24 in.). Bloom: June and July.

Iris foetidissima

Iris foetidissima seeds

Iris foetidissima 'Variegata'

Iris foetidissima 'Variegata'
This handsome, slow-growing clone produces grey-green leaves striped with white and pale cream. The flowers are pale beige-yellow. Height: 60 cm (24 in.). Bloom: June and July.

Series *Ensatae*

Like *Iris foetidissima*, *I. lactea* is the sole member of its series, *Ensatae*. Despite the series name, this iris is unrelated to *I. ensata* or Japanese irises. It is widely grown throughout China, where it is used as an ingredient for an herbal contraceptive and for animal fodder, and its leaf fibres are used in papermaking and for brushes. Three of the many variations have been named: *I. lactea* var. *lactea* has white flowers; *I. lactea* var. *chinesis* grows in Korea, Russia, and India as well; and *I. lactea* var. *chrysantha* has yellow flowers.

A tolerant plant, *Iris lactea* will grow in most types of soil including ones that are likely to dry out during the summer. It also tolerates salty areas and can be used as a soil improver.

Iris lactea var. *chinensis*

Iris lactea Pallas 1776
China
The flowers of this species range from pale blue to violet, and they are decorated with delicate veins. The upright leaves are usually soft green. Height: 30 cm (12 in.) tall. Bloom: May to August.

Rocky Mountain Iris
Series *Longipetalae*

Confusion surrounds *Iris missouriensis* and *I. longipetala*, both of which have been included in series *Longipetalae* in the past. The Species Group of the British Iris Society now lists only *I. missouriensis*, stating that the two species are one. As I am not a botanist, I shall describe both species, treating *I. longipetala* as a form or variation of *I. missouriensis*.

Iris missouriensis Nuttall 1834
Iris longipetala Herbert 1862
Western North America
The form originally known as *Iris longipetala* grows on the coastal hills of California. It has slender flowers with drooping white falls that are finely speckled with violet and upright, flaring, violet standards. One of

its parents could be *I. douglasiana*, the other *I. missouriensis*. More variable than *I. longipetala*, *I. missouriensis* is very similar in shape. In colour it ranges from pale blue to deep lavender. The veined falls have yellow signals. The flowers are carried on strong stems above long, slender, dark grey-green leaves that are semi-evergreen. *Iris missouriensis* is less evergreen than *I. longipetala*. It can be found growing from British Columbia to Mexico in damp meadows, along streams, and in forests. Although damp, the soil in these areas dries out during flowering time. The plant will grow in sun or partial shade and is sometimes known as Missouri iris. Height: 60 cm (2 ft.). Bloom: May to June.

Series *Tripetalae*

In the wild, *Iris setosa* is the most widely distributed iris species of all. It can be found growing across two continents in many different habitats, ranging from riverbanks to peat bogs, from moist meadows to light woodland. *Iris setosa* will adapt to a wide range of conditions with the exception of heavy clay soils that tend to dry during the summer. Because of its wide distribution, *I. setosa* is very variable. It will also hybridize with Siberian and Californian irises.

Iris setosa Pallas 1820
Newfoundland to Ontario and Maine, Alaska west to eastern Siberia, northeastern China and Japan
The flowers range from blue-purple to red-purple. They have round falls and short standards, and the hafts are usually yellowish white with purple veining. The broad, arching leaves tend to be purple at the base and grow into a thick clump. Most forms produce branched flower stems, but the smaller types have a singular

Iris setosa

Iris setosa

stem. Height: to 45 cm (18 in.) typically, but can reach 80 cm (32 in.). Bloom: June to August.

Winter Flowering Iris
Series *Unguiculares*

Once commonly referred to as *Iris stylosa*, *I. unguicularis* is now named from the Latin word for 'narrow fingernail' or 'claw', referring to the narrow base of the petal. The flowers are scented and can be found in many forms, blooming at any time from late October until February. If cut

Iris ruthenica Ker-Gawler 1808

Eastern Europe, Russia, Mongolia, Northern China

The violet flowers are fragrant, with slender, upright standards and white falls that are heavily marked with violet veins. Over these sit long violet style arms. The plant forms a tufted clump of grassy, bright green leaves. Height: 30 cm (12 in.). Bloom: May and June.

Subgenus *Nepalensis*

Iris decora (syn. *I. nepalensis*), the most frequently grown member of its subgenus, originates from a near-monsoon climate, in open pastures and forest clearings. In the garden it requires a site that becomes dry for at least six months, then gets water for the six months of the growing season. For this reason, *I. decora* is best grown in the controlled confinement of a bulb frame. As it is difficult to transplant, this plant is probably best raised from seed.

Iris decora Wallich 1832

Western central Himalayas into Yunnan (China)

This species produces rather flat, lightly scented, pale lavender-blue flowers with standards that flop down between the veined falls that are marked with yellow signals. The leaves are ribbed, and the roots, which are quite different from those of most irises, resemble the roots of *Hemerocallis*. Height: 60 cm (24 in.). Bloom: late June.

CHAPTER 16

Interspecies Hybrids

NATURE WILL CREATE its own hybrids, providing the plants are similar in makeup and grow close enough to one another to cross-pollinate. Man, being a curious creature has attempted to replicate this. During the late nineteenth century Sir Michael Foster carried out some of the earliest known crosses between different kinds of iris species. Very few of these were introduced, and all have since disappeared. Amos Perry, working from around 1910, followed Foster and was the first to give these various hybrids names that contained a combination of the two parent species. For instance, crosses between *Iris bulleyana* and *I. chrysographes* he named Bulleygraphes; *I. chrysographes* and *I. sibirica* he called Chrysobirica; and *I. chrysographes* and *I. douglasiana* he called Chrysodoug. From this latter cross he raised 'Margot Holmes' which won the first Dykes Medal in 1927. These were crosses between beardless irises. It is rare for a beardless iris to cross with a bearded iris.

Hybrids Between *Iris versicolor* and Other Members of Series *Laevigatae*

Crosses between members of the series *Laevigatae* are easy to grow. Although the species grow in moist soils in the wild, they establish well in most kinds of soil, including those that become dry in the summer. Their hybrids produce lavish amounts of foliage and graceful flower stems which make them ideal for edging ponds, wilder areas, or large borders.

Iris 'Berlin Tiger' (T. Tamberg 1988)
This hybrid is a more veined version of *Iris* 'Holden Clough' and *I.* 'Roy Davison'. The yellow flowers have falls that are patterned with brown lines. The blooms are borne on long, well-branched arching stems just above a thick clump of broad, deep green leaves. Height: 90 cm (36 in.). Bloom: June into early July. Parentage: a seedling of 'Holden Clough'.

Iris 'Berlin Tiger'

Iris 'Dark Aura' (J. Hewitt 1986)
The magenta-purple flower has triangular-shaped yellow signals with cream edges that are veined with magenta. The velvety falls have broad blades, the standards flare out, and the style arms are a soft rose-violet. The flowers are carried on black stems. The leaves are deep beet-red during the spring, a colour that remains throughout the year at the leaf base. Height: 107 cm (43 in.). Bloom: June and July. Parentage: *I. virginica* and *I. versicolor*.

Iris 'Enfant Prodige' (T. Huber 1996)
The flowers have lilac standards, white style arms, and violet-blue falls with deep yellow signals surrounded by deep violet halos. A long-flowering variety, this plant is technically known as a versata. Height: 110 cm (44 in.). Bloom: June. Parentage: *I. versicolor*, another versata named 'Oriental Touch' (Huber 1993), and *I. ensata*.

Iris 'Fourfold Blue' (T. Tamberg 1997)
Medium-blue flowers are borne on long stems above a clump of broad, deep green leaves. Height: to around 89 cm (35½ in.). Bloom: late June. Parentage: *I. versicolor* 'Mint Frost' (B. Warburton 1982) and a white *I. laevigata*.

Iris 'Holden Clough' (D. Patton 1971)
This very vigorous plant will grow in moist to dry soils. The flowers are yellow, veined with purple, and resemble *Iris pseudacorus*. Height: to around 66 cm (26½ in.). Bloom: late June. Parentage: When Sydney Linnegar registered this cultivar he commented that in form it resembled *I. pseudacorus* and that it was a cross between *I. chrysographes* and *I. pseudacorus*. Others, however, have said that it could be a cross between *I. pseudacorus* and *I. versicolor*, *I. ensata* or, since it tends to be evergreen, *I. foetidissima*.

Iris 'Dark Aura'. Photo by Jennifer Hewitt.

Iris 'Holden Clough'

Iris 'Enfant Prodige'

Iris ×*robusta* 'Gerald Darby'

Iris 'Fourfold Blue'

Iris ×*robusta* 'Gerald Darby' (Coe-Darby 1968)

The slender, violet-blue flowers are carried on long red-tinted stems that emerge from a vigorous clump of broad, deep green leaves. The leaves are washed with purple at the base. This variety was introduced after Gerald Darby's death and registered by Coe as having Siberian type flowers and the growth of the Louisiana iris, *Iris brevicaulis*. The plant has since been named *I.* ×*robusta*, but the older name continues to be used by most nurseries. Height: 76 cm (30½ in.). Bloom: June. Parentage: *I. virginica* × *I. versicolor*.

Iris 'Roy Davidson' (B. Hager 1987)

The bright yellow flowers are covered with a network of brown veins. The standards are reduced to small petals on either side of the style arms. The blooms are borne on slender, branched stems above a large bushy clump of long, lax, strappy, mid-green leaves similar to those of *Iris* 'Holden Clough'. If used in hybridizing *I.* 'Roy Davidson' will produce white seedlings. Height: to 86 cm (34½ in.). Bloom: June. Parentage: a seedling of 'Holden Clough'.

Hybrids Between *Iris pseudacorus* and *I. ensata*

For years hybridizers have tried to raise a yellow-flowered ensata iris. So far this has proved impossible. The Japanese hybridizer Mr Osugi began crossing the yellow water iris, *Iris pseudacorus*, with *I. ensata* to introduce the yellow element. These crosses were known as Pseudata hybrids, and Osugi's first introduction was 'Aichi-no-Kagayaki' in 1962. This plant was imported into the United States in 1977 and renamed *I. kaempferi* 'Golden Queen', a name already in existence.

Since then, a number of *Iris pseudacorus* and *I. ensata* crosses have been introduced. Some of the most noteworthy are from Hiroshi Shimizu in Japan. Shimizu, who began working in 1993, has raised a strain of irises he calls 'Eye Shadow' irises. The flowers have a dark halo around the signal, which bleeds into the falls, creating an eyelash effect.

The story of 'Eye Shadow' irises is an interesting one. Shimizu grew *Iris pseudacorus* from seed obtained from the British Iris Society and Species Iris Group of North America (SIGNA). He then mixed the pollen from several Japanese iris cultivars

and placed it on a 100 different *I. pseudacorus* clones. From the pseudacorus seedlings he selected one, which he named 'Gubijin'. This proved to be a very fertile pod parent, readily setting seed when crossed with *I. ensata* cultivars. When crossed with the white form of *I. ensata*, it produced seedlings with a similar blue halo around the yellow signal. These irises are muted in colour with slimmer petals similar to *I. pseudacorus* and mid-green leaves that form good thick clumps. In common with many early Pseudata hybrids these are sometimes tinged with yellow. They all bloom late in the iris season, from late June to late July.

These new cultivars are, at the time of writing, currently been trialled in Maryland, United States, at Carol Warner's nursery. Carol says that the plants raised by Mr Shimizu are taller, produce more flowers on well-branched stems, and have greener foliage than the earlier pseudata hybrids. Because I feel they have a great future, I have included a few cultivars to tempt the reader.

Iris 'Pixie Won' (Copeland 1997)

Readily available, this hybrid produces violet flowers with large round purple halos around its yellow sig-

Iris 'Roy Davidson'

Iris 'Pixie Won'

nals. The petals are veined with purple, and the style arms are cream coloured. The flowers are not produced profusely. Height: 60 cm (24 in.). Bloom: late June to July. Parentage: *I. pseudacorus* white seedling × *I. ensata* double purple seedling.

Iris 'Kinshikou' (H. Shimizu 2004 by Draycott Gardens)

At first the flowers appear to be peach, but on closer inspection the background colour of the flowers is yellow and heavily washed with rose-pink. On the falls sit deep yellow signals that are surrounded by rich dark wine markings that form eyelashes. The style arms and standards are soft yellow. The name of this plant means 'golden monkey'. Height: 96 cm (36-in.). Bloom: late June.

Iris 'Sarugaku' (H. Shimizu not yet registered)

Height: not recorded. Bloom: late June.

Iris 'Shirabyoshi' (H. Shimizu not yet registered)

The flowers are creamy white with large purple eyelash-like markings on the falls. Height: 80 cm (32 in). Bloom: late June.

Iris 'Shiunryu'

The flowers are deep purple with deep purple eyelash-like signals rimmed by purple. Height: not recorded. Bloom: late June.

Iris 'Kinshikou'

Iris 'Shiunryu'

Iris 'Sarugamku'

Iris 'Berlin Chrytosa'

Iris 'Shirabyoshi'

Iris 'Northern Pink'

Iris 'Sunny Red Wine'

Hybrids Between Series *Laevigatae* and Other Irises

Some of these crosses are trickier to establish in the garden than crosses between members of the series *Laevigatae*. Those that look more like *Iris setosa* than *I. chrysographes* are easier to grow. The hybrids that resemble *I. chrysographes* require a lime-free soil that remains moist for much of the year.

Iris **'Berlin Chrytosa'** (T. Tamberg 1993)
The mid violet-blue flowers have wide yellow veins that extend halfway down the falls. The standards and style arms are similar in height. The hybrid produces a low growing clump of leaves and slender stems that branch halfway up. This iris is known as a Chrytosa. Height: 127 cm (51 in.). Bloom: June. Parentage: 'Berliner Reisen' × *I. setosa*

Iris **'Northern Pink'** (T. Tamberg 1995)
Very similar to Siberian irises, this Sibtosa has short soft pink standards

and style arms of a similar height. The falls are pink-violet with golden signals surrounded by a deep pink halo. The spathes are tipped with red-brown. I grow this easy iris in a sunny position with moist soil. Height: 80 cm (32 in.). Bloom: June. Parentage: 'Pink Haze' × a lavender *I. setosa*.

Iris **'Sunny Red Wine'** (T. Tamberg 1998)
This tall iris produces soft wine-red flowers that look like a Californian iris. The flowers have ruffled edges that are rimmed a softer colour and buff-pink style arms. The falls are patterned in the centre with gold veins, and the flowers are carried on long stems that emerge from a clump of deep green foliage. A tough plant, I grow it in a well-drained, but heavy soil in full sun; in this position it grows taller than 36 cm (14½ n.). Height: 36 cm (14½.). Bloom: June. Parentage: includes a number of Californian irises and Siberian irises, some of which are tetraploids.

PART THREE BULBOUS IRISES

Bulbous irises can be divided into three sections: the small border or rockery types that provide colour from late winter to the middle of spring; the larger, summer-flowering ones, which have brilliant colours and are used extensively as cut flowers; and the Juno irises, or Junos as they are affectionately called, containing some of the loveliest members of the genus. Most Junos can be difficult to grow in more northerly gardens, while others, despite being easy, are less well known than the other bulbous irises. Botanists have argued about these three groups for decades. Some authorities feel that bulbous irises should be removed from the genus *Iris*; others include them. Junos in particular are usually treated separately from the other bulbous irises, but because their cultural requirements are similar and because they arise from bulbs, I feel it is right to include them here.

Iris danfordiae

CHAPTER 17

Reticulata Irises
Subgenus *Hermodactyloides*

LISTED UNDER THE DINOSAUR-LIKE sounding subgenus named *Hermodactyloides*, these small bulbous irises, usually just called Reticulata irises, are the earliest to flower. The name *reticulata* refers to the netted outer layer of the shiny bulb.

Most bulbous irises grow at high attitudes from mid Turkey to Iran and into central Asia and northwards from Israel into Russian Caucasus. The areas they grow in receive high rainfall during the spring and almost none during the summer. At this time the leaves die back and the bulb goes dormant. The plants flower around the same time as crocuses, producing the leaves before the blooms.

Although all reticulatas are lovely in gardens, only the hardier species can be grown in open borders or rockeries. As they disappear entirely after flowering it is a good idea to mark where they have been planted. They can also be grown in semi-wild areas and lightly wooded slopes. The types that take readily to garden cultivation are *Iris histrioides*, *I. reticulata*, *I. winogradowii*, and their hybrids. The other species, particularly the very early flowering ones, may be better in a raised bed, a bulb frame, or an alpine house.

Cultivation

Reticulata irises like a sunny spot with a light soil that drains well particularly during the summer. They dislike acid soils or those that stay wet during the year. The bulbs should be planted between 5 and 8 cm (2–3 in.) deep during the autumn. They can be planted in containers and brought indoors, but they resent being forced into flower. Each bulb will only produce one bloom, so it is preferable to plant groups of perhaps five or seven bulbs so they will make a colourful display. The bulbs should be spaced around 10 cm (4 in.) apart.

When it comes to feeding bulbous irises, they are like bearded irises, renewing their roots each year and therefore best fed in spring when the roots are growing. High-potash granular fertilizer, blood, and bone meal are suitable or liquid feed can be used. The time to lift and split bulbous irises is when the foliage dies back about a month after the blooms have finished. The dormant bulbs can be stored in a dry place until they are replanted. *Iris winogradowii* is an exception to this rule and should not be allowed to dry out before being planted.

The Sections

Over the years the bulbous irises have been botanically shifted around into different sections and subgenera. I suspect that in the years to come we will find them moved around again. At present the Species Group of the British Iris Society has divided subgenus *Hermodactyloides* into four sections. Section *Hermodactyloides* has produced many of the hybrids we know today and will hybridize with the species from section *Micropogon* but not the other two sections.

Section *Brevituba*: Bulbs with sharp basal leaf fibres and long flower stems. Found in Turkey. Includes *Iris pamphylica*.

Section *Monolepis*: Plants with channelled leaves. Found in the former Soviet Union and in central Asia. Includes *Iris kolpakowskiana*, *I. winkleri*.

Section *Hermodactyloides*: Classic reticulatas with, when sectioned, square leaves. Found in Turkey, Iraq, Iran, Lebanon, Syria, Israel, and Jordan. Includes *Iris bakeriana*, *I. histrio*, *I. histrioides*, *I. reticulata*, and *I. vartanii*.

Section *Micropogon*: Plants with

channelled leaves. Found in eastern Turkey. Includes one species only, namely, *Iris danfordiae*.

RETICULATA IRIS SPECIES

Iris bakeriana M. Foster 1889
Southeastern Turkey, northeastern Iraq, western Iran
This early flowering species produces flowers with light blue standards and violet falls that are marked with white. It grows in mountainous areas where the soil is heavy and stony, but despite this the species can be tender and might be better grown in a bulb frame or alpine house. Height: 8–15 cm (3–6 in.). Bloom: early March to late April.

Iris danfordiae Baker 1876
Eastern Turkey
This species is one of only two yellow reticulatas and is sometimes known as the Danford iris. The bright yellow, honey-scented flowers have small lime-green dots on the falls and large, feathered style arms that are as tall as the standards. This plant is not easy to keep perennial, as the small bulbs, once they have bloomed, tend to break up into even smaller bulbils. These do not always re-emerge the following year. Therefore *Iris danfordiae* is better treated as an annual, at best a biennial. The clone found in cultivation is larger than those in the wild. Height: 7 cm (3 in.). Bloom: February and March.

Iris histrio Reichenbach 1872
Lebanon, Israel, Syria, southern Turkey
The large soft blue flowers have falls with a large white spot on which sits a yellow ridge and deep blue blotches. There are three forms: the type, **subsp. *histrio*,** has fewer blotches but is rare in cultivation; **subsp. *aintabensis*,** has deeper-coloured flowers with darker blotches; and **subsp. *atropurpurea*** produces purple flowers with no markings. Generally this species is not considered hardy in Britain, although it has been known to grow outside in southern England. Therefore in colder, wetter areas the species is probably best in an alpine frame. Height: 10–15 cm (3–6 in.). Bloom: late January to March.

Iris histrioides G. F. Wilson 1893
Northern Turkey
This hardy species produces large blue flowers. The falls are decorated with a central white zone that is covered with a network of black veins. *Iris histrioides* 'Major' has no veining. The leaves emerge with the flowers, not before as with other reticulatas. The species and cultivar like humus-rich, limy soil. Height: 8–15 cm (3–6 in.). Bloom: March to April.

Iris reticulata Bieberstein 1808
Turkey, northeastern Iraq, northern and western Iran, former Soviet Union, Caucasus
The violet-scented flower comes in a range of blues, violets, and purple, all with an orange or yellow ridge on the falls. The form usually grown in cultivation has deep violet-purple flowers with short white stripes along side orange ridges. The leaves reach 30 cm (12 in.). This species is also known as netted or reticulated iris. Height: 5 cm (2 in.). Bloom: March to late May.

Iris winogradowii Fomin 1914
Former Soviet Union, western Caucasus
First grown in Britain around 1923, *Iris winogradowii* is slow to increase and expensive to buy. It is a very beautiful plant, named after P. Z. Winogradow-Nikitin, who first described it. The flowers are large, soft yellow with a golden ridge on the rounded falls that are also dotted with green. The style arms are feathered, upright, and as large as the standards. The flower is said to be scented, but I defy anyone to kneel low enough to smell it. The leaves, which emerge after flowering, grow to around 30 cm (12 in.). The plant is not difficult to grow provided the soil is moist during the growing season and the bulbs do not dry out after lifting. Height: 5 cm (2 in.). Bloom: April and May.

Iris reticulata. Photo by Sydney Linnegar.

Iris winogradowii

Iris 'Pauline'

Iris 'Purple Gem'

Iris 'Springtime'

Iris 'Pauline' (Hoog)

The flower has slim petals, wavy edges, soft purple standards, and velvety, black-purple falls that are decorated with a large uneven white patch. Parentage: *I. reticulata* × *I. bakeriana*.

Iris 'Purple Gem'

Similar to *Iris* 'Pauline' but with shorter falls, slimmer standards, and slightly bluer markings on the falls.

Iris 'Springtime' (Hoog)

The flowers have very slender petals, are slightly scented, and sit within sparsely produced tall leaves. The falls are deep blue-purple, the standards deep lilac. E. B. Anderson, writing in 1963, calls this *Iris* 'Spring Time'. Parentage: *I. reticulata* × *I. bakeriana*. Blooms: early spring (usually February).

CHAPTER 18

Dutch, Spanish, and English Irises
Subgenus *Xiphium*

THE TALL AND SLENDER IRISES of subgenus *Xiphium* are divided into three groups, each known by the common names of Dutch, English, and Spanish irises. All produce flowers on tall stems, blooms that last for many days, and narrow, deeply channelled leaves. The leaves of the Dutch and the Spanish irises emerge in autumn from pear-shaped bulbs that are covered with papery tunics, while the leaves of English irises emerge in spring from naked bulbs. The English irises are native to the Pyrenees, where they grow in marshy areas fed by the water from melting snow. Dutch irises are entirely of cultivated origin. All other Xiphium irises grow wild in southern Europe and countries around the Mediterranean, in areas that are hot and dry with very well drained soil. These are not hardy in northern Europe.

Xiphium Iris Species

Iris boissieri Henriques 1885
Northern Portugal, Spain
This species is difficult to grow in cultivation. It produces single deep purple flowers with a yellow flash on the falls. Height: 40 cm (16 in.). Bloom: May and June.

Iris filifolia Boissier 1842
Southwestern Spain, Gibraltar, Morocco, Tangier
This tender species produces red-purple flowers with orange spots on the falls. Height: 45 cm (18 in.). Bloom: June.

Iris juncea Poiret 1789
Southwestern Spain, Sicily, North Africa
This scented species has yellow flowers ranging from lemon to sulphur yellow. It comes from hot dry areas around the Mediterranean and therefore is not hardy in northern European countries. Height: 30 cm (12 in.). Bloom: June.

Iris latifolia P. Miller 1768
Northwestern Spain, Pyrenees
The common name for this plant, which was once known as *Iris xiphioides*, is English iris. In the wild it produces flowers that are mainly

Iris latifolia. Photo by Sydney Linnegar.

violet-blue. Sometimes it will produce white, violet, or purple blooms, but never yellow. However, the falls are decorated with a yellow spot. Height: 50 cm (20 in.). Bloom: June and July.

Iris serotina Willkomm 1861
Southeastern Spain

This blue-violet flowering species is better grown in a bulb frame. The petals are veined with a deeper colour, and the falls are marked with a yellow patch. Height: 60 cm (24 in.). Bloom: August.

Iris tingitana Boissier & Reuter 1853
North Africa

This tender species is better grown either in a bulb frame or lifted and stored like dahlias. It produces flowers in various shades of blue. Height: 60 cm (24 in.). Bloom: February and May.

Iris xiphium Linnaeus 1753
Spain, southwestern France, southern Italy, Portugal, Morocco, Algeria, Tunisia

Iris xiphium, or Spanish iris, is a variable species. The flowers range from white to yellow, blue, and violet. Some are self-coloured; others have softer-coloured standards, while others often have a yellow spot on the falls. Height: 60 cm (24 in.). Bloom: April and May.

English Iris Hybrids & Their Cultivation

The common name 'English iris' is misleading. It was adopted after a Dutchman saw certain irises in gardens around the seaport of Bristol in England. He assumed the plants to be native, when in fact they had been imported, possibly by sailors returning from trips abroad. At any rate, the plants thrived in the warm, damp climate of southwestern England.

The flowers of English irises, compared with Dutch or Spanish irises, are gentler in colour, with large round-ended falls that are decorated with a long sword-like flash. During the nineteenth century as many as 76 different cultivars were listed. Sadly, these have now dwindled so much that today the *RHS Plant Finder* lists only a handful of varieties: '**King of the Blues**', a dark blue-flowered form with dark speckling; '**Mont Blanc**', an old pure white form; and '**Queen of the Blues**', a blue form.

English irises like a cool, moist, humus-rich soil that is neutral or slightly acid. Unlike Dutch and Spanish irises, English irises do not mind semi-shade, and they will eventually grow into large clumps. The bulbs should be planted between September and October about 13 cm (5 in.) deep and about 30 cm (12 in.) apart. In the right conditions they can be left in the same location, undivided, for up to five years, and therefore they are an excellent border plant. If a clump becomes too large and overcrowded, it should be lifted and divided after the leaves have withered and the bulbs become dormant.

Dutch & Spanish Iris Hybrids & Their Cultivation

Dutch and Spanish irises have erect, rigid stems and flowers with firm, slender petals. The flowers can be as large as 13 cm (5 in.) across and vary in colour from white through yellow to grey-blue. There are no orange or red varieties. In height these irises can range from 45 to 90 cm (18–36 in.) tall, and outdoors in the garden they will bloom from April to June. Dutch irises will flower around two weeks before Spanish irises.

Spanish irises are selections of *Iris xiphium*. Although they are not hardy in northern European gardens, the

English horticulturalist Phillip Miller, writing in 1732, listed 16 varieties and stated that many more were coming onto the market each year. These were commonly grown for the cut flower market until the mid 1950s when they were replaced by the Dutch iris. Interestingly, however, Dutch irises are not mentioned in books on irises until the mid 1940s.

It is unclear which irises were used to raise the first Dutch irises. They certainly include the hardiest of the Xiphium species and probably selected varieties of Spanish irises. Two Dutch brothers named Hoog were the first to hybridize them. Working for van Tubergen nursery in Holland, their crosses produced plants with larger flowers, in a wider range of colours. Named Dutch irises, these were introduced during the early twentieth century. Because they are easy to force under glass and the flowers last for weeks in a vase, Dutch irises are now widely grown for the very profitable cut flower market; however, they also make excellent garden plants, particularly when grown in clumps. Spanish hybrids are far less available. In fact the current *RHS Plant Finder* does not list one variety. The plants described in this chapter are all Dutch irises.

Dutch irises require a warm, light, and well-drained soil that is preferably alkaline. In the summer, in common with all bulbous irises, their leaves die back and the bulbs become dormant. Dutch iris bulbs should be planted in September or October about 13 cm (5 in.) deep and spaced 10–15 cm (4–6 in.) apart. In colder, more northerly areas they may need to be lifted and stored over the winter. Lift them after the leaves have withered, storing the bulbs in a cool, dry place such as a box of dry sand. Replant the bulbs the following autumn.

Iris 'Apollo'

Iris 'Bronze Beauty'

Iris 'Blue Diamond'

Iris 'Bronze Queen'

Iris **'Apollo'**

This bicolour has white standards and yellow falls with deeper yellow spots. The flowers become bluer with age. The long, channelled leaves are shiny on the inside and arch elegantly. It is one of the earliest to bloom. Height: 90 cm (36 in.).

Iris **'Blue Diamond'**

The flowers are royal-blue with bright yellow flares on the falls. Height: 75 cm (30 in.).

Iris **'Bronze Beauty'**

This handsome variety has violet standards washed around the edges with bronze . The falls are also bronze and are highlighted with orange flares. Height: 45 cm (18 in.).

Iris **'Bronze Queen'**

This bicolour has bronze-blue standards. The bronze falls are painted with an orange spot. Height: 60 cm (24 in.).

Iris 'Casa Blanca'

The pure white flowers have very up-right standards and a V-shaped signal on the large, ounded falls. Height: 60 cm (24 in.).

Iris 'Frans Hals'

This variety produces open, royal-blue flowers with long falls and small round standards. Large golden signals decorate the falls. Height: 91 cm (36½ in.).

Iris 'Golden Beauty'

The pure golden yellow flower has short petals. Height: 91 cm (36½ in.).

Iris 'Golden Emperor'

The bright yellow flowers have up-right, slender standards and small, round falls marked with a deeper colour. The edges curl under themselves. Height: 91 cm (36½ in.).

Iris 'Hildegarde'

The soft blue flower has small yellow signals and tightly ruffled edges. Height: 75 cm (30 in.).

Iris 'Ideal'

The colour of this pure sky-blue flower veers towards violet. It has yellow signals on the round falls and

Iris 'Frans Hals'

Iris 'Golden Emperor'

Iris 'Golden Beauty'

Iris 'Casa Blanca'

Iris 'Hildegarde'

Iris 'Ideal'

long, round-topped standards. This is a sport of Iris 'Wedgwood', which is the blue form of I. 'White Wedgwood'. Height: 75 cm (30 in.).

Iris 'Purple Sensation'
This deep purple-blue flower has falls with yellow signals. Height: 30–60 cm (12–24 in.).

Iris 'Royal Yellow'
This neat, round flower is entirely yellow, but the yellow flashes are just visible on the falls. Height: 75 cm (30 cm).

Iris 'Sapphire Beauty'
The mid-blue falls carry broad yellow flares and deep blue standards. The style arms are ruffled around the edges. Height: 75 cm (30 in.).

Iris 'Silver Beauty'
The flowers have soft blue standards and blue-white falls decorated with yellow signals. The edges of the petals are tightly ruffled. Height: 75 cm (30 in.).

Iris 'Purple Sensation'

Iris 'Sapphire Beauty'

Iris 'Royal Yellow'

Iris 'Silver Beauty'

sand bed and covered with a good layer of grit to keep lichen and moss at bay, as well as aid water drainage around the bulb.

Watering is the key to success. In their natural state Junos are mountain dwellers and any water they receive comes from melting snow that passes around the bulb on its way down the slopes. Thus it is essential in cultivation that the base of the plant and the leaves do not get watered while they are growing, as this will cause the bulb to rot. Once planted, the dormant bulb should be watered only once and then just occasionally during the winter until it bursts into leaf the following spring. It should then be watered regularly until after flowering, a time when the leaves die back. Once the leaves have withered, do not water the plant again until early autumn.

IN THE GARDEN

It is possible to grow some Juno species outdoors in the garden. These include *Iris bucharica*, *I. cycloglossa*, *I. graeberiana*, and *I. magnifica*. Of these I have eventually successfully grown only *I. bucharica*. My first experience was in a sandy soil, but the plant disappeared after a few seasons. Later I planted another specimen in a very well drained, heavier, deprived soil that was full of brick rubble. In this situation it thrives with great vigour. Generally Junos require a warm spot with excellent drainage, perhaps between the warmed rocks of a rockery. Junos are also ideal subjects for containers, especially those made from frost-resistant terracotta, where they will live outside, undisturbed for a number of years.

Maintenance

Regular cleaning and repotting of bulbs grown in pots is essential. Failure to do this can lead to losses. Bulbs grown outside need dividing every three to five years, or they will either rot or fade away. To do this, lift the clump once the leaves have withered and split it using a knife to separate the bulbs. Replant the bulbs, taking care not to damage the roots, in new soil. A low-nitrogen, slow-release fertilizer may be added during the growing season. To prevent fungal diseases, it is necessary to remove the wilted flowers. Flowering times in the descriptions that follow indicate when a species blooms in the wild. In Britain, these species can be expected to bloom up to a month earlier.

JUNO IRIS SPECIES & THEIR COLLECTED FORMS

Iris aitchisonii Baker 1884
Pakistan, eastern Afghanistan
This species is found on moist, grassy slopes. Its flowers are either yellow or violet, or a combination of both. The form normally found in cultivation has yellow flowers. The flower stems are slender and branched. Height: up to 45 cm (18 in.). Bloom: March to April.

Iris aucheri Baker 1877
Southeastern Turkey, northern Syria, northern Iraq, western Iran
The flowers are usually pale blue with a yellow flash on the falls and spreading standards. Occasionally they can be found in any tone ranging from deep blue to violet or even white. Some outstanding named selections were raised from seed collected near Leylek Station in Turkey. These can be grown in a well-drained, sunny spot in the garden as well as an alpine house or bulb frame. Height: 35 cm (14 in.). Bloom: March to April.

Iris aitchisonii

Iris 'Leylek Ice'

Iris 'Leylek Purple'

Iris bucharica in a pot

Iris aucheri 'Leylek Ice'
This sweetly scented flower has transparent, white petals that are flushed with blue. The falls are decorated with yellow crests and a flush of blue. Height: 45 cm (18 in.). Bloom: March to April.

Iris aucheri 'Leylek Purple'
This very large ruffled flower is purple-blue with a white crest. Height: 45 cm (18 in.). Bloom: March to April.

Iris bucharica M. Foster 1902
Northeastern Afghanistan
One of the easiest Junos to grow and to purchase, this species produces flowers with lemon standards and bright yellow falls. Each flower has a raised ridge down the centre of the falls, and the standards droop down like little flaps between the standards. The blooms emerge from each light green shiny leaf. Height: 30 cm (12 in.). Bloom: April and May.

Iris cycloglossa Wendelbo 1958
Western Afghanistan
The soft blue flowers, coloured similarly to the bearded species *Iris pallida*, have distinctive white spots on the falls. Between these are seated flaring, broad, yellow standards. Each stem has three buds. The plant thrives outside. Height: 45 cm (18 in.). Bloom: May.

Iris fosteriana Aitchison & Baker 1888
Northwestern Afghanistan, northeastern Iran, former Soviet Union
This rarely cultivated species grows in dry grasslands high in the mountains. It produces translucent lemon flowers with bright lemon standards that dangle between the falls and are heavily flushed with purple. The flower sits within U-shaped, mid-green leaves lined with silver on the back. Height: only 9 cm (4 in.). Bloom: March and April.

Iris graeberiana Van Tubergen ex Sealy 1950
Central Asia
This species has not been seen in the wild since Paul Graeber collected it in central Asia. The Dutch bulb firm of van Tubergen initially distributed its seeds, and different colour forms or hybrids are currently available from specialist growers. It makes an ideal subject for growing in containers outside. The lavender-blue flower has a large white spot on the falls. Height: 40 cm (16 in.). Bloom: April.

Iris bucharica

Iris fosteriana

Iris cycloglossa

Iris graeberiana

Iris magnifica Vvedensky 1935
Central Asia

Together with *Iris bucharica*, this is the species most commonly encountered in cultivation. It is an easy and robust plant to grow in the open garden. The flowers are normally lilac with yellow on the falls around a white crest. White variants are known. Height: 60 cm (24 in.). Bloom: April to May.

Iris maracandica (Vvedensky) Wendelbo 1935
Central Asia

This species is similar in shape and colour but not size to *Iris bucharica*. It has soft yellow flowers, and its leaves are edged with silver. *Iris svetlanae* is also very similar and may be a variant of the same species. *Iris maracandica* is rarely found in cultivation. Height: 15 cm (6 in.). Bloom: March and April.

Iris nicolai Vvedensky 1935
Central Asia

This small species has cream flowers striped with purple and yellow. Various forms have been collected; all are very similar but some are more yellow than others. They have a distinctive peach fragrance. Height: 15 cm (3 in.). Bloom: February to April.

Iris orchioides Carrière 1880
Central Asia

Iris orchioides is similar to *I. bucharica* in many respects and often mistaken for it; however, the petals are a far more translucent, pale yellow, and the falls have distinctive wings on the hafts. This very variable species has many named forms varying from 15 to 30 cm (6–12 in.) tall. Height: 30 cm (12 in.). Bloom: March and May.

Iris magnifica. Photo by Sydney Linnegar.   *Iris nicolai*

Iris maracandica   *Iris orchioides*

Iris nicolai   *Iris pseudocaucasica*

Iris planifolia

Iris rosenbachiana

Iris persica Linnaeus 1753

Southern and southeastern Turkey, northeastern Iraq, Syria

One of the first Junos to be described, this species has been in cultivation for centuries and was listed by Philip Miller in his book of 1732. At that time it was grown indoors, as hyacinths are today, on the top of a glass jar filled with water. Today it is still difficult to buy probably because it is not the easiest Juno to grow. The flowers can be found in muted colours ranging from dull yellow to silver-grey with a yellow flash on each winged fall. Height: 5 cm (2 in.). Bloom: February to April.

Iris 'Sindpers'

Iris planifolia Aschers & Graeber 1906

Crete, Greece, Sicily, Spain, Portugal

The soft lilac-blue flowers have deep blue flushes on the falls, which are veined with yellow. The lightly scented blooms are hidden within the foliage. Known for centuries, this species is the Juno that can be found growing in Europe. Sadly it is not a long-lived plant and needs to be grown in a bulb frame. Height: 8 cm (3 in.). Bloom: early season (sometimes as early as December).

Iris pseudocaucasica Grossheim 1916

Southeastern Turkey, northern Iraq, north and northwestern Iran and Armenia

The wild plant grows in scree and on rocky slopes. The flowers are either pale yellow or pale blue with yellow crests on the falls and large winged standards. Height: 18 cm (7 in.). Bloom: April and June.

Iris rosenbachiana Regel

Central Asia

This species is similar to *Iris nicolai* both in cultural requirements and form. The flower is purple with deeper streaks down the side.

Height: 10 cm (4 in.). Bloom: March and April.

JUNO IRIS HYBRID

Iris 'Sindpers'

A cross between *Iris aucheri* and *I. persica*, this hybrid produces scented, bright sky-blue flowers with ruffled falls, which are deeper in colour along the edges. The deep yellow signals are covered with broken, purple lines. The standards are turquoise in colour. The broad style arms are long enough to cover half the falls. Height: 8 cm (3 in.). Bloom: March to April.

PART FOUR CULTIVATION

As described in previous sections, irises range in size from small to large. There are iris species for cool wet locations, well-drained soils, and shady spots, while others will survive in a hot dry spot; however, as all gardeners are ruled by the seasons, I have chosen to illustrate the growing of irises in the garden seasonally. The suggestions are quite naturally based on my own gardening experience, which is in the damp climate of Britain, but the same principles can be applied to many different climates. Likewise, the information on the relatively few pests and diseases that affect irises applies to all gardens around the world.

Siberian iris with hostas

CHAPTER 20

Growing Irises in the Garden

IRISES SHOULD BE one of the staple plants in any garden. They are versatile, colourful, largely trouble free, easy to grow, and rabbit- and deer-resistant. Having grown irises only in the middle of England, I can only describe each season from an English point of view. I hope that gardeners who live in colder or hotter climates that are largely continental will forgive me for describing irises in the garden this way.

Spring

For many gardeners, spring is the beginning of the gardening year. The days get lighter, the birds begin to court each other with song, and plants begin to stir. The first irises of the season emerge around late January. These are the Reticulata irises. Suddenly without warning they pop out of the soil.

Reticulatas should be planted in groups of at least six near the front of a well-drained border, on a rockery, or in a scree garden, in a position where they can easily be seen. They associate perfectly with other low-growing, early flowering plants such as crocuses, snowdrops (*Galanthus*), and small narcissi such as 'Tête-à-Tête', and they look wonderful poking up through a carpet of *Cyclamen coum*. The earliest Reticulata to flower is *Iris danfordiae*. The last to flower, around mid-March, include *I.* 'Cantab' and *I.* 'Natasha'.

By the time winter turns to spring, the leaves of the smallest bearded irises, the Miniature Dwarf Bearded irises, are beginning to shoot. These bloom around April. The very smallest cultivars are only really suitable for rockeries. In a border, larger plants can swamp them, and in general the soil in these locations is too rich for them to thrive. Reticulatas, the smallest, hardiest Juno irises, and Pacific Coast irises are also suitable for rockeries. All of these can be planted with other alpine plants such as *Aubrieta* and low-growing hardy geraniums.

From midspring until the beginning of summer the choice of irises in flower begins to increase. Standard Dwarf Bearded irises are coming into bloom. These can be placed at the front of a border where they will not be overlooked and where there is less competition from other plants. They can be planted with other early flowering perennials, including lungworts (*Pulmonaria* spp.) and narcissi. My current favourite lungwort, *Pulmonaria* 'Opal', and the late flowering, beautiful white *Narcissus* 'Thalia' look wonderful with soft blue Standard Dwarf Bearded irises. These irises can also be planted next to elephant's ears (*Bergenia* spp.), which come in a wide choice of varieties. All have large handsome evergreen leaves and produce upright stems of large bell-shaped flowers.

By midspring the Pacific Coast irises are beginning to bloom. In Britain these are not always hardy, but, given a humus-rich, acidic soil in a semi-shady, sheltered spot perhaps along the edge of woodland, Pacific Coast irises combine well with other late spring flowering plants such as bishop's mitre (*Epimedium* spp.) and carpeting, low-growing phlox. In Australia, Pacific Coast irises they can be seen in the National Rhododendron Garden growing on a large rockery near the shade of pine trees.

The Junos also begin to bloom in spring. Most of them are tender in Britain; those that will survive outside can be grown in a sheltered, very well drained spot such as on a rock garden or in borders that edge the sides of a house. Most Junos, like Dutch irises, die back and disappear entirely after they have flowered. Therefore, the gardener must either put up with an empty bed or choose carefully the partners that will produce a continuation of colour. Because Junos require a sunny, dry situation in Britain, the choice of companion plants is limited. Baby's breath (*Gypsophila* spp.) would be good, as the flowers bloom in July and cover the soil for weeks; however, they are suitable only for large borders. Rock roses (*Helianthemum* spp.) and thyme (*Thymus* spp.) could be used; they cover the ground and produce flowers later in the season.

Reticulata irises with *Helleborus foetidus*

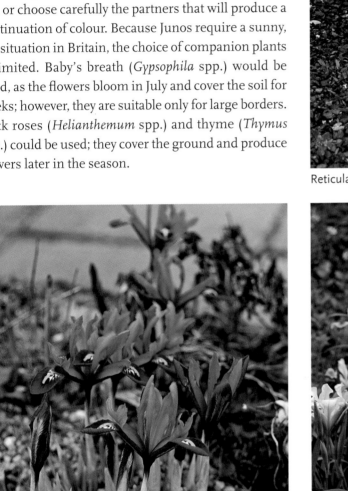

Iris 'Harmony' planted in paving

Pacific Coast irises in a rockery

Summer

Summer is the most important iris flowering season, with June being the peak month for bearded irises. Some of the taller varieties, including many of the Intermediate Bearded irises, will already have started flowering by late spring. Despite what some authorities say, bearded irises are valuable for mixing in borders with other perennials. They add colour, a focal point, and, after blooming, provide form with their leaves.

BEDS OF BEARDED IRISES

A bed planted entirely with bearded irises may be a luxury, but it can be the most effective way to show and cultivate these colourful plants. In larger gardens bearded irises have traditionally been planted in long, rectangular borders. Such borders can be edged by lawn or paving stones and planted with Tall Bearded irises alone. While this certainly makes an impact, providing a focal point to one area of the garden, within three weeks the bed is likely to be a sea of green leaves.

An alternative is to plant a mixture of varieties that flower at different times. In a one-sided bed, Standard

Iris 'China Moon' and *I.* 'World Premier'

Irises planted en masse

Dwarf Bearded irises, which flower around mid-May, can be placed around the edges, with Intermediate Bearded and Border Bearded irises behind them, and finally, at the back, a selection of Tall Bearded irises. In an island bed, the taller plants—Intermediate, Border, and Tall Bearded irises—could be mingled behind an edging of Standard Dwarf Bearded varieties. In both cases, by using a selection of different bearded irises, the iris bed will be in flower for up to six weeks. If re-blooming varieties are included, the bed will relight in late summer and flower well into autumn.

Bearded irises are incredibly diverse in their colours. If you are unsure what colours to choose for a large all-iris border, try to be conservative. Choose safe colours such as blues, white, blacks, pink, lilacs, and purples; or hot colours like yellow, orange, and brown. Brave gardeners may want to choose complementary colours such as orange and blue, purple and yellow, or even black and white. The combinations are endless, but I have found that browns and blues do not look good next to each other and that large blousy modern flowers distract attention away from the blooms of the older (pre-1970) hybrids.

MIXED BORDERS

Most gardens today are too small to have the luxury of planting bearded irises in a border of their own. For a plant collector like myself the idea of a garden dedicated to one genus is simply unthinkable. Therefore, I grow all my irises in the garden with other plants, usually perennials. It is important to leave a lot of space around the irises so that other plants do not shade the rhizomes and prevent them from producing blooms the following season.

Successful planting combinations for mixed borders have included the blue Border Bearded iris 'Blackbeard' with the beautiful early flowering, bright pink peony 'Honor' and columbines (*Aquilegia* spp.). I have planted the brown Tall Bearded iris 'Caliente' behind *Achillea* 'Moonshine' and next to a late summer flowering tickseed (*Coreopsis grandiflora*). In a part of the garden with slim, semi-circular beds, *Iris* 'Conjuration' sits prettily next to *Artemisia* 'Lambrook Mist', *Anchusa* 'Loddon Royalist', and *Penstemon* 'Sour Grapes'. In a similar bed I have *Aster amellus* 'King George' and *Liatris spicata*

with the big, frilly blue iris 'Yaquina Blue'. In wilder garden borders, one of the oldest hybrids available today, *Iris* 'Honorabile', associates perfectly with the yellow tree peony 'Souvenir de Maxime Cornu' and the silver foliage of *Stachys byzantina* 'Big Ears'. The possibilities are endless. Bearded irises combine well with lupins (*Lupinus* spp.), hardy geraniums such as *Geranium* 'Johnson's Blue' and *G.* 'Kashmir White', and the neatly mounding blue-flowered hardy salvias, such as *Salvia ×superba* 'Lubecca'. When bearded irises are mixed with the fluffy white or coral-pink flowers of common valerian (*Centranthus coccinea*), foxglove (*Digitalis purpurea*), and old-fashioned or English roses, they produce an attractive cottage garden type border.

Arilbred irises are ideal for gardens with very well drained soil, in full sun, where gardeners don't mind hiding the foliage. Arilbreds are some of the most beautiful bearded irises in both form and colour. Because their foliage is prone to leaf spot in damp climates, arilbreds are better planted behind other plants that can hide the leaves.

Iris 'Caliente' in border

Iris 'Dusky Challenger' in border

Iris 'Honorabile' in border

Iris 'Conjuration' in border

Iris 'Cherokee Heritage' with lupins at Schreiner's Iris Gardens, Oregon, USA

An unknown iris with *Stachys byzantina*

Irises with roses, *Potentilla fruticosa*, and *Santolina*

Irises with lemons

IRISES FOR A FOCAL POINT

Nothing provides a focal point to the garden in early summer like bearded irises. They can be placed along the edges of low, raised walls, along pathways, between shrubs, with a tree as a backdrop, or in a mixed border where other plants are yet to flower. In all these locations the choice of varieties can be as big and brash as you like. One combination I love is *Iris* 'Sable', an old blue-black iris, planted below a standard lilac (*Syringa*) with rich lavender flowers. Another combination that caught my eye, but one I cannot copy, was a bicoloured Tall Bearded iris sitting in front of a lemon tree. *Crambe cordifolia* produces large airy plumes of tiny white flowers and creates an excellent backdrop for any iris. In a semi-woodland border, *Iris* 'Jesse's Song', one of the first Tall Bearded irises to flower, can bring a border alive at a time when the leaves of trees are at their greenest.

Iris 'Jesse's Song' at Plotner's Iris Nursery, Oregon

Unknown iris with catmint (*Nepeta*) and roses

Iris 'Eleanor Clare' with *Asphodeline lutea*

Irises on a raised edge

An old iris cultivar with *Crambe cordifolia*

Irises as a focal point

IRISES FOR FOLIAGE & FLOWER

Foliage as well as flower is most important in a mixed border, and in some irises both are in perfect balance. Spuria irises are one such example. This group has some of the tallest irises. These begin blooming after most Tall Bearded irises, producing erect clumps of deep green leaves that provide a wonderful background for any mixed border. Spurias can cope with drier conditions, especially those found along the walls of a house. One member of the group, *Iris graminea*, is a little gem that should be more widely grown particularly as it produces upright tufted clumps of grassy, deep green leaves, which are perfect for the front of a border. Spurias combine well with other perennials that have completely different foliage, including ground-carpeting dead nettles (*Lamium* spp.) and low-growing hardy geraniums, such as *Geranium ×cantabrigiensis* with its bright pink flowers.

Siberian irises also form leafy, upright clumps that are less over powering in a border; however they need a moister soil than that required by spurias. Good companions for Siberian irises include single-flowered peonies and softly coloured, old-fashioned roses.

Siberian irises with roses and *Aquilegia*

IRISES FOR MOIST SOILS & WATER GARDENS

Water in a garden provides an exciting element which brings the garden to life and can be used to reflect colours and shapes. Bearded irises should not be grown in wet soil, as their rhizomes will rot; however, when planted along the edges of ponds that do not flood, they look very handsome.

Siberian irises are often associated with ponds and streams, but they are not water dwellers. They can, however, be grown along the margins of a pond or stream provided they are not kept wet year-round. Siberian irises look handsome when planted with large-leaved perennials such as hostas, ligularias, and tall, bog-dwelling primulas (for example, *Primula pulverulenta*). Other *Iris* species that can be used along the edges of ponds are *Iris setosa* and *I. versicolor*.

Japanese irises flower after Siberian irises and continue into early or mid-July. They like a soil that retains its moisture throughout the year, and they thrive in a wet and boggy soil. One of the most handsome sights I have seen recently was one with Japanese irises planted in a wild garden under the semi-shade of trees. It may be that they flower better with some overhead protec-

Iris laevigata 'Colchesterensis'

tion. In very hot climates the petals can be marked by the sun and by excessive rainwater. I feel that Japanese irises need no planting companions; however, if they are grown in with other plants, they can share the same partners as Siberian irises.

Iris laevigata and *I. pseudacorus* can be grown in bogs, but they can also be sunk into water. In fact, the only irises to thrive in water are those belonging to the series *Laevigatae*. *Iris pseudacorus* can be sunk more deeply than *I. laevigata*, but being a thug it should not be grown in a small pond. To stop these two species from filling the pond, plant them in deep buckets, then sink them into the pond. They are perfect in formal water gardens which require a focal point.

Other more unusual plants for moist soils include the Sino-Siberian irises, of which *Iris chrysographes* is an example. These delicate, slender-leaved plants like a soil that contains very little lime and also retains its mois-

ture. They are excellent near the edge of a small stream, where the soil may be moist but not wet.

Gardeners in Britain are not able to grow a wide range of Louisiana irises. A few hardy members of the group will grow in Britain; however, Louisiana irises tend to be large and, therefore, in common with many water-loving plants need a spot that allows them to stretch their feet.

IRISES FOR SHADY AREAS

Evergreen plants have always been popular with gardeners. Most evergreen irises are shade loving, a happy combination, and some, such as *Iris cristata*, can be used for groundcover. In Britain, the most useful shade-loving iris is *I. foetidissima*. It produces upright clumps of pointed leaves and in June bears unimportant flowers; however, it comes into its own in autumn, when it unveils bright red berries that can brighten a dull, shady

Iris 'Sapphire Hills' and *I.* 'Sam Carne'

Siberian irises with candelabra primulas

A water garden with irises, at Lelsey Blyth's, Melbourne, Australia

Iris confusa in semi-shade

Iris 'Knighted' in the shade of a hot Australian day

spot for months. A handsome combination for a shady spot includes Christmas and Lenten roses (*Helleborus* spp.) with *I. foetidissima*.

Iris japonica and many other crested irises do not seem to be fussy about the soil being a little dry or shady, provided it contains a reasonable amount of humus. These irises flower around the same time as Spuria irises, during late June and into July.

In very hot climates, bearded irises will flower in shade. In Britain, the only bearded iris that managed to bloom in my garden in semi-shade was *Iris flavescens*, an old soft lemon variety.

Irises at Heronswood, Melbourne, Australia

Arilbreds in a bed at Mid America Irises, Oregon

Dutch irises at Keith Keppel Irises, Salem, Oregon

IRISES FOR HOT, DRY AREAS

Another difficult situation for plants is one that is very hot and sunny and therefore very dry. I have seen bearded irises in the most inhospitable of places. They are so tough that they are ideal for municipal planting schemes, particularly in drier and hotter countries of the world where I have seen them on traffic islands and along footpaths. In these sites the soil is unattended most of the year and too hot to grow any competing weeds. Other irises suitable for hot, dry locations include bearded irises, particularly arilbreds and aril irises, bulbous Xiphium irises, junos, and spurias.

Irises at Melbourne Airport

Spuria irises near conifer trees, Kew, London

Autumn

By late summer—August in Britain—most irises have finished flowering. This is the time when reblooming irises come into their own, provided they have been adequately watered since they have finished their first flush of flowers. Most reblooming irises are vigorous bearded irises, but some of the species such as *Iris germanica* and *I. aphylla* have the ability to throw up the odd flower spike.

In most summers Britain is blessed naturally with lots of rain and therefore gardeners have no problem getting remontanting irises to rebloom. Different areas of the world, not to mention each country, will have different experiences when it comes to reblooming irises. In the year I am writing, the first bearded iris to rebloom for me was *Iris* 'English Cottage'. The first flowers were produced in early June and the second flush began in mid-August. The plant was still flowering in October. This is not uncommon; some remontant irises bloom each year for us in late October.

Occasionally Siberian irises rebloom, and although I am not as familiar with these, I can vouch for *Iris* 'Exuberant Encore', which not only flowered for six straight weeks from late June, but also produced a smattering of flowers well into October.

Winter

Coming into winter, the garden largely goes dormant. Shrubs and evergreen plants provide both structure and colour. The leaves of *Iris foetidissima* and its white-striped form 'Variegata' remain handsome, as do those of *Iris japonica*, but the queen of the winter months must surely be *I. unguicularis*. Commonly called the winter flowering iris, this species is easy to grow in Britain, perhaps less so in gardens that experience colder winters. *Iris unguicularis* originates from North Africa, and thus in gardens in Britain should be planted in a very sheltered spot, near the warm walls of a house or perhaps in a greenhouse. A delightful plant, this iris forms a rather straggly mound with slender leaves. Sometime during winter, bright violet flowers pop up through the foliage. *Iris unguicularis* can bloom on and off for many weeks, and if picked in bud, the flowers can be brought into a house, where when placed in a vase they will last for several days.

Irises in Containers

As modern gardens get smaller, containers become more popular. Placed on patios, in courtyards, or on flat roofs, containers allow millions of people to enjoy gardening who might not otherwise have the opportunity.

Irises are not naturally considered as container plants; however, a few of them adapt readily to being confined. Reticulata irises can be grown for outside or inside decoration. When grown for indoor decoration, they must not be forced, but they can be encouraged into early flower by being grown in a cold greenhouse. When grown for outdoor decoration, reticulatas can be planted in containers with heathers and crocuses.

Japanese irises are useful for cutting. Historically,

Iris graeberiana in a terracotta pot

many of them were bred for growing in containers. The plants were grown outside, then, as the bloom began to burst, they were brought inside. *Iris laevigata* can be grown in containers for putting in a pond. Therefore, there is no reason why, provided it is not allowed to dry out, it cannot be grown in a pot out of the water. Juno irises also are wonderful in containers. In fact, some varieties can only be grown this way in Britain. Jim Almond, who lives in the middle of England, grows *I. graeberiana* in a large container, which he leaves outside throughout the year.

The only irises I do not recommend for growing in pots are bearded irises. These do not always flower in the first year and they seem to resent the restrictions of a container, however large it might be. Furthermore, if bearded irises are not planted into open ground within a year, they fade.

Iris nicolai in a terracotta pot, sunk into a sand bed and grown under cover

CHAPTER 21

Pests and Diseases

MOST IRISES WILL NEVER SUFFER from any disease provided they are grown in the right conditions, kept tidy, and divided when they become crowded. As gardeners, however, we all try from time to time to grow plants that may not be wholly suited to our growing conditions.

Bearded irises, Britain's favourite iris, originate from warm, dry areas and therefore may, in Britain's warm, wet climate, occasionally suffer from fungal diseases. The most common of these are bacterial soft rot and fungal leaf spot. Slugs and snails also attack bearded irises.

In this chapter I have indicated which type of iris is most likely to be affected by a particular disease; however, diseases are fickle and may attack plants I am unaware of. In such situations, local knowledge is everything.

When it comes to chemicals I have suggested only that a fungicide or insecticide should be used. This is because today so many are being removed from garden centre shelves that any advice given may be redundant in a few years' time. When looking for a chemical to control whichever disease or pest, seek advice from either your local garden centre or an iris society. Remember that, because iris leaves are waxy, it is necessary to use a wetting agent when applying a spray, so the spray will adhere to the leaf.

Diseases That Attack the Roots

Bacterial soft rot (*Erwinia carotovora*) affects all bearded irises, although it has been known to affect Japanese and Siberian irises. Also known as wet rot, this horrible disease turns the rhizome into a mushy, evil-smelling mess. The first signs of it appear when the base leaves begin to yellow and eventually fall off. There are several causes, but the main one is likely to be too much moisture, although high-nitrogen fertilizers, insects, or careless cultivation can also be causes. To prevent this disease from spreading further, lift the rhizome out of the soil and cut out the soft, mushy part. Disinfect the wound with either sulphur or a solution of one part bleach to nine parts water. Once the wound has dried out, replace any soil that was removed.

Botrytis rhizome rot (*Sclerotina convoluta*) affects bearded and Siberian irises. Not common, this disease occurs in cool conditions, mainly in spring. The rhizomes at first look mouldy, then become dry and brown inside. Finally they refuse to grow. To control this fungus, drench the rhizomes with a fungicide or destroy the entire plant. Botrytis among Siberian irises occurs when a large number of plants are grown together and in heavier soils in warm wet weather.

Crown rot (*Sclerotium rolfsii*) affects bearded, Japanese, Siberian, and Spuria irises. Similar to bacterial soft rot, crown rot attacks the rhizome, rotting it where the leaves join. The leaves become yellow at the tips, and then fall over. The disease occurs in warmer, more humid parts of the world including the subtropics and among plants that are grown in either rich or very poor soils. To control crown rot, follow the treatment for bacterial soft rot.

Ink disease affects Reticulata and Xiphium irises. At one time this disease almost destroyed all the reticulatas in cultivation. It is simple to spot. If a plant looks as though it is fading away, lift it, and examine the bulb. If the bulb is a mere shell and full of a black sooty dust, or the skin marked with black blotches, then it has ink disease. The disease is contagious to all other reticulatas. The bulbs should be destroyed. If the bulb can be rescued, lift it and soak it in a solution of fungicide or dust it with the dry powder. Any remaining bulbs that are healthy should be lifted and stored in a dry place until they can be replanted in a different part of the garden. The soil where diseased bulbs have been lifted from should be sterilized with a fungicide. Because, however, many Reticulata and Xiphium irises are inexpensive, it may be easier to purchase fresh bulbs. Be sure to plant them in a different spot.

Among the other bulb rot problems are **fusarium rot** (*Fusarium oxysporum*), a fungus that causes the bulbs and roots to rot, and **penicillium bulb rot** (*Penicillium corymbiferum*). The latter causes bulbs to become mouldy and usually occurs while the bulbs are being stored. If either disease affects bulbs, the bulbs should be destroyed.

Diseases That Attack the Leaves

Bacterial leaf spot (*Xanthomonas tardicrescens*) affects bearded irises, Japanese irises, Siberian irises, *Iris cristata*, *I. tectorum*, and *I. tenax*. Also known as bacterial leaf blight, this disfiguring disease causes long, irregularly shaped brown blotches that appear at first towards the top and edges of the leaves. In warm, wet weather, the blotches continue to rapidly spread down the leaves, eventually killing them off. Bacterial leaf spot is not as common as fungal leaf spot.

Fungal leaf spot (*Didymelina macrospora*) affects bearded irises, Siberian irises, and Louisiana irises. A common fungal disease, it attacks plants grown in areas with high humidity and ample rainfall and is easily recognized by the small yellow and brown spots that appear on the leaves. The spots gradually cover the whole leaf and eventually, but not inevitably, turn it brown. In severe cases this fungus will cause the rhizome to rot. It may be more noticeable when the leaves die back in the autumn. To prevent fungal leaf spot, regularly clean away old iris leaves and nearby weeds, both of which might harbour the spores. Remove the leaves or, if the problem is constant, spray the plants with a fungicide. At my nursery, we use two sprays alternately to prevent the fungus from becoming resistant to one fungicide. If leaf spot is persistent, spray plants early in spring to help prevent the disease.

Mosaic virus affects all irises. Spread by aphids and/or infected tools, the virus affects different irises in different ways. On the whole, if a plant is affected, it will show no symptoms unless it is under stress, such as during very dry spells or in spring and in the autumn. Then leaves appear mottled and the flowers become puckered and deformed. There is no cure for this virus. If a plant is badly affected, it should be dug up and destroyed.

Rust (*Puccinia iridis*, *P. sessilis*) affects bearded irises, Louisiana irises, bulbous irises, and *Iris tenax*. This unsightly disease causes red-brown spots that may eventually cover the entire leaf. It occurs at times of high humidity and can be exacerbated by overhead watering. Plants affected can be sprayed with a fungicide.

Scorch affects bearded and Siberian irises. It is uncommon in Britain and, in the United States, only affects irises grown in the more southerly states. It usually first shows up on newer leaves. These die back from the tips, until eventually the whole leaf turns a rust-red colour. The roots also die off. Scorch is caused by a bacteria carried by leaf-sucking insects, but it will not affect the surrounding soil. Little can be done to prevent or cure it.

Pineappling, though not a common problem, is a mysterious disease that causes the rhizome to grow, but not the leaves. The flower stems are malformed. Pineappling may occur in plants that are transplanted from a cold climate into a warm one. The only treatment is to destroy diseased plants.

Pests

Slugs and snails are the most likely pests to attack irises in Britain. They quickly rasp their way across the succulent foliage, leaving unsightly holes where diseases can get in. I favour using biological methods to get rid of these pests. Slugs and snails can easily be picked off plants using gardening gloves. A beer trap is another useful control. To construct a beer trap, fill a cup or glass jar with beer, then sink the jar to ground level. Slugs simply cannot resist beer and will drown in the solution. Chemicals also are available for killing slugs.

Aphids can be a nuisance and are responsible for spreading diseases, particularly viruses. These tiny, juicy-looking insects tend to hide between leaves, or sit in huddles on the surface of the leaves. One of the most effective methods of controlling aphids is to physically spray them off the leaves with a forceful jet of water or by frequently drenching the leaves with a soap-and-water solution. Another method is to use a systemic insecticide.

Iris borer (*Macronoctua onusta*), the larva of a native American night-flying moth, is restricted to the central and eastern United States, where it is a common and serious pest. It is unknown in Europe or in the southern United States. The life cycle of this pest begins when eggs are laid in autumn, usually among decaying iris leaves and other leaf debris. In spring the grubs hatch. They are light greyish white with a shading of red, hairless, and have a dark brown head. The larvae chew their way into the leaf, causing the leaves to 'bleed', and create notches, then work their way down to the rhizome, eventually growing to over 2.5 cm (1 in.) long. The first signs of borers are wet, slimy patches on the leaves or notched edges to the central leaves. Eventually the leaf fan collapses and the rhizome rots.

The best way of dealing with the problem is to catch the larvae before they descend to the rhizome. To prevent the borer from laying eggs anywhere near the plant, remove decaying leaves in autumn. A sharp eye will detect the borer before it enters the leaves. When spotted, the grubs should be destroyed. Otherwise the plants can be sprayed with a systemic insecticide.

Other iris pests are very localized and probably do not effect gardeners in most countries. **Eelworm** (*Ditylenchus destructor*) is a nematode that causes bulbs to rot. **Leaf miners** (*Liriomyza urophorina*) attack beardless irises, eating the bud and flower. **Iris thrips** (*Iridothrips iridis*) in their early stages feed on young leaves, causing dark patches and stunted growth. **Iris snout weevils** (*Mononychus vulpeculus*), also known as iris weevils, are small, long, and black; they eat the flowers and feed on seeds still in the pod.

CHAPTER 22

Hybridizing and Growing Irises from Seed

IRIS LOVERS MIGHT BEGIN hybridizing for any number of reasons. Curiosity could be fuelled by the enthusiasm of another hybridizer, or it may be that seeds sown from a bee-pollinated flower have produced something interesting. Whatever the reason, hybridizing is easy. I have no intention of covering the topic in any great detail, as other books, such as *Iris* (Köhlein 1987) and *The World of Irises* (Warburton and Hamblen 1978), do so in great depth.

Choosing Parents for Hybridizing

Whether you choose bearded, beardless, or bulbous irises, the principle of hybridization is the same. There are a few points, however, that should be remembered. Bearded and beardless irises do not cross-pollinate easily, although it is not impossible. Also attempting to cross plants that contain different numbers of chromosomes is difficult, as many crosses will not produce seeds. The most modern iris varieties do not readily cross with the oldest ones. This applies particularly to bearded hybrids, the most commonly hybridized group. The beardless group is a large one, however, with endless possibilities. In the past, crossing *Iris pseudacorus* with *I. ensata, I. laevigata,* and *I. versicolor* has raised plants. Other successful crosses include *I. chrysographes* with *I. douglasiana* and *I. setosa,* and Siberian irises with *I. setosa* and Pacific Coast irises.

Choosing the parents for hybridizing should be very personal. Human beings are creative beasts, and the reason we hybridize plants is because we want to create something new and different. Iris breeders with many years of experience may tell you to use only the most up-to-date varieties as they believe that very few advances can be gained by retracing old steps. I do not necessarily agree with this point of view. It may be that by going back we can come forward again, perhaps along a different path to create new plants with a different set of qualities that are as yet unknown. One thing to remember is that the breeding of plants does not always lead directly to new introductions. Experienced hybridizers frequently keep plants that may not be good enough to introduce, but that may have some special quality that can later be used in further crosses.

The Method of Hybridizing

The hybridizer is simply replacing the bee for the purposes of pollination. The bee, or any insect that is small enough to crawl into the iris bloom, enters the flower to retrieve nectar and, in doing so, pollen becomes attached to its back. The insect then flies into another flower, brushing the pollen onto the stigma of the new flower. The stigma is the lip that can be found just under the style crest, which is at the top of the style arm. The pollen makes its way down the tunnel to pollinate the ovaries, and the seeds are formed.

Iris pollen can be white, yellow, or blue, and it is ready to use when it brushes off, in the form of powder, onto your fingers. The stigma is receptive to the pollen when it looks sticky. Remove the stamen from one of the parents, now known as the pollen parent, with a pair of tweezers or by gently pulling it between your fingers (the method I prefer), and then gently brush the pollen across the stigma of the second parent, now known as the seed parent. Before brushing the pollen onto the seed parent, you can remove the lower petals from the seedpod parent to prevent insects from landing on the flower and adding more pollen from a different source. After making your cross, label the pod. I use small white tags attached to string. The name of the seedpod parent, then the pollen parent should be written on the label before it is attached to the stem near to the flower.

The seed should begin to swell fairly soon, in about 10 to 14 days for bearded irises. If it does not, and you intend to continue pollinating, remember to note down which crosses have not taken so that you do not waste your time later on. Recording crosses is something that can never be underestimated because it provides information for future crosses. When the pods have reached maturity, the seed can be collected and sown.

Seedpod of a tall bearded iris

Seedpod of a Spuria iris

Seedpod of a Louisiana iris

Iris pseudacorus seedpod

Seedpod of a Siberian iris

Growing Irises from Seed

One of the most satisfying horticultural tasks is seed sowing. All irises can easily be raised from seed. If you are collecting seed from your own plants, remember that only species irises are likely to come true, provided they have not been cross-pollinated by a neighbour of a different kind.

COLLECTING THE SEED

Collect seedpods as they mature. Each type of iris will reach this point at a different time. If you wait for the pod to open, the seeds will likely have been dispersed by the time you get to them. Therefore, it is better to collect seedpods just before they split. If you are unsure when a pod is about to burst, squeeze it gently; if it is soft the seeds are mature enough to be collected. The pods can be opened and the seeds removed. Sow the seeds immediately or store them in a paper bag to sow later.

SOWING THE SEED

Iris seeds vary in their form and their germination requirements. For instance, desert dwellers such as Aril irises may take longer to germinate than many other irises simply because in their natural location they may not receive water for some years. The seeds of Louisiana irises have an unusual, thick, cork-like covering that allows them to float. This covering can be removed before sowing to aid easier germination.

In general, seeds germinate more easily if they are sown when they are fresh. Purchased or donated seeds are likely to be dry. The seed coat of dried seeds contains an inhibitor that delays germination until the right conditions for germination have arrived. Therefore, it may help to prepare dry seeds before sowing by soaking them in a jar of water for up to a week to remove the germinating inhibitor. Alternatively, some people scratch the seed covering gently with fine sandpaper and then chill the seeds in a fridge for a month before sowing them in spring.

Seeds should be sown in good soil-based compost in shallow trays or, in the case of deep-rooted species, such as arils and Xiphium irises, in deep pots with sandy soil where the seedlings can remain for a year before being transplanted. If sowing a large number of seeds, it might be easier to sow them directly outdoors into a seedbed that has been thoroughly prepared. Most seeds can be left outside over winter, but it may be better to keep them in a greenhouse, where watering is controlled and the compost monitored so it does not dry out or become too wet. Dry compost will prevent or delay germination; wet compost will rot the seeds.

Germination is likely to be erratic. Some seeds sown in the autumn will germinate immediately; others even in the same tray will not appear until the spring. Patience is needed with other seeds, such as arils, which may take several years to germinate.

TRANSPLANTING SEEDLINGS

In theory, seedlings can be put into pots when they are big enough to be handled; however, I recommend leaving them in the seed tray or container until the roots are large enough to be seen through the base of the pot. This is because if seedlings are potted too soon, they have fewer resources to survive on and, particularly in the case of bearded iris, are liable to root off. Seedlings can either be potted into larger, individual pots or, if they are large enough, planted straight into the ground. Some of the smaller irises, such as Pacific Coast irises, are better transplanted into pots. Seedlings do not usually flower in the first year, although occasionally the seedling of a spring-germinated seed will produce a flower spike in autumn of the same year.

SOURCES

IRISES ARE BEST PURCHASED as bare-rooted plants. Many specialist nurseries throughout the world grow an enormous number of varieties and usually produce detailed catalogues that are often extravagantly illustrated. Some of these have been in existence for several generations, and many raise their own hybrids. During the flowering season, nurseries tend to be open to visitors, and it is a marvellous way to choose irises. Irises are always despatched when it is the correct time to plant them. Container-grown plants can be bought from garden centres as well as nurseries, although garden centres tend to stock the older varieties. For newer hybrids or a particular plant, you should buy through mail order or from a nursery that grows irises.

There are far too many iris nurseries in existence around the world for me to list each one here. Every year new ones open, some close down or are sold. Therefore I have mentioned only those that have gained, what I consider, to be a reliable reputation within the world of irises, or currently have a unique collection of irises.

Iris Societies

American Iris Society:
  http://www.irises.org
British Iris Society:
  http://www.britishirissociety.org.uk
Canadian Iris Society:
  http://www.members.rogers.com/
  cdn-iris
Italian Iris Society:
  http://www.irisfirenze.it
Species Iris Group of North America
  (SIGNA): http://www.signa.org

Iris Nurseries

AUSTRALIA

Iris Haven
P.O. Box 83
Pennant Hills
New South Wales 1715
http://www. irishaven.com.au

Tempo Two
P.O. Box 1109
Pearcedale
Victoria 3912
http://www.tempotwo.com.au

Rainbow Ridge
8 Taylors Road
Dural
New South Wales 2158

BRITAIN

Broadleigh Gardens
Bishops Hull
Taunton
Somerset TA4 1AE
http://www.broadleighbulbs.co.uk

Claire Austin Hardy Plants
The Stone House
Cramp Pool
Shifnal
Shropshire TF11 8PE
http:www.claireaustin-hardyplants.co.uk

Croftway Nursery
Yapton Road
Barnham
Bognor Regis
West Sussex PO22 0BQ
http: www.croftway.co.uk

Tempo Two, Pearcedale, Victoria, Australia

Kelways
Langport
Somerset TA10 9EZ
http://www.kelways.co.uk

Lingen Nursery
Lingen
Bucknell
Shropshire SY7 0DY

Rowden Gardens
Brentnor
Near Tavistock
Devon PL19 0NG

CANADA

Chuck Chapman Iris
R.R. 1
8790 Highway 24
Guelph, Ontario N1H 6H7

Claire Austin Hardy Plants, Shropshire, England

FRANCE

Bourdillon Iris
B.P. 2
F-41230 Soings en Sologne
http://www.bourdillon.com

Cayeux Irises
B.P. 35
45501 Gien Cedex
http://www.cayeux

Iris en Provence
Chemin des Maures
83400 Hyères

ITALY

Iride
Via San Pietro
126-15020 Gabiano (AL)
http://www.biancoiride.com

UNITED STATES

Aitken's Salmon Creek Garden
608 NW 119th Street
Vancouver, Washington 98685
http://www.flowerfantasy.net

Argyle Acres
910 Pioneer Circle East
Argyle, Texas 76226
http://www.argyleacres.com

Bay View Gardens
The Irises of Joe Ghio
1201 Bay Street
Santa Cruz, California 95060

Bois D'arc Gardens
Rusty Ostheimer
Bud McSparrin
1831 Bull Run Road
Schriever, Louisiana 70395
http://www.bois-darc.com

Cape Iris Gardens
822 Rodney Vista Blvd.
Cape Girardeau, Missouri 63701

Chehalem Gardens
P.O. Box 74
Dundee, Oregon 97115

Contemporary Gardens
7204 North Council Road
Blanchard, Oklahoma 73010

Cooley's Gardens
P.O. Box 126NT
Silverton, Oregon 97381
http:www.cooleysgardens.com

Vicki and Jim Craig
16325 SW 113th Avenue
Portland, Oregon 97224
http://www.aphyllaspecialists.com

Draycott Gardens
16815 Falls Road
Upperco, Maryland 21155

Ensata Gardens
9823 East Michigan Avenue
Galesburg, Michigan 49053
http://www.ensata.com

Keith Keppel Irises
P.O. Box 18154
Salem, Oregon 97305

Gormley Greenery
6717 Martha Drive
Cedar Hill, Mo 63016
http://www.gromleygreenery.com

Iris Colorado
10918 Sunshine Drive
Littleton, Colorado 80125
http://www.iriscolorado.com

Joe Pye Weed's Garden
Jan Sacks and Marty Schafer
337 Acton Street
Carlisle, Massachusetts 01741

Mid America Gardens
P.O. Box 9008
Brooks, Oregon 97305
http://www.mid-americagarden.com

Iris 'Aztec Burst' growing at Sutton's Iris Gardens, Porterville, California

Nicholls Gardens
4724 Angus Drive
Gainesville, Virginia 20155
www.nichollsgardens.com

Sans Souci Nursery
3819 Beatty Road
Monkton, Maryland 21111
http://www.irises.com

Schreiner's Iris Gardens
3625 Quinaby Road N.E.
Salem, Oregon 97303
http: www.schreinersgardens.com

Superstition Iris Gardens
2536 Old Highway
Cathey's Valley, California 95306

Sutton's Iris Gardens
16592 Road 208
Porterville, California 93257
http://www.suttoniris.com

Wildwood Gardens
William Plotner
P.O. Box 250
Molalla, Oregon 97038

Tony and Dorothy Willott
26231 Shaker Blvd.
Beachwood, Ohio 44122

Winterberry Gardens
1225 Reynolds Road
Cross Junction, Virginia 22625

Zebra Gardens
9130 N 5200 W
Elwood, Utah 84337
http://www.zebrairis.com

Schreiner's Iris Gardens, Salem, Oregon

GLOSSARY

Amoena An iris with white or whitish standards and differently coloured falls

Apogon iris A beardless iris

Beard The strip of hairs that sits at the back of the falls. Largely confined to bearded irises, it is a pollinating guide for insects.

Bicolour An iris with falls of one colour and standards of another

Bitone An iris with falls and standards of the same colour, but in two different tones

Blend An iris flower with petals of two or more colours. Often the colours are too complicated or unusual to place the flower elsewhere.

Chromosome A little rod-shaped body in the nucleus of a cell that carries the genes

Crest The raised ridge on Evansia irises

Cultivar A cultivated variety. The names of cultivars are always enclosed with single quote marks.

Diploid A plant with twice the basic number of chromosomes

Falls The three lower petals

Flare, Flared petals Petals that are more or less horizontal to the flower stem

Fluting, Fluted petals Petals with gentle dips along the edges

Forma A plant with minor variations to the species

Genus A group of species

Haft The base of the petal where the petal narrows or constricts. Also referred to as the shoulders

Horns Long extensions from the end of the beard

Hybrid The offspring of two different species

Lacing, Laced petals Petals with serrated edges. Lightly laced petals have serrated edges; flowers with heavy lacing have crinkled edges

Luminata An iris with white or nearly white style arms and white or yellow veining on the falls

Neglecta A blue- or purple-flowered iris with standards a lighter colour than the falls

Plicata An iris with colour speckled, stippled, or stitched on the petals over a different background colour

Pogon iris A bearded iris

Reblooming, Remonting, Remontant irises Irises that bloom twice in one season. Sometimes the term is used to refer to plants that bloom on and off over a long period

Rhizome A swollen flower stem that creeps along the surface of the soil and produces roots. In some iris groups the rhizomes can be large and very noticeable, in others they are less so.

Ruffles, Ruffled petals Petals with undulating edges

Self An iris having one colour only

Signal A patch of contrasting colour that surrounds or forms a flare on the falls and functions as a signal for pollinating insects

Spathe The covering on a bud that in some irises eventually turns brown and papery

Species A plant found growing in the wild that is not a hybrid

Standards The three upper petals

Style arms The slender, petal-like structures that sit between the standards and above the falls

Style crests The upward curved tops on the style arms

Subspecies A division of a species comprised of plants which differ slightly from the species

Substance The thickness of the petals

Tetraploid A plant with four times the usual number of chromosomes

Variety A selected or man-made plant grown in cultivation

Variegata An iris with yellow standards and red falls

BIBLIOGRAPHY

American Iris Society. Bulletins from 1985 to 2004.

American Iris Society Web site. http://www.irises.org.

Anley, Gwendolyn. 1946. *Irises: Their Culture and Selection*. London: W. H. and L. Collingridge.

Berrisford, Judith M. 1961. *Irises*. London: John Gifford.

British Iris Society. Yearbooks from 1984 to 2003, plus 1961 to 1966, and 1957.

British Iris Society Web site. http://www.britishirissociety.org.

Broadleigh Gardens Web site. http://www.broadleighbulbs.co.uk.

Cassidy, G. E., and S. Linnegar. 1982. *Growing Irises*. Reprint, 1987. London: Croom Helm.

Cave, Lesley. 1951. *The Iris*. London: Faber and Faber.

Cave, Lesley. 1960. *Irises for Everyone*. London: Faber and Faber.

Dykes, W. R. 1913. *The Genus* Iris. Cambridge: Cambridge University Press. Reprint 1974. New York: Dover Publications.

Dykes, W. R. 1924. *A Handbook of Garden Irises*. London: Martin Hopkinson and Company.

Glasgow, Karen. 1996. *Irises: A Practical Gardening Guide*. Portland, Oregon: Timber Press.

Grosvenor, Graeme. 1997. *Iris: Flower of the Rainbow*. Kenthurst, Australia: Kangaroo Press.

Köhlein, Fritz. 1987. *Iris*. Portland, Oregon: Timber Press.

Linnegar, S., and J. Hewitt. 2003. *Irises*. RHS Wisley Handbooks. London: Cassell.

Lynch, R. Irwin. 1903. *The Book of the Iris*. London: Bodley Press.

Mathew, Brian. 1981. *The Iris*. Portland, Oregon: Timber Press.

McEwen, Currier. 1996. *The Siberian Iris*. Portland, Oregon: Timber Press.

Miller, Philip. 1732. *Gardener's Dictionary*.

Pesel, L. F., and R. E. S. Spender. 1937. *Iris Culture for Amateurs*. London: Country Life.

Price, Molly. 1973. *The Iris Book*. New York: Dover Publications.

Randall, Harry. 1969. *Irises*. London: Batsford.

Royal Horticulture Society. 2003. *RHS Plant Finder 2003–2004*. London: Dorling Kindersley.

Shear, William. 2002. *The Gardener's Iris Book*. Connecticut: Taunton Press.

Society for Louisiana Irises. 2000. *The Louisiana Iris: The Taming of a Native American Wildflower*. Portland, Oregon: Timber Press.

Species Group of the British Iris Society. 1997. *A Guide to Species Irises: Their Identification and Cultivation*. Cambridge: Cambridge University Press.

Species Iris Group of North America (SIGNA) Web site. http://www.signa.org.

Stebbins, Geoff. 1997. *The Gardener's Guide to Growing Irises*. Portland, Oregon: Timber Press.

Waddick, James W., and Zhao Yu-tang. 1992. *Iris of China*. Portland, Oregon: Timber Press.

Warburton, Beatrice, and Melba Hamblen. 1978. *The World of Irises*. American Iris Society.

INDEX